THE LISBON LIONS

THE
LISBON LIONS

The Real Inside Story of
Celtic's European Cup Triumph

**Billy McNeill, Jim Craig,
Tommy Gemmell, John Clark,
Willie Wallace, Stevie Chalmers,
Bertie Auld and Bobby Lennox**

with Alex Gordon

BLACK & WHITE PUBLISHING

First published 2007
by Black & White Publishing Ltd
99 Giles Street, Edinburgh EH6 6BZ

1 3 5 7 9 10 8 6 4 2   07 08 09 10 11

ISBN 13: 978 1 84502 161 0
ISBN 10: 1 84502 161 4

A CIP catalogue record for this book is available from the
British Library.

Typeset by AJT
Printed and bound by Creative Print and Design Group Ltd

To Gerda, my wife, who has now become a fan of the Lisbon Lions. And, of course, the Lions themselves – great lads, one and all.

Alex Gordon

CONTENTS

AUTHOR'S NOTE

The date 22 May 1967 is one that will live with me forever. The one three days later is fairly memorable, too! At the age of fifteen, I started work as a messenger at the *Daily Record* on 22 May all those years ago. I wanted to get my foot in the door and see where my career would take me. Luckily for me, I was in the right place at the right time and I enjoyed twenty years with the *Daily Record* and then seven with the *Sunday Mail*, where I was Sports Editor.

On Monday, 22 May 1967, however, when I turned up at Hope Street, in Glasgow, where the *Daily Record* offices were situated at the time, I was in a real quandary. My working hours were from 9 a.m. to 5.30 p.m. I knew Celtic would kick off against Inter Milan in Lisbon at 5.30 p.m. three days later. My starting wage of £4 per week (£3.50 after tax!) would hardly cover the hire of a Leer Jet to get me from the city centre to my home in the south side of Glasgow. I wasn't about to throw a 'sickie' either. That wouldn't have looked too impressive in my first week in the job and might have taken a bit of explaining.

My gaffer was a bloke called Robert Melvin, who was sympathetic to my pleas, and I will be grateful to him to the end of my days. Robert, who still works at the *Daily Record*, allowed me to have a half day on Thursday, 25 May and I was sitting in front of the television in plenty of time for the start of the Lisbon game.

If the Martians had decided to invade Glasgow between 5.30 p.m. and 7.15 p.m. that evening they would have thought they had found a deserted part of the planet – no one was in sight. Televisions were switched on everywhere with everyone witnessing Celtic Football Club making history against the might of Inter Milan in a truly extraordinary encounter.

They say you should never meet your heroes for fear of being disappointed. Believe me, that is not the case with the Lisbon Lions. They are everything you would expect them to be and more. If I urgently required company in a trench, I know who I would call.

Alex Gordon

FOREWORD

BY DAVIE HAY

I was born three years too late. I am not wishing my life away but I wouldn't have minded making my entrance on to this planet on 29 January 1945 instead of 1948. Then I might have been in with a chance of playing in Lisbon. Where in that wonderful team, I don't know, but I would have been thrilled simply to have been part of that experience.

I signed for Celtic in April 1965, the month before Jock Stein returned as manager. Actually, Tommy Docherty was interested in taking me to Chelsea at the time but, as soon as Sean Fallon told me Celtic, too, wouldn't mind signing me, there was only going to be one winner and that was the club from the east end of Glasgow. So, as a nineteen-year-old I was on the staff back then as Celtic swept through Europe and got to the final where they would meet Inter Milan on 25 May 1967. I knew Celtic had plans to take some of their younger players to Portugal to give them some experience of football at that level.

You could say I was just a wee bit excited at that prospect. Sadly, it was not to be, though. The travelling squad was announced and the name Davie Hay wasn't on it. I had left it too late to make travel arrangements or even get a ticket so the next best thing was to watch the big game on the television. What a game! I was transfixed to the set and I kicked every ball. I was exhausted at the end!

As people said at the time, it was a magnificent achievement and it helped to reverse the trend of thinking that only defensively minded teams could be successful. Inter Milan had, of course, built their reputation on spoiling, negative tactics but they were blown away in Lisbon. The score was 2–1

xi

going on 6–1. The main thing is, though, that Celtic were rightly acclaimed European Champions and it was a title they thoroughly deserved. No one could say otherwise. It was a triumph applauded by everyone.

I learned a lot from mixing with the Lisbon Lions. Just to be around these guys in training was a bit special. Billy McNeill always had a special presence about him. If you walked into a crowded dressing room, you would have immediately picked out Big Billy as the Celtic captain. He just had that aura about him. Big Jock was different class too, of course, and, if I couldn't learn a thing or two from this guy, then I was surely wasting my time.

I could go through the whole team – Ronnie Simpson, Jim Craig, Tommy Gemmell, Bobby Murdoch, Billy McNeill, John Clark, Jimmy Johnstone, Willie Wallace, Stevie Chalmers, Bertie Auld and Bobby Lennox – and, without doubt, every one of them was a star in his own right. They all had different abilities and it took a great manager such as Jock Stein to take all that varying talent and shape it into a side that would conquer Europe.

We shouldn't forget the other guys who helped the club get to Lisbon but didn't play against Inter Milan. John Hughes, for instance, played in five of the nine games during that successful run. Willie O'Neill played in four and Charlie Gallagher and Joe McBride in two. Nor should we overlook the input of Sean Fallon, as Big Jock's right-hand man. All these guys and others played their part in helping Celtic to become the most successful side in Scottish footballing history.

I did play for the club in a European Cup Final three years after Lisbon but, unfortunately, we were beaten 2–1 in extra time by Dutch side Feyenoord. They scored their winning goal three minutes from the end and, if they hadn't, it would have gone to a replay (penalty kicks to decide the winner hadn't been introduced back then). You'll have to take my word for it but we would have won that second game and Celtic would have had two European Cups in their trophy cabinet. Feyenoord surprised us in the San Siro Stadium in Milan but they wouldn't have done so in a replay.

It would have been nice to have had a European Cup winner's medal in my collection. Still, I've got the next best thing – the wonderful memory of Celtic Football Club conquering Europe in that maverick, attacking style that was their trademark. If only I had been born three years earlier!

PROLOGUE

Date – 28 April 1965
Venue – East End Park
Result – Dunfermline 5, Celtic 1
Team – Fallon; Gemmell and O'Neill; Clark, McNeill and Brogan;
Johnstone, Murdoch, Hughes, Maxwell and Lennox

Fast forward to . . .

Date – 25 May 1967
Venue – Estadio Nacionale, Lisbon
Result – Celtic 2, Inter Milan 1
Team – Simpson; Craig and Gemmell; Murdoch, McNeill and Clark;
Johnstone, Wallace, Chalmers, Auld and Lennox

Fast forward to . . .

Date – 23 March 2007
Venue – 7 Day Press, West Nile Street, Glasgow

Tommy Gemmell has popped into our offices for a cup of coffee and a choccy biscuit. We're making observations and having a general chat about the official book to mark the fortieth anniversary of the Lisbon Lions. How do you dig up something fresh on such a momentous occasion that has been covered time and again over the past four decades? What possibly could be new on Scottish football's most historic occasion? Are there any nuggets out there that haven't, as yet, come to the surface?

Tommy takes a look at the team list that had been decimated by Dunfermline all those years ago. As succinct as ever, he remarks, 'If anyone had told me after that game that Celtic would win the European Cup two years later, I would have made sure they were put on the best medication for the rest of their lives. Honestly, how could you start to dare to dream that conquering Europe was going to be even a vague possibility for this team? Let's get serious. We've just been taken apart by Dunfermline. Humbled and humiliated – not even at the races. If I had gone up to Big Billy or Wee Jinky in the showers afterwards and told them I thought we would lift Europe's most prized trophy in two years' time, they would have had me locked up for my own good – and I wouldn't have blamed them.'

Gemmell peruses the line-up again. He looks up, shakes his head and exclaims, 'Good God! I've just realised that only two of that team didn't figure at all in our European run – Hughie Maxwell and Jim Brogan. Eight of the others played at some stage or another while John Fallon was reserve goalkeeper to Ronnie Simpson for all nine games in the competition.

'Brogan would have been standing by as cover if there had been any injury problems on the left-hand side of the defence where he could have slotted in for, say, John Clark or Willie O'Neill earlier in the run. Poor Hughie! Jimmy McGrory bought him from Falkirk where he had been something of a goalscoring inside left who was a bit of a penalty expert. There wasn't much of him – tall but almost painfully thin. You would play a guy like him up at Inverness Caley Thistle on a windy day at your peril. You might never see him again. Actually, he didn't last too long during Big Jock's regime. If memory serves correctly, he was bought from Falkirk for something in the region of £15,000 in mid November, sold to St Johnstone for £10,000 in the summer and that was the end of his short spell as a Celt. Football can be so cruel.'

Exactly twenty-nine days after Celtic had been dismissed by Dunfermline, Inter Milan collected their second successive

European Cup by overcoming Portuguese giants Benfica 1–0 in their own San Siro Stadium with a goal from Jair in the forty-second minute.

'That makes it even more remarkable, doesn't it?' asks Gemmell. 'We actually beat the team that had ruled Europe for two years. Us – a team that was gubbed at East End Park. In fact, I also recall a 6–2 hiding by Falkirk at Brockville around the same time.'

A quick check of the record books do, indeed, show Celtic being toppled by Falkirk in an old First Division encounter only a fortnight before their Dunfermline debacle. Three days after the Brockville embarrassment, Celtic slumped at home to Partick Thistle, beaten 2–1 in front of their own fans.

'How could anyone think we were capable of what we achieved in Lisbon?' asks Gemmell with that trademark beaming smile. 'Three successive league games, three defeats and thirteen goals conceded. Not too impressive, eh?'

It hadn't all been doom, gloom and disaster, though, for the Celtic fans back in April 1965. There were wild celebrations at a packed Hampden Park when captain Billy McNeill soared above friend and foe to thump a header beyond the stranded goalkeeper Jim Herriot to give Celtic a 3–2 triumph over Dunfermline in the Scottish Cup Final. It was just four days after that when the Fifers exacted their revenge with that 5–1 win at East End Park but no one seemed to notice – or care.

That Scottish Cup victory, with Celtic coming back twice with equalisers from Bertie Auld before McNeill made his indelible mark, was the club's first piece of silverware since season 1957/58 when, in one of the most astoundingly one-sided Old Firm games in history, the club overwhelmed Rangers 7–1 in the League Cup Final. After that, Celtic embarked on a seven-year trek through a series of out-takes that are better forgotten. Before the Lisbon Lions, the club somehow managed to win through to the semi-finals of the European Cup-Winners' Cup in 1964 where they met Hungary's MTK Budapest over the two legs. Celtic coasted to a 3–0 victory in Glasgow with two goals from Stevie Chalmers and one from Jimmy Johnstone and it looked to all of Europe, if not the world, as though they had booked their place in the cup final against Sporting Lisbon in Brussels. The second leg was just a formality, surely?

MTK Budapest 4, Celtic 0 is a scoreline that still haunts older Celtic supporters. How could it happen? John Hughes, who played that miserable evening in the Hungarian capital, says, 'Bob Kelly was our chairman at the time and it was no secret that he, and not manager Jimmy McGrory, picked the team. He believed that Celtic should always put on a show, home or away. We were three goals ahead but he demanded that we still attacked our opponents. A wonderful and admirable philosophy, of course, but maybe just a wee bit naive, wouldn't you say? MTK couldn't believe their good fortune as they swarmed down on us and got the four goals they required.'

Drastic changes were urgently required. Enter Jock Stein in March 1965 – and things were never to be the same again.

Pre-Stein it would be fair to say the players were becoming more than a shade disillusioned and disaffected. Billy McNeill was being wooed by Tottenham Hotspur. Bobby Murdoch was tinkering with the idea of emigrating to Australia. Bobby Lennox had been the subject of two enquiries from Falkirk. Even more alarming was the news that Jimmy Johnstone was seriously thinking about giving up senior football to return to the juniors where he would have assuredly disappeared without trace. To one observer at the time, it was more of a 'probability than a possibility'.

Two years later, all four of them were picking up European Cup medals.

1

A DARK NIGHT IN LISBON

Picture this extraordinary scene: Footballers stumbling around in the dark around midnight. It's pitch black and the sportsmen and their manager are stepping over loose stones, fallen rocks and all sorts of other debris lying scattered around the hillside. They are wading through a stream and trying not to get scratched to bits by wild shrubbery. They are clambering over a derelict fence with rusty nails dangling at dangerous angles. This is Celtic Football Club a mere eighteen hours or so before they play in the biggest game in the club's history – the European Cup Final against Inter Milan in Lisbon on Thursday, 25 May.

Tommy Gemmell recalls, 'When we were in Estoril preparing for the match, Jock Stein was trying all sorts of things to prevent us from getting bored. Put a lot of young men together away from home for a reasonably lengthy spell and you can get a wee bit frustrated. There are only so many crosswords you can do. Jock worried about everything. He didn't want us spending too much time in the sun. Our visits to the outdoor swimming pool were curtailed too. There were fans everywhere and, for once, he wanted us to keep them at arm's length.

'We met up with a bloke called Brodie Lennox – no relation to Wee Bobby – and he had been a top amateur golfer for Scotland in his day. Brodie owned a golfing complex and had a place situated high in the hills about a thirty-minute walk away from our hotel. England were due to play Spain in an international on the Wednesday night at Wembley and he invited all the players to his place to take in the action. Jock thought it was a great idea and absolutely perfect for us to take our minds off our own game.

'So, after our evening meal, we took off up this long and winding road to Brodie's place. We were all fit guys, of course, so there was no problem in getting to the complex although, to be honest, it was a fair old hike. Anyway, we reached our destination, watched England win the match 2–0 and, after a few soft drinks, decided to wend our merry way back to our hotel.

'Neilly Mochan, who was our trainer at the time, decided we should take a short cut. He pointed to our hotel and said to Jock, "I reckon we can cut about ten minutes off our trip, Boss. Let's go down through the fields." Jock, rather amazingly when you consider he had wrapped us up in cotton wool beforehand, agreed to the notion. We found ourselves wandering around in the dark with no lights in sight. All you could hear was an "Ouch!" or something a bit more earthy as we tried to find our bearings. I felt some rocks go from under my weight a couple of times and I thought, "Wouldn't it be so typical to reach the European Cup Final and get injured walking down a bloody hill!"

'Jock, too, must have felt the strain because he had walked with a fairly heavy limp ever since injury had ended his football-playing career. We stuck it out, though, and reached the safety of our hotel around midnight. Honestly, someone could have picked up any sort of injury. Someone could have turned an ankle or worse. Thankfully, we were all OK but, on reflection, it wasn't the brightest thing to do on the eve of such an important match. I couldn't imagine the Inter Milan players being asked to carry out such a task. I wonder what the likes of Ronaldinho, Thierry Henry, Paolo Maldini, Cristiano Ronaldo and all the other superstars of today's football would have made of that rather bizarre situation. What would they have said if they were told to undertake such a trip at midnight? "No way!" would be one of the more polite responses, I think.'

Jim Craig added, 'I recall we had to clamber over a fence in the dead of night. All this on the eve of the final. Anyone could have broken a leg. It was just that sort of innocence, though, which was our great strength.'

No one was unduly surprised that Jock Stein never repeated the exercise – despite the fact that it was followed by an over-whelming success the next day.

2

THE LISBON FINAL

Thirty-one seconds . . . one throw-in . . . six passes . . . a thundering shot –that's all it took for Celtic to turn football on its head on that magical, memorable, exhilarating day in Lisbon on 25 May 1967.

For over an hour the marauding green-and-white legions had battered away at the Inter Milan goal without success. Goalkeeper Giuliano Sarti had been seen as a possible weak link in the Inter Milan defensive armoury which was otherwise festooned with seasoned internationals. But his was an extraordinary act of defiance that day; an impressive one-man barricade standing in the way of Celtic and destiny. He repelled raid after raid with one of the most astonishing goalkeeping performances ever witnessed. On the rare occasions when he was beaten, the angels appeared to be on his side. Bertie Auld, sensing a rare opening, clipped the crossbar with a cunning left-foot effort while running at speed. Shots and headers rained down on the black-clad No. 1 who dealt with everything with an annoying assurance. Jock Stein ventured to the touchline, his massive left paw pointing the way for his troops. 'Keep going,' he urged. 'Keep moving forward.'

Sixty-one minutes – still Sarti and Inter are standing firm. Sixty-two minutes – still nothing doing. Sixty-three minutes – Celtic have a shy thirty yards from the goal line on the left. Willie Wallace, confronted with the giant frame of Giacinto Facchetti, is looking for a team-mate in a good position. Facchetti, blocking his view, holds his ground. Wallace shapes up to throw it and changes his mind. Gemmell looms into view to offer an option. The ball duly drops at his right foot. There's a quick switch across the park to Jim Craig on the right. Craig rolls it inside for Bobby Murdoch who is crowded out on the edge of the box and the ball is retrieved by Jimmy Johnstone, on the left. He touches it back to John Clark who thrusts it forward again to Murdoch, this time in the old inside-left channel thirty yards from goal. The Italians, methodical as ever, are refusing to be put off their stride. They regroup, cover, pick up a man, shut down space.

Celtic continue to show commendable patience as they pass the ball around. Murdoch slips a simple pass in front of the galloping Craig. He controls the ball as he gathers momentum, heading for the danger zone. Another touch – three in all – before squaring across to Gemmell. There is no break in his stride as he reaches the eighteen-yard box with precision timing before clubbing the ball high past Sarti. The unbeatable is beaten at last. Hallelujah!

Thirty-one seconds . . . a throw-in . . . six passes . . . one thundering shot – that's all it took.

Liam Brady, who had the unique distinction of serving both Celtic and Inter Milan, recalls watching the game on television in his native Dublin. 'Inter actually started quite well. Sandro Mazzola, who was a director when I was at the club, had a good chance but Ronnie Simpson made an important diving save. We were all outraged when the referee awarded Inter a penalty kick in the seventh minute. Jim Craig's challenge on Renato Cappellini seemed good but, looking at it again, you could see it was very much a penalty kick.

'Mazzola was Inter's star player around that time and he accepted the responsibility of taking the penalty kicks. Credit where credit is due; he took that one against Celtic very well and scored quite comfortably, sending the keeper the wrong way. What was very interesting, though, was the way Celtic's players kept interchanging as they continued to move forward. Jimmy Johnstone was everywhere and even came close with a header which was well saved by Sarti. Willie Wallace and Stevie Chalmers had the ability to drop deep and Bobby Lennox continually switched wings.

'Celtic got the neutral fans on their side with their flair. They played with such skill and commitment to going forward. They seemed to be strong in all departments, especially in centre midfield where they had Bobby Murdoch and Bertie Auld, of course. These two guys really complemented each other. Bobby was up and down, from penalty box to penalty box – a real dynamo. He was a great passer of the ball with either foot. Bertie could put his foot on the ball when the pace needed to be slowed down. He had a great footballing brain.

'I was also amazed at how far forward the fullbacks were against the Italians. They were popping up on the edge of the penalty box all the time. I remember Tommy Gemmell, in particular, having a helluva shot and Sarti making a tremendous save from his volley in the first half. It was a real screamer but the keeper got down to his left to push it away.'

Brady, a player of exquisite footballing ability who spent two years at Inter Milan as a player and just over two years at Celtic as manager from 1991 to 1993, could hardly believe what was unfolding in front of his eyes as he watched the action. 'I think goalkeeper Ronnie Simpson showed how vigilant he was inasmuch as Celtic were pushing up in the search for the equaliser and were always open at the back and vulnerable to one long ball that could present danger. That's precisely what happened when a defender thumped one straight down the middle from just inside his own box. Ronnie raced out of his area and gave everyone heart failure when he back-heeled the ball to John Clark with an Inter Milan player breathing down his neck. It was an unbelievable bit of skill and, I suppose, in a way, epitomised the spirit of the Celtic side that day.

'There was to be no goal for Celtic in that first half, of course, but I believe Jock Stein would have told his players to carry on doing what they were doing. "You've got Inter Milan on the rack," he would have said. I think he might have encouraged more shots from outside the box because it was becoming increasingly more difficult to get in behind the Inter Milan defence. Several times it looked as though Celtic would score, only for Sarti to keep them out. He made some truly stupendous saves that day and none more so than his one-handed save after the ball had been deflected past him from a shot by Tommy Gemmell. Somehow he got back to stop the ball right on the line. Celtic claimed a goal but it was a truly superb save.

'The second half was more or less played in Inter's half which was quite amazing when you consider their reputation for counter-attacking. Obviously, it was something they were very good at because they played that way week in, week out. They got plenty of practice. Mazzola and Domenghini were especially dangerous going forward. But the Celtic players simply never allowed them to get out. The patience in Celtic's play in that game was something to be admired. They never got panicky because they were a goal down. They never got carried away. The unrelenting spirit throughout the team, as I have said, was magnificent.

'They kept passing away, coming forward and probing, looking for openings. And, in fact, it was good possession football that led to the equaliser. Again both fullbacks were well forward with Jim Craig laying the ball back for Tommy Gemmell and he just buried it past Sarti. There was no way the goalkeeper was going to keep that effort out of his net. It was interesting to see how many heads went down among the ranks of the Inter Milan players when they went forward to restart the game. They knew it was going to be very, very difficult to stem the tide with twenty-seven minutes still to go. I think they knew then that the game was up.

'There was a move shortly after the equaliser when Tommy Gemmell got down the left again and his ball inside eventually broke in front of Bobby Murdoch about twenty-five yards from goal. He demonstrated the awesome shooting power he possessed in both feet when he hit it first time with his so-called weaker left foot and Sarti was forced to make another miraculous save. Later in the second half, we saw a cross from far out on the left by Tommy Gemmell. I hope I am not doing Tommy an injustice by saying it was a cross – he might say he was trying for goal – and Sarti made one of his few mistakes when he lost the flight of the ball. He misjudged it completely but it hit the bar when it could so easily have dropped behind him.

'One of the most impressive things for me in that performance was the technique each and every player had. They were of a very high quality. I can remember watching a lot of football back then – it was like a drug to me as I was growing up. I watched a lot of Manchester United and Tottenham Hotspur on the television. I used to marvel at players such as George Best, Bobby Charlton, Denis Law, Pat Crerand, Jimmy Greaves, Pat Jennings and so on. The BBC used to show a lot of English football but then along came this Celtic team and suddenly we were all Celtic fans!

'Few teams had the technique that Celtic possessed right throughout the side. This was undoubtedly a conscious decision by Jock Stein to get each and every one of his players to perform at a certain level. I still believe Celtic should have been ahead even before Stevie Chalmers scored the winner. They were denied a legitimate claim for a penalty kick, as far as I am concerned. I remember it vividly. Tommy Gemmell got the ball across and Sarti and his defender got in a terrible mix-up and the ball broke to Willie Wallace. He was just about to knock it into the empty net when the goalkeeper wrapped his arms around one of his legs and quite deliberately pulled him down. No one could believe the referee didn't immediately point to the spot.

'Well, the second goal just had to come, hadn't it? Without going overboard, it would have been a tragedy if Celtic hadn't won. I have never seen a team dominate a match so much. It could have been 5–1 or 6–1 at the end and no one could have complained. However, with about five or so minutes to go, it was Tommy Gemmell once more getting down the left and again showing his wonderful ability at taking on players. He pushed the ball inside for Bobby Murdoch and he let fly. Stevie Chalmers was right in line with the effort and he guided it in with his instep from close range. The Italians actually appealed for offside, as you might expect, but film showed Stevie was well on.

'Justice was done. It was a victory for the good guys. It was a victory for football. Everything that Inter Milan stood for was wrong. It was wrong for them to deny their exceptionally skilful players such as Mazzola, Suárez and Jair the opportunity to express themselves in games. However, when they got a goal ahead, they fell back into deep defence and put up the shutters. It was all so negative.

'Helenio Herrera versus Jock Stein was an intriguing contest on a coaching level. Thankfully, Jock's philosophy won the day. Celtic really stopped the domination of European football by these stifling, frustrating, unattractive and unimaginative tactics. They did Europe a real favour in Lisbon. They put the smile back on the face of football.'

3

BILLY McNEILL

Stirling Albion's Jim Kerray gave me a harder time at Celtic Park in November 1966 than Inter Milan's Sandro Mazzola at the Estadio Nacionale in May 1967. Jim who? Well may you ask. I hope Big Jim doesn't mind me making this observation but he was a journeyman centre forward playing in a fairly average side. We all know who Sandro is, though, don't we? A year before we faced Inter Milan in Lisbon, Mazzola had played for the Italian World Cup side in England. Three years after Lisbon, he would lead the attack in the World Cup Final against those wonderful Brazilians in Mexico.

Jim? I can't recall him ever being mentioned for a possible call-up for his country. However, what I do remember is an evening in Glasgow six months before we played in the European Cup Final and Stirling Albion, who always seemed to spend their time battling relegation when they were in the top division, stuck three past Ronnie Simpson in a league match. If my memory serves correctly, Kerray got two that night. As he was my direct opponent, I couldn't have been too satisfied with my own performance. Mind you, we scored seven at the other end to win the match but Stirling Albion and Kerray had let us know we were in a contest. In fact, so much so that I missed our next league game, a 1–1 draw with St Mirren, through injury – the only league encounter I sat out that season.

I mention Big Jim simply because he gave me such a difficult ninety minutes that Wednesday night. Now I look back at Lisbon and I can honestly say that was the easiest match of the entire season. I really mean that. John Clark and I were rarely under any pressure because the other guys in the middle and up front were doing their jobs so well. My biggest problem that day was whether to pass it out of defence to Bobby Murdoch or Bertie Auld. I would gather the ball and suddenly there was a shout in unison, 'Give it here, big man!' I would look up and there was Bobby and Bertie urging me to pass the ball to them and let them get on with it. If only all games had been such a cakewalk – I could still have been playing today!

We discovered fairly swiftly on our travels that reputations meant little or nothing in this game. Some of the biggest names, the so-called superstars of their era, often disappointed. But guys such as Jim Kerray were honest, hard-working pros who went about their job with phenomenal enthusiasm and genuine determination. I remember Dunfermline scoring four and three against us that season. Hibs also netted three. Strangely, we won all three of those games – 5–4 at East End Park, 6–3 in a League Cup tie at Celtic Park and 5–3 at Easter Road. In the league game at East End Park, where a certain Alex Ferguson got right in about it for the Fifers, they were leading 4–2 at one stage. Other teams would have folded, but we didn't possess such a thing as a white flag. We kept plugging away and claimed the three goals that gave us the points. We were prepared to go through any pain barrier for the cause of the club.

That quality was fairly evident in the journey through Europe. There were a few occasions when you felt you were right up against it, that the pressure was really on, but, at other times, you knew you had arrived at the level you craved. Let's talk about the Palacio Hotel in Estoril, for a start. Situated in the beautiful little coastal town to the west of Lisbon, it was to be our HQ. It was perfect as we prepared for the European Cup Final. Let me tell you, it was breathtaking. Five-star? It was more than that – out of this world. I, for one, had never witnessed such opulence. What a place and it made us feel big-time. The club hadn't stinted on lavishing big money on the place where we would be spending the next two days before the biggest match in our history. It was luxury from start to finish and it made you feel important. It all seemed so right.

What made us feel even more welcome was the sight of large lanterns in their expansive gardens that just happened to be painted green and white. When they were lit up at night it made you feel right at home. It looked as though the complete jigsaw had been put together with great care. You know, I went back there a few years ago and the lanterns have now gone. I wonder if they just put them up for us! We relaxed, played cards, read books and generally just took it easy. There was a magnificent pool at the hotel and Big Jock would only allow us thirty minutes to go for a swim. He would point to the sun in the clear blue sky and say, 'That is your enemy, remember that. It will sap your energy. Be careful what you do.'

Before I go any further, may I state here and now, once and for all, that I was not, repeat not, Jock Stein's blue-eyed boy. I know a lot of folk have said he never gave me a rollicking because I was the captain and he wouldn't belittle me in anyone else's presence. Fair enough but I can only say, 'Why on earth would you have a go at someone who was always completely blameless and never ever made a solitary mistake in any of the games in which he played?' Seriously, though, I would like to think Jock and I had a special relationship. I would hope it was the same for everyone at the club at the time.

However, I have to say that there were occasions when he might point out a thing or two to me. I never took it personally, believe me. Everything he did was for the good of Celtic and I was well up for that. I found him most helpful. I never forgot the fact that he had also played in my position at centre half for many more years than I had and had a lot more experience. So, if he had a little gem of knowledge to impart that would make me a better player, then I was more than willing to listen.

Big Jock, of course, was blessed with more than his fair share of common sense. You know what they say about common sense, don't you? It's not that common! But The Boss had the ability never to complicate things. He saw football as essentially a simple game. He had the wonderful knack, though, of finding someone's strengths. He could look at a player and have the ability to immediately see where they could improve their game. It could be simple little things. Bobby Lennox was an outside left when Big Jock arrived. Lemon wasn't bad on the flank but just take a look at what he contributed to the club when he came inside. What an improvement! His pace was breathtaking and I honestly wonder just how many legitimate goals the Wee Man scored that we never got because of dodgy offside calls. He finished his career at Celtic with 273 goals from 571 games – an absolutely fantastic return. How many were wiped out by bad refereeing decisions because of Bobby's speed off the mark? Probably another 100! I can think of one referee, who has since passed on so I won't bother naming him, who must have chalked off about fifty himself!

Bobby Murdoch, too, benefited from the arrival of Big Jock. Bobby started off as an old-fashioned inside right but The Boss thought he would be better off at wing-half. He made the switch against other people's perceptions of the player and, once again, was justified in his decision-making.

Big Jock also had a presence about him that told you he was the boss. He may be thought of as being a strict disciplinarian – and certainly he wouldn't tolerate any nonsense – but he could have a laugh and joke with the lads too. He was once asked in one of the many European hotels we stayed in at the time if he was Stein. Because of the accent – I think it was Spanish – it came out something like 'Steeyin'. Jock, quick as a flash, replied, 'No, I'm leaving on Thursday!' He was in no way aloof – he was far too down-to-earth for that – but you always knew he was the gaffer.

He never asked anyone to do anything he believed was outwith their capabilities. That may sound fairly obvious but I still watch football today and see players in positions that clearly don't suit them. You've got wingers whose defensive knowledge is negligible playing at fullback. You've got guys who might be better in defence playing up front and leading attacks. Jock would take a player aside and say something like, 'Look, I don't expect you to be top goalscorer at the club so just you leave the shooting to the others.' Or he might point out, 'I don't want to see you taking on an opponent. Think about passing quickly and accurately and don't bother running with the ball – that's a job for someone else.' Another manager might have taken route one and said, 'You're shooting is bloody awful.' or 'You dribble like an old lady.' I'm not sure that would get the best out of a player. Jock's approach was simple, but so effective.

All the players were treated alike by The Boss. There were no superstars although, I suppose, Wee Jinky could have walked into the first team of just about any side on the planet. But he, too, realised he would get a lacing if Big Jock thought he wasn't pulling his weight. Jinky, of course, was special but, if he turned up late for training in the morning, he could expect to be sent home and told to return and train on his own in the afternoon. It happened a few times, as I recall!

I never saw Jimmy McGrory in a tracksuit. Of course, he was the boss before Big Jock arrived but he was always immaculately turned out – suit, shirt and tie – with that famous pipe sitting at a jaunty angle at the corner of his mouth. Jock arrived, though, and the next thing he was out there at Barrowfield with the training gear on and making a big difference in all our thinking. He would give you some leeway during training but, if he thought we were just fooling around, he would step in and bark, 'Right, that's enough of that. Get on with your work.'

Footballers are always at their happiest when they are working with the ball. Lapping tracks can get a bit monotonous and Big Jock knew that. Our practice games could get a bit competitive back then. Remember, we all shared a winning mentality and that was obvious too in these so-called bounce games. Big Jock would be watching everything, making certain some things didn't get out of hand. Wee Jinky, for instance, loved shoving the ball through your legs and running round you. It's something you can get a bit fed up with when it happens time and time again. 'Jinky! Behave!' would come the bellow from the sidelines. If two players clashed – and it would surprise you just how often that actually happened – The Boss would wait and see if they were calming down. Training with a competitive edge is fine but not if it gets out of hand and there's the risk that someone might pick up an injury. If the two guys didn't get their act together, then we'd all find ourselves lapping the track again. Big Jock would always get his message across, one way or another!

I have to say I had all the time in the world for the Big Man. I took it as an enormous compliment when someone said I was the centre half Jock Stein wanted to be during his playing days. I don't think he scored too many goals but he always encouraged me to go forward for set pieces. 'Get up there, Billy,' he would shout from the dugout. 'It's time you used that head of yours.'

He was also the master of psychology and he proved that once more before kick-off in Lisbon. He and the rest of the backroom staff, including substitute goalkeeper John Fallon, came on to the pitch after we had been led out. Celtic were listed as the home team for the game and Jock and Co., naturally enough, headed for the bench on the touchline allocated to the home side. Jock was confronted by Inter Milan manager Helenio Herrera and his backroom boys who were already seated and waiting for kick-off. Big Jock was having none of that. If the wily Herrera had thought he was putting one over on our gaffer he was swiftly put right. 'You're in the wrong place,' said Jock. Herrera understood all right but he was simply looking at our manager with a typical Latin quizzical expression. Shoulders were shrugging this way and that, hands were splayed out and, of course, the Inter Milan boss was innocence personified. Jock refused to back down. He would be sitting on that bench or there were going to big problems for the officials before the start of the 1967 European Cup Final.

Jock called over my stand-in, centre half John Cushley, to have a word with the Inter staff. John wasn't stripped for the game, of course, because only the goalkeeper could be used as a substitute but it is no exaggeration to say Big John wasn't unlike the Incredible Hulk without the green dye. If he hadn't been a fine footballer he would have been in great demand as a minder for some sort of celebrity. He must have made his considerable presence felt. After a few words, Herrera and his entourage decided it would be wise to beat a hasty retreat and walk the considerable distance to the away bench. Now, all this was going on while we were out on the pitch warming up. We were aware that something was happening at the side of the pitch and we witnessed Big Jock making his stance. It was very interesting to see the Inter Milan bench capitulate and move on. They didn't look a happy bunch as they picked up their kitbags and were forced to shift. One up to us before a ball had been kicked!

Actually, I was quite surprised when I was looking back on that extraordinary year in 1967 to see how many goals I scored. Frankly, I was just a little bit disappointed to note how many I claimed in the league games. Not one. Zero. Zilch. However, I did get one in that European Cup run and, even if I do say so myself, I couldn't have timed it better. I know the manager and all the lads rated Vojvodina Novi Sad as by far the best team we'd met that year, including Inter Milan in the final. The Yugoslavs were superb technically but were also fairly adept in what you might call the not-so-finer points in the game. There were also some memorable mind games going on off the pitch between The Boss and their manager Vujadin Boskov, who went on to coach at some of the biggest teams in Europe, including Real Madrid, two years after playing us.

Big Jock clearly wasn't impressed by Boskov's pre-match prediction. The Slav boss stated quite clearly and emphatically that he believed Vojvodina would win by 'at least two goals'. 'Oh, really? We'll see about that,' said Jock. When they won by a solitary effort from Stanic, Boskov came out again and declared he hadn't been too impressed by Celtic and his team would win again in Glasgow. Now if Boskov was trying to get Jock fired up for the return, he couldn't have done a better job. The Big Man was well prepared when they flew into Glasgow. 'We'll be ready for them,' he said. He went public, too, with the Yugoslav press and went on record as saying, 'Vojvodina are a very good team but we are better and we will win in Glasgow.' It was sheer bravado because we all realised just how difficult the Slavs would be in the return leg.

Boskov and his players turned up at Celtic Park the night before the game and they wanted a work-out on the pitch under the floodlights. It was normal practice for teams to go through this routine as it made a lot of sense for them to get a feel for the conditions they would encounter twenty-four hours later. They would want the training to start at roughly around the same time as the kick-off, giving them the opportunity to see how light or dark it might be at such-and-such a time. Boskov, then, wasn't best pleased when Big Jock gave him the news they wouldn't be placing a foot on the pitch at Celtic Park. 'Sorry, there's been too much rain recently,' Jock informed them. 'We can't take the chance of the pitch cutting up.' He did have a point but Boskov was far from convinced. He made all sorts of protestations – he would take it up with the Celtic chairman, he threatened. Jock waved it away in his usual fashion. 'You can train at Barrowfield and I'll make sure the lights are switched on. Off you go.'

To say the Slavs were not amused would be putting it rather mildly. They were fizzing but, at least, Boskov and his boys got the drift that Jock Stein was, indeed, the man in charge at Celtic. As far as football matters went, there was no higher power. Vojvodina, who had beaten a strong Atletico Madrid team to reach the quarter-finals, were out to make sure they would have the last word at Celtic Park during the game. Like I say, they were an extremely talented and resilient outfit and they weren't slow to hand out a wee bit of punishment every now and then.

We had to endure close to an hour of frustration before we got our own back when Stevie Chalmers made it 1–1 on aggregate after a typical lung-bursting run and cross from the left by Tommy Gemmell. As a matter of fact, I was delighted for Big Tommy because he had taken most of the blame for our 1–0 defeat in Novi Sad in the first leg. He was short with a pass back and the ball ended up behind Ronnie Simpson. Tommy looked crestfallen. He was always a chirpy character and we can only thank the Good Lord that there wasn't such a thing as karaoke back then. Tommy, of course, looked a bit like an American comedy actor who was all the rage at the time and was always first to the microphone to belt out a Sinatra number or something from the charts. I remember we were in Miami on one of our American trips in the sixties and we were in this place where Tommy decided to go into one of his routines. I heard this female voice from behind me blurt out, 'Gee, is that Danny Kaye? He's really good!'

So it was smashing to see the big chap all smiles again after he helped set up that all-important leveller. I've always been a great believer that the best time to get a winning goal is as near to that final whistle as possible. There is no way back for teams at that point. Look at the 1974 World Cup Final between West Germany and Holland in Munich, for instance. The Dutch got a penalty kick inside a minute without a single player from the host nation getting a touch of the ball. The Dutch lads stroked it around until the magnificent Johan Cruyff produced a marvellous burst of speed to get into the box and he was hauled down. And, no, it wasn't Berti Vogts who was the offender – it was, in fact, Uli Hoeness. Mind you, the Tartan Army will probably still blame Berti anyway. Johan Neeskens duly scored and it was a perfect start for Holland but it also gave West Germany eighty-nine minutes to get back into the game in front of their own fans. That's exactly what they did, of course, and, at the end of the day, it was their name on the trophy after a 2–1 comeback victory.

I have been told that the referee blew for time-up two seconds after the restart following my goal against Vojvodina – now that is a late, late goal. I'll always recall Big Jock waving us all up for one last assault on Ilija Pantelic's goal. In those days, there was no extra time. The game would have gone to a replay at a neutral ground – Rotterdam, I believe. Charlie Gallagher, who had a sublime touch, raced over to the right wing to take the corner. Actually, I think Charlie was about to take a short one but a Slav defender raced to cut it off and Charlie changed his mind. Thank God!

Charlie was left with no option but to put the ball into the mix. There was the usual barging and jostling as I made my way forward. The Slavs had marked me very well at set pieces and I hadn't really had a sniff at goal. On this occasion, though, the timing was just absolutely spot-on. Charlie swung it in, I kept my run going, the ball hung in the air, I got a good leap and made superb contact and the next thing I saw was the effort soaring high into the net. Pantelic had strayed a bit from his line and they had a defender on the goal line who did a fair impersonation of a goalkeeper as he leapt up with his left arm to try to keep the ball out. He was wasting his time – that was a goal all the way as soon as it came off my napper.

Actually, I scored quite a few goals after getting great service from Charlie at dead-ball situations. He was supremely accurate with corner kicks, in particular, and could vary his ball into the box. Sometimes he would float one in with precision and then he would follow that by shelling one in at pace. It was difficult for defenders to anticipate what was coming next. We didn't have any pre-arranged signals or anything like that. I would just trot forward and do my level best to get something on it when Charlie sent it in.

Remember, it was good old Charlie who sent over the corner kick – this time from the left – two years earlier when I scored the winning goal in the Scottish Cup Final against Dunfermline at Hampden. So, we had a good thing going but, ironically, I don't think Charlie would have been playing that night if it hadn't been for an injury to Bertie Auld. Normally, Big Jock would go with Bobby Murdoch and Bertie in the main midfield roles and overlook Charlie. However, he was a fine footballer and his delivery that night couldn't have been better.

Vojvodina went crazy when the referee awarded the goal. They were convinced I had fouled Pantelic. I can hold my hands up all these years down the line and tell the world I didn't even touch their goalkeeper. However, you might ask Stevie Chalmers if he had blocked their keeper! He may have taken a half-yard step in front of the big goalie when he was leaving his goal line in an effort to cut out the cross. So what? It was all part of the game back then as it still is today. Believe me, the Slavs weren't slow in getting in front of me any time I came forward. But, thanks to Charlie's dead-ball accuracy, there was nothing anyone could do to prevent me from making contact on that occasion and managing to do some damage.

I knew it was late in the game but, honestly, I had no idea that it was quite as late as that. As I ran back to take my position in the heart of the defence, I shouted over at John Clark, 'Keep concentrating, Luggy. We're not going to lose a goal now.' Luggy just looked at me and said, 'What are you talking about, big man? The game's finished. It's over and we're through.' Seconds later it was, indeed, well and truly over and our great adventure was still on track. I remember the Vojvodina players cracking up as they kicked off and the ref blew for time-up. Actually, one of their own players raced into the melee and started shoving his team-mates all over the place to get them to calm down. He was a big lad too and, thankfully, they did as they were told. It could have been very interesting going up the tunnel that evening. That tunnel could tell a tale or two, that's for sure. These were the days before TV cameras seemed to spring up everywhere and sometimes there could be some 'sorting out' done in the darkness of that tight, little area that led to the dressing rooms. Not that I ever got involved myself, you understand!

Funnily enough, our next game afterwards was a Scottish Cup tie against Queen's Park at Celtic Park and our fans rolled up in their thousands, still on a high from our midweek success and the news we would play Dukla Prague in the semi-finals. As I recall, Sean Connery, James Bond himself, turned up too and had his photograph taken with the Celtic team before the game. The crowd was still filtering in when Tommy Gemmell scored an own goal for the Queen's in the first minute! He turned the ball behind a startled Ronnie Simpson and we all looked at each other. Surely, there wasn't another Scottish Cup shock on the cards for, remember, Rangers, then the holders, had gone out at the first hurdle, beaten 1–0 by little Berwick Rangers a couple of months earlier. We recovered our composure quickly, though, and I believe it was Big Tommy who equalised before we went on to win 5–3. But it was a game that hammered into us the fact that, if we were to do anything in football, concentration would have to be our watchword.

We had that in abundance in Lisbon, you better believe it. It may seem a strange observation to make but Inter Milan scoring so early with that penalty kick was one of the best things that could have happened to us. It was their natural style to try to hold on to anything they had. They had a goal to protect and they seemed quite content to filter into their own half and do their best to keep us out. Although I was a central defender, it was not the way I was brought up to play football. It certainly wasn't the Celtic way. Our supporters wouldn't have tolerated that and, in any case, we all knew the fans deserved better. I said it then, I'll say it now and I'll say it again – those guys on the terracings were absolutely brilliant. They were our twelfth man and we never, ever took them for granted.

We were invited to take the game to the Italians and it was an invite we so readily accepted. We really should have been in front by half-time but their goalkeeper, Giuliano Sarti, was quite outstanding. When we got in at the interval, we couldn't wait to get out to restart the second half. The penalty-kick decision really inspired us. We were all rattling on about the injustice of it and there was no way we were going to be beaten by a dodgy refereeing decision. Cairney – as Jim Craig was known – won't thank me for this but, having watched the incident several thousand times, I now think the referee called it right. Back then, though, we were all united in believing the match official had done us no favours whatsoever. I know Cairney will still argue that it was never a spot kick but let's just say it certainly acted as a catalyst for us to get out there and turn them over.

I recall it was actually quite calm in our dressing room at half-time. There were no histrionics and, of course, we didn't have any prima donnas in our team. Big Jock simply repeated, 'Keep doing what you are doing and we'll be OK.' He did make one telling observation, though, when he asked our wide men to think about pulling the ball back closer to the edge of the penalty box because Inter were crowding into the six-yard area as they tried to protect their goalkeeper. When you look again at our first goal, you'll see how good that advice was. Cairney was calmness personified when he came racing into the box on to Bobby Murdoch's pass. His cutback for Tommy Gemmell was just right and Tommy simply belted one of his specials high into the net. Sarti had no chance. Eleven Sartis would have had no chance! We were on course and nothing could stop us taking our place in history.

Before that game, the European Cup was a trophy that belonged to other teams – to glamorous sides from other parts of Europe. Only Real Madrid – six times – Benfica – twice – Inter Milan – twice – and AC Milan – once – had won the most prestigious prize European football had to offer. British football merely had its nose pressed up against the window, wanting to get in but being completely ignored. Celtic, in Lisbon, opened the door. We proved it was possible. The mystique was stripped away. The barrier had been broken. And, by God, did it feel good!

Stevie Chalmers duly knocked in the winner with about five minutes to go and Inter Milan were out of it. They were a beaten team. If, by some chance, they had equalised, then the game would have gone to thirty minutes of extra time. Believe me, those guys didn't want to endure another half hour of what they had already been through.

Another injustice – and, this time, the perception is 100 per cent accurate – that really motivated us in Lisbon was the fact that we had gone so close to playing in the European Cup-Winners' Cup Final the previous season. We had faced Liverpool in the semi-final and beaten them 1–0 going on 4–0 or 5–0 in the first leg at Celtic Park. Bobby Lennox was our scorer that night with a typical whiplash close-range effort that left their keeper, the Scot Tommy Lawrence, helpless. We pummelled them that evening but just couldn't add to our tally. A one-goal advantage seemed scant reward for the amount of possession and effort and endeavour we had put in.

We went to Anfield for the return match and I can tell you we were not one bit afraid. We reasoned we had played them off the park in Glasgow and we could do something similar on their own patch. Everything seemed to be going OK until they were awarded a free kick on the hour mark about thirty yards out. As I recall, it was a filthy night on Merseyside and Tommy Smith stepped up to take it. He fired the ball goal-wards and, unfortunately for Ronnie Simpson, it took a wicked bounce off the muddy pitch. Ronnie looked as though he had it covered but it actually seemed to pick up momentum as it hit the turf in front of him and flashed low into the corner of the net. We couldn't believe it. We were level.

It got worse five minutes later when Geoff Strong got up really well to power an unstoppable header away from Ronnie. There was nothing flukey about that effort – I would have happily claimed it as one of my own. However, the real controversy was just around the corner. Near the end, Bobby Lennox turned the ball wide of Tommy Lawrence and left back Gerry Byrne on the goal line and into the net – a goal, surely? Alas, not according to the man who mattered, the Belgian referee Josef Hannet. He ruled it out for offside which was a fairly strange decision when you consider they had a fullback behind their goalkeeper. In actual fact, there is absolutely no way the goal shouldn't have counted. We didn't get any consolation much later when Hannet admitted, after watching reruns of the incident, that he had, in fact, got it wrong. Thanks, ref – that was just another for the growing Bobby Lennox collection of injustices!

Yes, we were furious. So, too, unfortunately were our fans and a few bottles were thrown. I would never condone such actions but their frustrations were understandable. They had just seen a perfectly legitimate goal ruled out and their team was out of Europe. What made it even more galling was the fact that the European Cup-Winners' Cup Final was due to be played at Hampden Park that season. Can you imagine the scenes if we had played in that game? Dear old Hampden would have been rocking to its foundations. As it turned out, Liverpool took our place and I think they must have used up all their luck against us in the previous games. They lost 2–1 in extra time to the West Germans of Borussia Dortmund and, ironically, the winning goal came from Ron Yeats, who was one of my main challengers for the centre-half slot in the Scottish international team at the time. I remember a Borussia Dortmund player, a guy called Reinhard Libuda, lobbing Tommy Lawrence and the ball hitting the crossbar. Ron Yeats, running back in an effort to clear off the line, couldn't get out of the way of the rebound and it came down, struck him and bounced over the line. Trophies are won and lost in such bizarre moments.

So, a year later, when we turned up at Lisbon, we were a team on a mission. That European Cup had our name on it, we were certain of that. But, as I said right at the start, John Clark and I couldn't have had a more comfortable ninety minutes. Inter simply had no answer to our pulsating, attacking play. There is absolutely no way they would have encountered anything like that in their league matches back in Italy. Inter Milan, and we should remember they also won the World Club Championship in 1964 and 1965, were top dogs – hugely successful – and, therefore, it made sense to some coaches to copy their methods. However, we may have changed a few mindsets after our performance in Lisbon, eh?

To my mind, the greatest thing about our European Cup victory is that we did it in the Celtic manner. We always wanted to play with flair, adventure and style. We were determined for people to remember us for our attacking philosophy. I would like to think we managed that in Lisbon. It was a breakthrough for British football. It was marvellous for Scottish football. However, the main thing for everyone connected with the club – the manager, his assistants, the players and tea ladies – was that it was truly wonderful for Celtic Football Club.

4

JIM CRAIG

I fully admit to making life difficult for Jock Stein. I am also sure he found me a bit awkward. Either way, it made sure life as a Lisbon Lion was never dull.

Right from the start, Big Jock could never get his head round the fact that I had a job outside football. I was a qualified dentist – surely the only one who has ever won a European Cup medal! – and he wasn't prepared to accept that I could concentrate 100 per cent on being a footballer while I had outside interests. I told him many times that I could, indeed, do both jobs equally well but he was never convinced. It would be fair to say we had a few run-ins during our time together.

Don't get me wrong – Big Jock was a very talented man. An exceptional, ground-breaking manager. Football to him was everything and, if he thought you weren't eating, drinking, sleeping football too, he believed there was something wrong with you. You got the impression you should park your brain at the door outside Celtic Park and pick it up on your way home. I had other interests but I would defy anyone to say I wasn't committed to the Celtic cause. When I pulled on that green-and-white shirt, I was as ready to go as anyone. Jock and I had a problem, though, because of our differing attitudes. I'll admit I could be deliberately destructive. I had an inquisitive mind – still do, I hope – and I would ask questions. This was something that was new to Big Jock and something he didn't embrace with any enthusiasm, believe me.

I was the guy who would query this, that and the next thing while most of my colleagues bit their tongues and kept quiet. He would point to the tactics board and go through a lengthy routine. Some of us took it in and others didn't. How could you tell Jimmy Johnstone how to play? I would ask a few questions and make a point or two and Big Jock plainly didn't welcome such intrusions. He was a meticulous planner – probably the first of his kind. He would go through our line-up and tell us exactly what he expected us to do. He rarely dwelt on the opposition. He concentrated mainly on us and what we should do on the day. I thought it was only right and proper that I should ask a question or two just to clear up any possible misunderstanding. If Plan A wasn't working, what was Plan B? Jock didn't like that. He was a big fan of the master–servant relationship and, naturally, I didn't agree with that mode of thinking. For a start, I was halfway through my dental studies and that's a job where, quite literally, you have to think on your feet. You have to make decisions very quickly. You are very much your own man. So, I have to admit, when I turned up at Celtic Park and found I didn't have a mind of my own, it was extremely difficult to accept. Big Jock would wave you away with that big left hand of his. 'Oh, just do as you're told,' he would say. OK, he was the boss but that didn't mean I had to touch my forelock every time I spoke to him. In fact, I was never a massive admirer of authority figures. I'm afraid that still applies!

But I was a seeker of knowledge and I don't think that is a bad thing. I wanted to know what was going on inside Big Jock's head. I'll also admit that I did sometimes go over the score and I'm sure he knew it. For instance, there was one particular day when The Boss was going through his usual routine before a big match. We were all taking it in, listening to his instructions, but I noticed one individual who looked as though he couldn't give a stuff. When Big Jock was pointing to the blackboard, this guy was looking at the ceiling, clearly totally unimpressed by proceedings. I won't name the player but, suffice to say, he was never a great believer in tactics and such like. He played totally off the cuff and that's what made him such an entrancing, exciting individual. Football, to him, was completely instinctive.

You could say he was a free spirit. I guess you'll have worked out by now who I am talking about!

At the end of this talk-in, I had, as usual, a few questions to put to the manager. Again I was waved away. 'Just do as you're told', I was instructed for the umpteenth time. However, as we were filtering out of the room, Big Jock got a hold of me and pulled me back in. 'OK, what is it now?' he asked. I told him I knew what I was supposed to do but wondered if everyone else was taking in what he was saying. He knew what I was talking about OK and he just laughed. I reckon he, too, realised there was little you could do with this player. You could hammer all sorts of instructions into him but he would just go out and do his own thing anyway. And he did it very well too, I hasten to add.

Big Jock, as everyone knows, was a huge admirer of attacking football. He always believed in entertaining the punters. We could be three goals ahead but he would demand four. If we were four in front, he would look for five. Ironically, as a player, he was a centre half who rarely ventured across the halfway line. As a manager, though, he liked nothing better than to have his team playing with flair and adventure. I suppose his philosophy was that attack was the best form of defence. No team was going to score from their own half, after all. However, Big Jock wasn't against letting the opposition know you were on the field. If he thought you were up against a particularly dangerous individual, he actively encouraged you to 'lean on him'. That was a euphemism for giving him a wee dunt just to see how his heart stood up to it. You would be amazed at the amount of players who disappeared off the radar after a fairly solid challenge. I don't think you could ever categorise me as a dirty player but I can now admit that I could put it about with the best of them.

Not that long ago, they were showing the Jimmy Johnstone film at a theatre in Glasgow when yours truly appeared on the screen with what looked like a fairly vicious tackle on an opponent. Well, I almost separated the guy's torso from his legs and there was a sharp intake of breath among the audience. To say I was just a tad startled would be putting it mildly. I could hardly believe I was the guy up on that film who had made such a crude challenge. Yes, I was a bit embarrassed but anyone who watched me in action back then would say that wasn't typical of Jim Craig. I hope so, anyway.

People have often approached me to say they thought I was the quiet man in the Lisbon Lions line-up and I would accept that as a fair assumption. I'm not a particularly noisy character and, in a busy dressing room, it was never easy to get a word in edgeways anyway – especially with guys such as Tommy Gemmell and Bertie Auld around. I preferred to do my talking when you could actually be heard although, as I have already stated, Big Jock probably would have been a lot happier if I had kept my trap shut from day one!

I didn't go overboard in my protestations when the referee awarded Inter Milan a penalty kick in Lisbon after my tackle on Renato Cappellini. What would have been the point? The referee was hardly likely to change his decision once he had pointed to the spot. Let me say here and now, though, that it was never a penalty kick – absolutely no way. It doesn't matter now, of course, but I still hold the belief that the referee got it totally wrong. Folk have said I tackled with the wrong foot. Others have said I should have tried to play the Inter Milan centre forward offside. Everyone is welcome to his or her opinion but, forty years down the road, I am as convinced as I was back then that it was no penalty kick. Cappellini was a big bloke but he went down like a sack of tatties when I challenged him. Of course, he was looking for a penalty and the referee didn't disappoint him. He couldn't wait to point to the spot. I've lost count of the times I have replayed that incident in my mind and I always come to the same conclusion – the referee made a bad call.

You could say that I helped to make a game of it! How would the remaining eighty-three minutes have panned out if Inter

Milan hadn't got that penalty kick? Who knows? But it certainly handed the impetus to Celtic and we knew exactly what we had to do in an effort to turn things around. I think we achieved our goal fairly well. One interested spectator that day at the Estadio Nacionale was my dad. He was a manager in the furniture department of Glasgow South's Co-op and, as a result of this, he worked on a Saturday and could only get to midweek matches. However, he really floored me by saying that he did not want to go to Lisbon. I couldn't believe my ears and asked him why. He was quite honest about it. He said he thought Inter Milan would be too strong for us and he did not want to go over there and see us being beaten. I accepted that but, just in case he changed his mind, I held a ticket for him and booked a seat on the plane. As the days passed, I worked hard on Dad but he only changed his mind at the last minute. However, I had the ticket and the seat all ready so off he went on the great adventure.

Dad couldn't have been too happy when I was involved in the penalty incident, that's for sure. I had been assured that Cappellini was, in fact, all left foot so, when he ran in on goal, I assumed that at some point he would want to put the ball to his stronger foot. I decided that I would block any attempt to do so but, when the challenge came, he went down rather like an ageing actor and I believe the referee was completely conned by it. A question I am often asked is, 'What does a player think about in a time like that?' Well, in my case, I can assure you that my thoughts were with my dad up in his seat. I had spent time persuading him to come over against his better judgement and now he had to sit through it all.

Dad told me afterwards, 'I didn't think it was a penalty kick, to be quite honest, because the Italian player wasn't going towards goal and I think he had overrun the ball. Probably, the referee was as nervous as the players and overreacted. What worried me more was that it might be the only goal of the game and my son would get the blame for the defeat. In retrospect, it probably helped a lot because the Italians just fell back into defence and Celtic were allowed to take control.'

Actually, I still laugh at the recollection of Big Jock at half-time. Of course, we were all disappointed to be 1–0 down despite bossing the first half after that goal. I wasn't too enamoured by the fact that I had been adjudged to have given away the penalty kick. Jock came over, threw an arm around me and said, 'Don't worry, Cairney, that was never a penalty. Never in a million years. Don't worry. Don't blame yourself. Put it behind you. Show them what you can do in the second half.'

At the end of the game, though, Big Jock sidled up to me and said, 'What on earth were you thinking about at the penalty? What a stupid challenge. You almost cost us the European Cup with that daft tackle.' Thanks, Boss! That was so typical of Big Jock, though. He knew the right buttons to push at the right time. That was part of his make-up and I suppose that's what made him so special. He could have taken me apart at half-time but that would hardly have done my morale or confidence any good. He waited until that silverware was heading for the Celtic Park trophy cabinet before he told me what he really thought. I still don't believe it was a penalty, though. And, at least, I had the satisfaction of laying on the equalising goal for Tommy Gemmell. In fact, if you are going to talk about penalties, can I mention the one we didn't get when their excellent goalkeeper Giuliano Sarti hauled down Willie Wallace in the second half? Sarti actually grabbed Wispy's leg and pulled him to the ground as he was about to roll the ball into a gaping and inviting net. It was like something out of WWF but, on this occasion, the match official, a certain Herr Kurt Tschenscher, was not impressed and waved play on. Yes, it was an injustice but it simply made us all the more determined to win that match. Nothing was going to prevent us – nothing and no one.

I was on £30 per week back then. I think I was the poorest paid player of the Lisbon Lions. The rest, I believed, were picking up £40 per week with Billy McNeill getting an extra £10 for being captain. That meant a difference of £20 between me and Big Billy and, believe me, that was one helluva differential. You know, I can't remember how I spent my £1,500 bonus for winning the European Cup. I know some of my colleagues bought cars, put down deposits on houses or went on luxurious holidays. Me? Can't remember but I do know I would have enjoyed spending it. If you are earning £30 per week then you are bound to go just a little bit crazy when you suddenly pick up something in the region of a year's wages. I was rich beyond my wildest dreams!

Getting to Lisbon, of course, was a wonderful journey. It was a huge learning curve and just one superb experience. You have to say we thoroughly merited our European triumph – just take a look at the sides we had to overcome on our way to the final. They were all top quality. Those were the days when you actually played the champions of their country. It really was the European Champions Cup. Nowadays you can get teams winning Europe's premier trophy when they aren't even the champions of their own nation – something odd there, I think.

We opened by playing FC Zurich and it would be fair to say Switzerland was a strong footballing nation at that point. For instance, the Swiss played in the World Cup Finals the previous year in England. Remember, too, there were only sixteen countries competing for the trophy back then, unlike today where there seems to be a cast of thousands, a real Cecil B. de Mille job with all the extras. Then we took on Nantes and France, too, had made it to the World Cup Finals in 1966. Then it was on to Vojvodina Novi Sad and they were by far the best team we faced in Europe that season. It tells you everything when you note they were champions of Yugoslavia when Partizan Belgrade had played against Real Madrid and lost narrowly 2–1 in the European Cup Final the previous year. Dukla Prague were the biggest team in Czechoslovakia and, of course, that country had played Brazil in the World Cup Final in Chile in 1962 and, like the others, had a strong footballing pedigree. These were also the days before the influx of so many foreign players plying their trade in different countries from their birthplace. So, how the nations performed on the international stage was fairly indicative of how healthy their club competition was at home. Playing teams from Switzerland, France, Yugoslavia, Czechoslovakia and then Italy underlines Celtic's achievement in 1967. It was no easy ride, take it from me. We earned everything we got.

We faced a lot of excellent individual players, too. The guy who gave me most bother was Vojvodina's Stanic, who got their goal in the first leg in Novi Sad. He was skilful and tricky but I remembered Big Jock's words – 'Lean on him and see if he has a heart the size of a pea.' So, dutifully, I 'leaned' on Stanic at one point. Lo and behold, he suddenly thought it was a better idea to go and play somewhere else on the field – problem solved. Vojvodina were a fabulous team, though. They played in a typical controlled Eastern European fashion and were superb at keeping possession. You can run for miles with the ball at your feet but it's not so easy when you are chasing around trying to get it back. That can be exhausting and the Slavs put a lot of emphasis on retaining possession. We may have lost that game 1–0 but we weren't disheartened. Simply put, we believed we could overturn their advantage in Glasgow. And so it proved – but we did leave it a bit late, didn't we?

I thought we played well that night and, unfortunately for yours truly, I was on the right touchline next to Big Jock in the dugout throughout a dramatic second half that was fraught with anxiety. All I could hear above the din of almost 70,000 fans was 'Cairney, do this' or 'Cairney, do that'. It wasn't easy playing right back when Big Jock was in full flow. I used to look round every now and again and shout, 'Why don't you have a go at Bobby or Wee Jinky?' Luckily for them, they were probably out of earshot and were spared the verbal volleys from the manager. Big Jock would also yell at you to pass on instructions.

Aye, right! I simply concentrated on my own game – that was enough to be going on with.

Looking back on that so special day in Lisbon, I have to chuckle at how different it was from the day I made my Celtic first-team debut. I remember it well. It was on 7 October 1965 against Dutch side Go Ahead Deventer in the European Cup-Winners' Cup at Celtic Park. Big Jock, as thoughtful as ever, had a habit of selecting games in which younger players could get a chance without too much pressure on them and he chose well with this one – Celtic were 6–0 ahead from the first leg in Holland! Bobby Lennox with a hat-trick, Jimmy Johnstone with two and a single from John Hughes had made certain Celtic would be in the next round. The evening before the home tie, I was told I would be playing. I was twenty-two years old at the time and still doing my dentistry studies while playing part-time. Excited? You can bet on it. I will always recall waiting for a bus in Argyle Street along with a bunch of Celtic supporters to take me to the east end of Glasgow. I was sitting among these guys and they were talking about who might be playing for Celtic that night. No one took a blind bit of notice of me. I was totally unknown. I felt like telling them I would be turning out at right back for their favourite team but they probably wouldn't have believed me. A Celtic player on a bus? Just an hour or so away from kick-off? Don't be daft!

However, I did indeed make my first appearance in those famous hoops and a single goal from Joe McBride gave us a rather emphatic 7–0 aggregate triumph. I would like to say I played my part in that victory! I must have impressed Big Jock – I was promptly put back in the reserves with Ian Young returning to the No. 2 berth for the next game, a 5–2 win over Hearts. However, I came back on 13 November in a 4–1 win over St Johnstone and played another thirteen first-team games after that. Big Jock might not have given it his blessing but I was coping well enough with combining my studies with my football. Actually, I might have missed out on Lisbon entirely because I wasn't involved in the opening four games against FC Zurich and Nantes, home and away. Tommy Gemmell was at right back with Willie O'Neill at left back.

I could hardly complain as I had missed out on the team's summer trip to the States because I had dentistry exams at the same time. So, I sat out that tour as the team bonded. They played eleven games, won eight and drew three. They scored a remarkable forty-seven goals in the process with Bobby Lennox claiming nineteen of them. They played a strong Spurs team three times, beat them twice and getting a draw in the other game. They also drew with Bayern Munich and Bologna. However, they did come up against some inferior opposition too and they walloped a Bermuda Select 10–1, a Hamilton Select 11–0 and St Louis All Stars 6–1. So it was a worthwhile exercise all round but, unfortunately, I had to miss out.

Big Jock started the 1966/67 campaign with Tommy Gemmell in the right-back berth and he played the first five league games before Ian Young came in for the 3–0 win over Airdrie on 15 October. Remarkably, that was Ian's only league outing that season. I came in for the 1–1 draw with St Mirren on 5 November at Parkhead after Tommy moved from his usual berth to take over at centre half for the injured Billy McNeill. Sadly, there were no fireworks from Celtic that afternoon but I do recall Dennis Connaghan having a very good game in goal for the Paisley outfit. He eventually joined up at Celtic five years later. After the Saints game, I dropped out. With Billy fit again, Big Tommy was switched back from central defence. I got the nod once more, though, on 7 January 1967 in a 5–1 victory over Dundee at Parkhead and, apart from a 3–2 triumph over Dunfermline on 18 March, I played in every other league game. As far as Europe was concerned, Big Jock changed things around when he put Tommy over to the left and went for me on the other flank for the matches against Vojvodina and I stayed there all the way to Lisbon.

It made a lot of sense for Tommy to play at left back despite the fact he was mainly right-footed. Coming in from the left on his favoured foot often gave Tommy the opportunity to have a go at goal. Playing on the right, he would probably pass the ball inside to the likes of Bobby Murdoch to have a pop. He was in his element, though, on the left and, of course, scored some spectacular goals for the club. In fact, just about every outside player chipped in with goals with the exception of John Clark who was our defensive rock. His nickname was Luggy but he was also known as The Brush to the fans. He would sweep up deep in our own half and he did it so very well. His concentration never wavered and he was absolutely brilliant at reading play coming towards him. He rarely got the headlines but that didn't bother him as he put in solid displays on a match-by-match basis – a great team man.

I don't suppose I was your typical right back way back then. A lot of fullbacks were merely that. They didn't display much enthusiasm for getting across the halfway line. They were defenders first and foremost. The forwards could get on with their job of plonking the ball in the opposition's net. However, just like Tommy Gemmell over on the left, I liked to get forward and join up with the attack. Tommy often described me as an athlete and I took that as a compliment. Yes, I was exceptionally fit during my playing days and I also took care of myself. I never dived into tackles, either. I am 6ft 1in tall and there was a long way to get back up if I mistimed a tackle and the forward got away from me. I preferred to jockey my opponent and make my move when I was absolutely certain the timing was spot on.

Most of the time, the guys in front of me on the right-hand side of the team were Bobby Murdoch and Jimmy Johnstone. Bobby, of course, could slice open any rearguard with one of his searching, probing passes. He was the master at unlocking defences. Like Tommy, he could also score from long-range with his excellent shooting prowess. His natural desire was to go forward. Jimmy Johnstone was in front of me, too, as our natural outside right and we all know about his immense talent. But the Wee Man was never going to become famous for his ability to track back. Actually, if Jinky put his mind to it, he could tackle with the best of them. It was just about getting his mindset right on the day. Jinky may have only been 5ft 4in but he was incredibly well built. He had huge shoulders and good upper-body strength. Big defenders who thought they could scare off the Wee Man swiftly had that notion knocked out of them. He was so brave too. I've said it often enough and no doubt I will repeat it. Folk talk of Jinky's outstanding talents but they often overlook the sheer bravery of the player. It takes a man with a big heart to continually get bowled over and keep getting back to his feet knowing some of the same is waiting for him. Some players would go and hide, simply disappear into an air pocket somewhere, but not Jinky. He just kept on running at defenders and was completely fearless. Have a look at his display against Atletico Madrid in a European Cup tie at Celtic Park back in 1974. The Spaniards had three players sent off and ended up with eight men after one of the most brutal games in memory. They hacked Jinky to pieces and his legs were scarred and black and blue afterwards. Not once, though, did he complain. He just kept on going and underlined what we all already knew – nothing on a football field frightened him.

You couldn't help but love the Wee Man but he was a bit of a scamp at times. We used Seamill as our HQ quite a lot back in the sixties and seventies as we prepared for big games and a lot of us fancied ourselves as budding Jack Nicklauses and Arnold Palmers. We took our golf clubs with us to help us relax. Jinky, though, wasn't interested in getting the sticks out and he would often hide behind a bush or a tree when we were playing. You would look quite pleased with yourself when you hit a good, direct shot down the fairway from the tee. While you were congratulating yourself on a reasonable effort, a wee ginger-haired figure would suddenly flash into vision, pick up the ball and throw it into the rough or, even worse, a bunker. I never could see the funny side of that!

I've often been asked who I thought Celtic's man of the match in Lisbon was. Wee Jinky? Bertie Auld? Bobby Murdoch? Modestly, I believe the two fullbacks, me and Big Tommy, did rather well. Seriously, though, it was all down to team work. We had some smashing individuals but Lisbon on 25 May 1967 was a time and place for all of us to stand up and be counted. No one shirked his responsibility and we won as a team. However, I don't think Jinky ever received the credit he deserved for his performance that day. He didn't seem to be involved in the key points of the game but, take my word for it, Wee Jinky was immense. He dragged their player, Burgnich, all around Lisbon to make openings for others. It was a totally unselfish, magnificently professional performance from the Wee Man. We, the players, knew what he contributed against Inter. He was at his happiest racing down the wing on one of those unbelievable, mesmerising runs, leaving defenders tackling fresh air. However, he sacrificed all that in Lisbon for the cause of the team. No one will ever forget him.

His courage in battling the motor neurone disease that eventually took him from us was awesome. He never let his head go down – not once. How do you cope with something like that? The Wee Man actually realised there was something wrong back in November 2001. He turned up with Bertie Auld at the funeral of my father and Bertie remembers Wee Jinky telling him that day that all was not well. He probably revealed it in that matter-of-fact manner of his and I know he was convinced he could overcome the illness. Sadly, it was one battle even the Wee Man couldn't win. Let's not get weepy, though – Jinky wouldn't have wanted that. Let's just offer up a special thanks for all the wonderful memories he left with us. Quite rightly, he was voted the greatest-ever Celtic player a few years ago. There may have been many worthy candidates for the award from the supporters but I didn't hear one dissenting voice when the accolade went to Jimmy Johnstone. That tells you everything.

I've already said the Wee Man had a wicked sense of humour but Ronnie Simpson could be quite funny, too. He was fairly droll and could make the odd caustic comment when he thought it was required. I remember one day when I mis-hit a pass-back and Ronnie, in fact, had to make a very smart save. Those were the days when you could actually pass the ball back to your goalkeeper to pick it up without being penalised. On this occasion, though, I got a bit too much oomph behind my pass and Ronnie had to look alert. I expected a rollicking but it didn't come immediately. However, as I was lining up on the goal line to defend a corner kick, I heard Ronnie growling, 'Cairney, if you want to score a bloody goal, will you please do it at the other bloody end?' Point taken!

Neilly Mochan, our trainer, was nicknamed Smiler because of the way his face used to light up when he scored a goal during his playing days at Celtic. Neilly had a ferocious shot on him and could thump the ball past keepers from all sorts of ranges and angles. He wasn't smiling, though, on the afternoon of the European Cup Final. I was in my room, trying to get some rest, when the door opened and there was Neilly, scowling and very definitely not smiling. 'Cairney, you're a real nuisance,' he said. 'Oh, what have I done now?' I asked. Neilly answered: 'We have just signed a deal with Adidas for the match and you are the only one who wears Puma boots. Now I have got to take your boots, paint out the white flash with black paint and then put in three stripes!' As the match wore on, I could see the white stripes slowly disappearing and the white flash showing through. Thankfully, no one at Adidas noticed and we got our money!

Of course, I have many memories of that European expedition but not all of them were happy. I recall feeling just a little bit ropey after our 0–0 draw with Dukla Prague in the Czechoslovakian capital that earned us a 3–1 aggregate win and a place in the Lisbon final. I should have been celebrating with the rest of the troops but I felt awful. I had not been feeling good all day although I had been able to play against the Czechs without any great problem. Soon after, though, my temperature started to fluctuate – cold one minute, hot the next. By the time I took my seat on the plane, all my joints were sore. I was kept away from the rest of the players as much as possible and, on arrival in Glasgow, was whisked home and went straight to bed. To say I was worried would be an understatement. I was desperate to play in our next game which was only four days away – a little matter of the Scottish Cup Final against Aberdeen at Hampden. Thankfully, though, the bug disappeared as swiftly as it arrived and I was able to turn out against the Dons. Willie Wallace scored two fine goals to give us a 2–0 victory and the silverware. We were still waiting to clinch the league title – which we managed by drawing with Rangers 2–2 at Ibrox a week later – so it was a matter of three down, the Scottish Cup, League Cup and Glasgow Cup, and two to go as we chased a clean sweep.

Of course, we brought the curtain down on a wonderful season with the triumph over Inter Milan. I'll always remember both teams lining up to go out before the game. Bertie Auld started belting out 'The Celtic Song' and we all joined in, giving it pelters. It was a surreal moment, no doubt about it. There were rather gallus Glaswegians on one side with bronzed, smooth, but clearly startled, Italians on the other. I'm sure they thought we were all off our heads. This was no way to act before a European Cup Final, surely? I'm pretty certain it's not the way Real Madrid or Benfica acted before they played Inter Milan in the finals of 1964 and 1965. The Italians won both those games but our off-key singing must have unsettled them. It certainly showed them we were not afraid.

After the match it was pure pandemonium – and a bit disappointing. The fans' fervour boiled over at the end and thousands raced onto the pitch to applaud their heroes. I lost shirt, boots and socks to supporters, eventually reaching the dressing room, firmly holding on to my shorts and jock strap. Those Celtic fans were always there when needed. They got solidly behind the team whenever we were down and were often regarded as our extra man. However, with the supporters swarming all over the place, it meant we could not be awarded the trophy on the pitch. Goodness knows where the most prized trophy in European football might have ended up. On top of a cupboard in a Glasgow flat possibly!

It would have been wonderful for the players to have been awarded the European Cup and been allowed to take a lap of honour – not just for the fans present in Lisbon, but for the many thousands watching on television throughout Europe. The presentation of our medals was also anti-climactic, to say the least. At the banquet following the game, an official came up and placed two containers of medals on our table. We more or less helped ourselves to them. It was a rather strange end to such a fantastic, unforgettable adventure.

But, hey, we were the champions of Europe and, at the end of the day, that was all that mattered.

5

TOMMY GEMMELL

Think of Lisbon and it immediately conjures up wonderful, unforgettable images of a deliriously happy bunch of guys in green-and-white hoops cavorting around the Estadio Nacionale, looking very pleased with themselves. It was an exhibition of joyful pandemonium in the Portuguese capital on a gloriously sunny evening. Fans were racing across the moat on to that lush green pitch to celebrate with the players as Paradise came to Lisbon.

After all these years, let me tell you another story of that fabulous day – a side of the well-told tale that no one caught on camera or tape. We were snarling, growling, arguing and spitting blood at each other all the way to my equaliser in the sixty-third minute. Birth certificates were to be checked en masse following the game after what we'd called each other. Expletives abounded all around the picturesque ground as emotions reached an all-time high. No one was auditioning for Charm School that day. John Clark – Luggy to his mates – would be screaming at me for venturing too far forward and I would be shouting back at him for being too slow in picking up an opponent. Billy, the good captain that he was, was sending out a steady stream of instructions and no one was missed if he wasn't content with what we were producing. It went all the way through the team. We fired each other up and it kept us right on our toes. If you were caught slacking, you would swiftly realise that your colleagues were never going to tolerate it. Quite rightly, too.

However, if you look at those spectacular pictures on film, all you can see is players filled with unbridled happiness. If they could have slapped a tax on smiling, we would have written off the national debt in one fell swoop. There would have been big trouble, though, if it hadn't quite worked out. Let's get this straight – the Lions loved each other and still do. We were friends and buddies off the pitch. On it, it was a different ball game entirely. Those Lions could snarl, believe me. We were all winners and couldn't tolerate anything else. I think that's what made us a bit special. We could rant and rave at each other throughout the game but, afterwards, it was all forgotten. There were no grudges or backstabbing. That was not our style. Everything was said to your face and there were plenty of clear-the-air views back then. We all knew where we stood with each other. Big Jock actively encouraged that side of our game and it didn't do us any harm, did it?

Travelling back in time, though, I must point out two players who have never received any credit for our victory in Lisbon. The names Armando Picchi and Angelo Domenghini may not be instantly recognisable to the Celtic supporters but I can assure you that these individuals played a significant, if unwitting, part in the club's history. Let me explain. As we prepared for Lisbon, Big Jock took me aside and told me, 'You'll get the freedom of the left wing. That Italian Domenghini won't chase back – he doesn't know how to tackle. I know what his game is all about. He'll want to do his tricks and flicks at the other end of the pitch. The hard work will be left to the guys behind him. You're going to enjoy this game.'

Sure enough, Big Jock, as usual, was absolutely spot on. Domeghini was a seasoned and gifted Italian international and, yes, he was exceptionally dangerous going forward but he didn't want to know about defending. When I received the ball, I never had to look over my shoulder. He would simply be standing there, hands on hips, waiting for one of his colleagues to get the ball off me and feed it forward to him.

He was a bit precious, as they say in football – porcelain, even. Around my part of the world, we would have labelled him a lazy beggar! He may have possessed bundles of skill but he would never have been in any Celtic team managed by Jock Stein, that's for sure. So, certain in the knowledge that I would be unhindered throughout the ninety minutes, I launched into as many assaults on the Inter Milan defence as was possible before complete and utter exhaustion might have set in.

In domestic games, it had become a bit of a habit for rival teams to pick me for special marking attention. I suppose I should take it as the extreme compliment but it was a pain in the backside. It was difficult enough being a defender so, when you got the opportunity to get forward, you would want some freedom. Once I got a bit of a reputation, though, I suddenly found these sorties being blocked. Wingers were being asked to defend first and attack only if they got the opportunity. That's why I thoroughly enjoyed Lisbon. I could join the attack, safe in the knowledge that Domenghini would not be tracking me and, basically, making a nuisance of himself.

Armando Picchi? Yes, he's another for whom Celtic should have a special medal struck. I can't recall how many times I have replayed my equaliser over and over in my head. I've seen it countless times and, on each and every occasion, I offer up a wee thanks to Picchi. Why? If you watch that goal again, keep your eye on the Inter Milan No. 6 who charges out from defence as Jim Craig passes the ball inside for me. Picchi comes at me at pace but, for whatever reason, he hesitates and turns his back just as I am about to pull the trigger. As I said, I have watched film of that goal over and over again and I have to admit that, if he had kept his momentum going, then there would have been every chance he might have blocked my effort. If he had come out with his foot up or to the side, he might have made contact with my shot. Maybe he was thinking of his manhood, marriage prospects or whatever but, thankfully, he had a swift change of mind and got out of the way.

In fact, I should actually thank him twice because there is every possibility that his aerial acrobatics also blinded their excellent goalkeeper Giuliano Sarti, who had looked unbeatable that day. He was immense throughout and sometimes you start to believe it is just not going to be your day. We hit him with everything but he thwarted us time and time again. I was beginning to hate the sight of him as he patrolled his area with so much confidence and composure. He looked pompous and even a wee bit arrogant. I recall him trying to ridicule Stevie Chalmers who had claimed a goal before the keeper stretched back to claw the ball off the line.

Stevie was convinced my effort had been good but Sarti was having none of it and got to his feet and belted the ball back up the field. Then he made a rude gesture to Stevie that, basically, meant he thought he wasn't right in the head. Insulting a Lion? I wasn't having any of that. I have described my effort that day in great detail over the past four decades but I saw it again when I was at Celtic Park for the Champions League last-sixteen encounter with AC Milan. I was invited along to a corporate box to witness the action and, as we were having something to eat, the television was on and SKY were showing old footage of the game in Lisbon as a scene-setter.

I noticed that Picchi definitely was in Sarti's line of vision. The goalkeeper would not have got a great view of the shot until it was too late. He still made a spectacular effort to keep it out, though – I'll give him that. Actually, I thought then – and I still do now – that my shot was a goal all the way. It was destined to hit the net. You instinctively know these things. I belted it right on the money. It was a sweet strike all right and, of course, I had been fortunate enough over the years to knock in a few from distance. Most of the times, you know there is nothing the goalkeeper is going to do to keep it out.

It took us until the sixty-third minute to get that goal and, yes, as legend has it, I did swear at the gaffer shortly afterwards. He was yelling from the touchline, 'Keep it tight – we'll get them in extra time.'

I looked over and shouted back, 'Fuck off, Boss, it's eighty-five degrees out here and we're going to finish it here and now.'

Thankfully, that's what happened and Big Jock never once mentioned our little bout of touchline verbals afterwards!

Again, when you examine that goal, you can see how spoiled for choice Jim Craig was as he came into the box with that loping gait of his. Stevie Chalmers, Bobby Lennox and the others seemed to be swarming all over the place. The Italians didn't know who to pick up as everyone got into scoring positions. There was no way they were used to such a situation in an Italian league game when they generally concentrated on in-depth defence.

As I recall, I was screaming at Cairney – as Craig was known – to put the ball in front of me. I was timing my run and I didn't care one whit if Domenghini was with me or not on this occasion. Nobody and nothing were going to get in my way. At last, Cairney put the pass in – perfectly weighted, may I say – and, well, the rest is history. Wonderful, wonderful history. I'll let you into a little secret – I still get a tingle when I witness that effort. Four decades down the line and I still can't prevent myself from smiling when I see that shot whizzing high past Sarti and the ball strangling itself in the net.

If you get the opportunity to see film of that goal again, just witness the amount of Celtic players who are in the Inter Milan penalty area as I scored. I saw it recently and could hardly believe my eyes – there were seven of us in there. SEVEN! Count them – me, Craig, Chalmers, Lennox, Wallace, Auld and Murdoch. You would be lucky these days to have seven players in the opposition's half, never mind their own penalty area in an away European tie. OK, Simpson had to remain in goal but where were Big Billy, John Clark and Wee Jinky when we needed them!

Again, you could see how much Jinky meant to that team by the completely unselfish part he played in that goal. He was actually wide on the left and that, naturally, wasn't his favoured position. But Inter had placed the tenacious Tarcisio Burgnich on him right from the kick-off and this bloke just stuck to the Wee Man like glue. His reputation was as a man-marker so it was no surprise when he immediately moved to Jinky's side straight from the off. Big Jock had already said that was exactly what their coach Herrera's plan would be.

The left back who played that day was Giacinto Facchetti and Herrera was not going to even contemplate allowing the club's most illustrious player to be put in a position where he could have had a nightmare with the rest of Europe looking on. Facchetti was a tall, slender guy who, like yours truly, enjoyed getting forward every now and again. He was known as one of Europe's best attacking fullbacks before we met in Lisbon but, try as I might, I can't remember him crossing the halfway line all day. A couple of years earlier, he had scored with a long-range lob against Scotland in a World Cup qualifier in Naples. That cemented his reputation as a fullback who had an eye for goal and, strange as it may seem these days, that was highly unusual.

Herrera watched Celtic in person just before the European Cup Final when we played Rangers at Ibrox and clinched our second successive championship with a 2–2 draw. Jinky was immense that day and scored both our goals. What made that achievement even more remarkable was the fact the entire game was played in a downpour. The heavens opened that day in Govan and I'm sure I saw a bloke in a large ark floating by at one point!

Jinky, though, was in his element. He should have disappeared in the quagmire but he decided to turn it on. His shirt was drenched and sodden and just about falling off him but nothing was going to deter him taking centre stage. Up against him that day was Davie Provan, who, like Facchetti, was a tall, rangy guy. Herrera must have noted that the Rangers player was being torn apart by Jinky. Inside, outside, through his legs – it didn't matter to the Wee Man. He was in the mood and he was unstoppable. The Inter Milan boss must have winced as he witnessed all this unfolding before his very eyes.

If he had arrived in Glasgow believing Jimmy Johnstone was merely a run-of-the-mill outside right who could provide a telling cross or two, then he left with different ideas. Jinky capped a wonderful display – easily one of the best I have ever seen by an individual anywhere – with a soaring left-foot shot into the roof of the net from about twenty-five yards. Norrie Martin was in the Rangers goal that afternoon and he took off in determined fashion but there was no way he was going to prevent that effort from rattling the rigging. By the way, I did say *left* foot. A lot of folk thought that was the one Jinky used for standing on but, take it from someone who used to get tied in knots trying to stop him in training, he could use both feet with equal ability.

Herrera didn't know it at the time but he was watching the side that would play in Lisbon, man for man. He had us watched again a week or so later when we beat Kilmarnock 2–0 at Celtic Park, but he wouldn't have gleaned a lot of knowledge that evening. For a start, Jock played Big Billy alongside John Cushley as twin centre halves, something he had rarely, if ever, done before. It may have baffled the Italian spy but I think our gaffer was doing a favour for West Ham manager Ron Greenwood, an old friend of his. Greenwood was looking for a new central defender to play alongside the great Bobby Moore and he wanted to run the rule over Cushley. With the league already won, Big Jock duly obliged. Greenwood must have been impressed – he immediately bought our player for something in the region of £30,000 which was good money back then. Not a bad bit of business for Celtic as I believe that was Cushley's one and only appearance in the first team that season!

Wee Jimmy used to tell me how disappointed he was with his own performance in Lisbon. He really wanted to go out there and just take over. As we all know, he was a cocky little character and he knew this was his sort of platform. The European

Cup Final was invented for Jinky – that was just his sort of stage – but it is to his eternal credit that he sacrificed himself that day for the team. He roamed here, there and everywhere, taking the redoubtable Burgnich with him. It wouldn't have been how he thought or dreamed it would turn out but he saw the team as being a lot more important than himself and he just got on with putting in a marvellous shift.

He dragged Burgnich all over the place and, when he did that, holes opened up behind the Italian. That's where the likes of Chalmers, Lennox and Wallace poured in and started rattling the cages of the back lot. Remember, this was a team that had built its reputation on resolute defence but you could sense fear within their ranks as we stormed forward. Sarti would have broken the hearts of other teams. We weren't just another team, though, and we proved that in Lisbon. I will always recall Jinky in the dressing room at half-time when he turned to me and asked, 'Tam, are we really losing? Are we not winning 10–1? Why are we not winning 10–1?' And, with a shake of the head, he sat down; baffled but unbowed. The answer, of course, was Sarti, who was having the game of his life. I said I thought he was arrogant but I had to take that back when I met him at a Lisbon Lions function in the eighties. He was flown over as a special guest for the evening and he turned out to be a charming individual and he had the good grace to concede that we deserved to win. He told me, 'Your victory was a triumph for sport.' It takes a big man to make such an admission and we all greatly appreciated it. But, by God, did he make us work hard to achieve it.

When I stormed into Inter's half, I knew my backside would have been well and truly booted all the way back to Glasgow if that move had broken down and the Italians had taken advantage. Big Jock's plans were fairly straightforward. If Jim Craig was overlapping on the right, I had to hold my position on the left alongside Big Billy and John Clark in defence. It was like there was an invisible rope attached to the four of us, if you can imagine that. Jim went forward down the right and we would all be pulled over a bit. I admit I gambled against Inter. I shouldn't have been there but, och, you get nothing in this life if you don't take a risk or two. I threw the dice and won. Or, at least, equalised.

I also remember we got a free kick about thirty-five yards out near the end of the game as we were all willing the referee, a German called Kurt Tschenscher, to blow for time up. Bertie Auld sidled up to me in that wonderful gallus manner of his. 'What are you thinking of doing, Tam?' he asked out of the side of his mouth. I just gave him a look that told him I was about to send the ball into orbit and hope that it stayed up there until it was full-time. Actually, I once read that Geoff Hurst had tried to balloon the ball out of the ground during England's World Cup win in 1966 when he was racing through on goal with his country 3–2 ahead and the minutes were ticking down in extra time. If you recall, he just clattered the ball straight into the roof of the net with the West German keeper not even moving a muscle. It looked like a fantastic effort but at least he was honest enough to admit later it was a complete and utter fluke. If my late free kick had flown into the Inter Milan net I would have happily accepted the accolades that went with it. However, in truth, it came closer to knocking out some spectator in Row Z! Picchi didn't have to bother getting out of the way of that one.

Inter Milan didn't know how to handle us at all that day. I know their manager Helenio Herrera – revered as The Magician in Italy – was a little bit concerned about the Celtic attack. Honestly, it had never occurred to me but he made the very valid point that each of our five frontline players – Jimmy Johnstone, Willie Wallace, Stevie Chalmers, Bertie Auld and Bobby Lennox – had all been wingers at some stage in their careers.

We all knew about Jinky and Lemon, of course but Herrera must have done his homework on the other lads. I believe Wispy Wallace had played on the right wing for Stenhousemuir, Raith Rovers and Hearts before joining us – Willie was the only player in the Lisbon Lions line-up Big Jock had to buy. Stevie had also played as an outside right but, with Jinky coming through, Big Jock utilised his blistering pace in the middle of the attack. Wee Bertie had started off as an outside left and played there in his first spell at Celtic and then at Birmingham City before his return to Glasgow.

Bertie was wasted out on the wing, no doubt about it. The foxes fled when they knew Wee Bertie was in town, as I told him more than once. He was as wily as they come. There wasn't an awful lot of him but he was terrified of nothing. All the way to Lisbon, teams tried to put the frighteners on Bertie. They were wasting their time and energy. Bertie used to knock big guys out of the way to get into a fight. He came from Maryhill in Glasgow and you got the impression he'd learned very swiftly how to look after himself on those mean streets and I hastily add that is no disrespect to the good people of that area.

Big Jock realised Bertie was of far better use to the team in a midfield role where he excelled alongside Bobby Murdoch. These two guys had it all. Vision, range of passing, movement, shooting – just all-round intelligence. I've said it many times over the years and no doubt I'll repeat it again but it was an absolute pleasure and privilege to play alongside these guys. Every game was an experience and every encounter an adventure. They were good fun off the pitch too, as I recall! How much would they be worth in today's ridiculous transfer market? How high is up? There is no answer but it would be fair to say that both were invaluable to Celtic. They fitted right into Big Jock's ideal framework of how football should be played. Flair and flamboyance? Both had it in abundance. Grit and tenacity? Ditto.

Alas, Bobby was the first of the Lions to pass on but he left us with great memories. He was known as Chopper and not a lot of people ever realised why. I'll tell you – he was Wee Jinky's on-field minder. If the Wee Man was getting a particularly torrid time from a defender, Bobby would let them know it might be a good idea to desist. Obviously, he wasn't a dirty player but he was never going to stand back and allow Wee Jinky to be belted all over the place. To be honest, the Wee Man knew how to look after himself too. He was incredibly brave – a superb man to have at your side – and, of course, we've also now lost Jinky. With Ronnie Simpson in goal, they must have some team in heaven. I am not going to get mawkish – that's not my style. Suffice to say, I have a warm glow inside when I think of these guys. They played such an enormous part in my life and they will never be forgotten.

As I said earlier, Helenio Herrera had obviously done his homework on Celtic before 25 May 1967 but even this so-called master tactician, who was hoping to lead his club to their third European Cup success in four years, couldn't have anticipated what transpired in Lisbon. Simply put, we were a team that was not going to be beaten. We were never there to make up the numbers. We were never going to be bit-part players. Try telling guys such as Big Billy and Wee Bertie or anyone else that they had to accept being second best. We had done all the hard work in the earlier rounds and we were now at the business end of the competition. We were in Lisbon to win.

Inter Milan? Frankly, I was disappointed in them. When I equalised you could see their heads drop on to their chests. They were a spent force – completely out of it. I looked around and all I could see were faces of a beaten team. None of them were rolling up their sleeves or cajoling one another. They knew it was only a matter of time before we got a second goal and lifted the trophy. Too many of them disappeared and, when you realise that this team actually beat the holders, Real Madrid, on their way to the final, I think we can only take that as a massive compliment to Celtic.

We all got a bonus of £1,500 for entering the history books and it didn't stay in the Gemmell bank account too long, I can tell you. Once taxes were deducted, I was left with the handsome sum of £720. I paid £500 to buy a Ford Cortina from Skelly's in Motherwell, where my mum worked, and £120 on a superb Rolex – the genuine article, I hasten to add– from Laing's in Renfield Street in Glasgow. I also gave £100 to Anne, my first wife, and that, my friends, was the cash spent – done and dusted. By the way, I've still got the watch but I fear my gleaming Cortina, once my pride and joy, may just be a pile of rust by now.

On our superb journey through Switzerland, France, Yugoslavia and Czechoslovakia to Lisbon, there may have been occasions when I might not have been at my best but I always gave it my all. Things, though, didn't always go according to plan. Take our quarter-final first leg against Vojvodina Novi Sad in Yugoslavia, for instance. We were performing on a treacherous pitch but holding out against an extremely talented and skilful bunch of guys. Then, with only twenty minutes to go and with us looking like we'd do enough to stop them from scoring, I misplaced a pass. It fell between Bobby Murdoch and John Clark and a Vojvodina player latched on to it, passed to a guy called Stanic and he knocked the ball beyond the exposed and helpless Ronnie Simpson. I felt dreadful. One bad pass and we were smack in trouble – all our good work had gone for precisely nothing. I knew we would be up against it in Glasgow in the second leg.

To set the scene, I should illustrate just how good Yugoslav football was at the time. The previous year Partizan Belgrade had reached the European Cup Final and, rather unluckily according to some observers, had lost 2–1 to the legendary Real Madrid. The year after Lisbon, their national side got to the European Nations Final – now the UEFA Championship – where they went down 2–0 to host nation Italy in Rome in a replay after a 1–1 draw in the first game.

Vojvodina were a class act and I had presented them with a one-goal advantage. How do you go out and rectify a situation like that? Simple, really – I had to play out of my skin in the second game and, as ever, give everything. I was determined to atone for my error. My team-mates exonerated me completely, I must add. There was a frost on the pitch in Novi Sad and I must say their stadium had more than a passing resemblance to the shambolic Cliftonhill where I later had two spells as manager of Albion Rovers. Their surroundings were not befitting a team of such footballing stature.

However, that was the least of my worries when they came to Glasgow a fortnight later. I wanted to bomb forward at every opportunity but Big Jock had drilled into us the need for discipline and concentration. We were up against a team with the ability to pick us off with laser-beam passes if we left any gaps at the back. As I remember, their defenders were as comfortable on the ball as most of the creative midfielders we faced in Scottish football week in, week out. They exuded confidence and never looked flustered. Our front guys would chase them into corners and in Scotland you would see the defender simply hoof the ball into the stand – not this lot, though. They always tried to retain possession and were exceptionally well drilled.

We were approaching the hour mark and, to be honest, it was getting a bit exasperating. No towels were being thrown in but we were beginning to wonder where the opening was going to come from. Their goalkeeper, Ilija Pantelic, was rated one of the best in the world and there was talk afterwards of Big Jock being interested in taking him to Celtic. Like my old mate Sarti afterwards, he was giving everyone around him the impression he was in complete charge of all he surveyed. And, up until that sixty-minute mark, that was undoubtedly the case.

Then I saw my opportunity to get down the left wing. Big Yogi – John Hughes – was playing that night and, to his credit, he took a defender out of the road and acted as a decoy. He came inside as I moved into the wide position, had a quick look up and, for once, could see an unmarked team-mate, Stevie Chalmers. I sent over a left-wing cross and Pantelic, who, as I said, had been immaculate all night, decided to try to cut it out. As he stretched to his left, Stevie, another player who was as brave as they come, threw himself forward. A defender stopped in his tracks, fully believing his goalkeeper would deal with the danger. But not this time – the ball dropped to Stevie and he could hardly believe his luck.

Pantelic was grounded and out of position and Stevie gleefully stroked the ball into the inviting net. You might just have heard my sigh of relief above the 69,374 spectators crammed into Celtic Park that evening. Of course, no one would be satisfied until Pantelic picked the ball out of the net again and Big Billy duly delivered the goods but I'm certain he will want to tell you that himself! How do you even start to explain your feelings at such a time? With a minute to go, you are absolutely shattered and out on your feet. A handful of seconds later and you are ready to jump over the main stand. The adrenalin rush is simply unbelievable. Suddenly there is life in that tired old torso and those spent legs and you are ready to run a marathon. Aches and pains are immediately replaced with elation. I'm telling you, if Big Billy had taken off on a lap of honour anywhere on the planet that night I would have caught him. Caught him? I would have overtaken him!

People look back on the Lisbon Lions and they talk about how well drilled we were and how skilful this guy was and how strong this bloke was and so on. First of all, we were fit. Big Jock always believed there was no point of having all the talent at your disposal if you couldn't last the ninety minutes. I might not have agreed at the time when he put us through some punishing training exercises but, looking back, I obviously do now. When you came back from your summer break, you knew there was nothing but agony and pain awaiting you. I'm a big guy and it was worse for me. Some blokes such as Stevie Chalmers and Bobby Lennox could come back after six weeks or so off and look as though they had never been away – lucky beggars!

I took over from Jim Kennedy as left back in the team a couple of seasons before Jock arrived. The Prez, as Jim was known, was the man who normally got the nod up until I moved in, making my debut in January 1963 in a 5–1 win over Aberdeen.

Jim and Willie O'Neill also shared the duties until the end of that season until I finally broke through the year after. Younger Celtic fans may not have seen a lot of footage of Jim in action but you'll have to take my word for it that he was never the most adventurous of left backs. He was there to defend and he did it very well too. When I got a chance, though, my natural style was to get forward and help in attack. I had a reasonable shot in me at the time and I was quite happy to let fly every now and again.

Goalkeepers must have just loved it when I careered forward. If I had a shot on target and they spilled it, you could be sure the likes of Chalmers, McBride, Lennox and Wallace would be charging in looking for the rebound. They won't thank me for this analogy but they were like little bees buzzing around the honey pot. I couldn't even start to count the number of goals we scored like that. Bobby Murdoch, too, would have a go from all sorts of distances and the unfortunate goalkeeper must have known what was coming next if he didn't collect the ball cleanly. It was all fair and above board, of course, but our front guys were predators and a goalkeeper would normally pay a high price for not clutching the ball first time. I've got a mental image of a picture that was used in the newspapers back then of Hearts keeper Jim Cruickshank, a superb shot-stopper, performing at Celtic Park. He is lying in the mud after fumbling an effort and there seems to be about seven Celtic players swarming all over him without a Hearts defender in sight. Talk about protecting your goalkeeper!

Actually, and this will probably surprise you, I well remember games when I was being ordered back by the management when I wanted to cross the halfway line. Sean Fallon, in particular, used to go apoplectic if he saw me venturing too far into enemy territory. He would scream at me to get into my defensive position. Naturally, I completely ignored those pleas. Poor Sean – he must have thought I was deaf!

I had always been a bit of a maverick. I wasn't a big fan of a ball-and-chain role shackling me within the team structure and I always wanted the opportunity to express myself. Maybe I was a frustrated centre forward! When I heard Big Jock was coming back to Celtic I was overjoyed. I had a fair inkling that he liked his team to go forward and I realised he would encourage his fullbacks to push on. That wasn't something that had been overly encouraged by previous backroom staff at the club.

I was talking to Davie Hay not so long ago and we were recalling the days when he played on the right and I was over on the left. Jock simply ordered you to go forward with your first touch. He wasn't a great admirer of a fullback taking a touch and pushing the ball inside. If you wanted a rocket and a severe ear-bashing from The Boss that would have been a fair way to go about it. Jock didn't want his fullbacks playing the ball inside to his central defenders. It was our job to turn defence immediately into attack and get our opponents going backwards after their own move had broken down.

It worked a treat too. You would be amazed at the amount of opponents who did not pile forward because they knew the ball would be in their half as soon as we got hold of it. There was none of that passing it around the back four that these days allows teams to get back into their own half and into defensive positions. We did everything at pace and rivals were simply swept off their feet if they couldn't keep up.

I had a laugh when there was a suggestion from some dubious South American sources that we must be on some sort of stimulants before we played Racing Club of Argentina in the World Club Championship Final. The least said about that lot the better but they did try to stir it up before we played them over the two legs that eventually would be settled in the infamous play-off in Uruguay. We lost 1–0 but I'm only prepared to talk about football and those guys don't fall into that category. I hope they found a suitable place to shove that trophy.

Someone did make the observation that long- and middle-distance runners tended to be slight figures from African nations who could run all day without upsetting their metabolism. I was over 6ft and weighed in at around 12st or so but do you think that would have washed with Big Jock if I had said I couldn't do the job he wanted me to do in the team? Not a chance! I could have been built like Billy Bunter and he would still have expected me to gallop up and down that wing all day in all conditions to help Celtic. I never argued; the Big Man talked my kind of language. Well, most of the time, anyway.

Looking back, I can only smile at the entire adventure. A bloke from Craigneuk whose one-time major ambition was to play for Motherwell. Yet, there, in Lisbon, was yours truly helping to upset the aristocrats of Inter Milan and getting my hands on the most glittering prize club football had to offer – the European Cup. All these years down the line, I still find it utterly remarkable.

You know, as I was doing a bit of research recently, something occurred to me that hadn't surfaced before. I scored Celtic's first-ever European Cup goal when we defeated Swiss outfit FC Zurich in Glasgow on 28 September 1966. The time of that goal? Most historians give it as sixty-four minutes – just sixty seconds off my effort in Lisbon. So, that demonstrated Celtic's fitness and never-say-die spirit. Jock always had us primed for those ninety minutes – or more, if extra time was required. Teams must have loathed us because they knew they were going to have to put in a full shift. It would be fair to say the supporters got their money's worth.

I ran amok against FC Zurich who, would you believe, were better against us in Glasgow than they were in Switzerland. I got two more goals as we eased to a 3–0 second-leg victory and I was delighted to become the first player to get a European Cup hat-trick for Celtic. OK, it wasn't technically a hat-trick with the goals spread over two games but you wouldn't take that honour away from me now, would you? Europe might not have sat up immediately at Celtic beating the Swiss champions 5–0 on aggregate but they might have taken a bit of notice that we had walloped in six in two games against French outfit Nantes, winning 3–1 home and away. We were on a roll.

I suppose I will always be remembered for that goal in Lisbon. I'm hardly likely ever to complain about that but I would like to think I did my fair share of the work at the back too. If not, I'm sure someone would have had a word in my ear. Being a Lisbon Lion is a bit special – I have to admit it. And, yes, I love everything that goes with that honour. I was a bit bemused when a bunch of travelling football supporters were in Glasgow not that long ago. They were bedecked in red scarves and one came up to me while I was having lunch and asked if he could get his photograph taken with me. I agreed and the next minute his mates, all seven or eight of them, were also there wanting a photograph. They turned out to be fans of Spanish side Osasuna who were due to play Rangers in a UEFA Cup tie that evening at Ibrox. I looked at these guys. Their average age was around twenty-five and they were from a place called Pamplona, tucked away somewhere outside Madrid. How on earth did they know who the heck I was? I suppose I haven't aged too badly in the past forty years although I do agree my figure is a tad fuller these days! Football fans never fail to astound me.

Football, in fact, never fails to astound me. It's been a truly memorable experience all the way through. All the twists and the turns – the wonderful, the woeful, the delight, the dejection. I can look back on that truly precious day in Lisbon and I can also have a quiet chuckle at the evening I was at a board meeting at Cliftonhill when I was manager of Albion Rovers. I was trying to persuade the directors to buy a centre half from the juniors. The fee? A princely £200. And, no, I didn't get the money or the player.

Aah, memories are made of this.

6

JOHN CLARK

It took utter humiliation in Hungary to make absolutely certain there was going to be a lot of partying in Portugal when we lined up to face Inter Milan.

As we prepared for the European Cup Final on 25 May 1967, I couldn't help but cast my mind back to Budapest three years earlier when we blew the opportunity of playing in the European Cup-Winners' Cup Final. We arrived for the second leg on 29 April with a handsome three-goal advantage from the first semi-final leg at Celtic Park. Stevie Chalmers (2) and Jimmy Johnstone had scored against MTK Budapest and we believed – stupidly, not arrogantly – we held an unassailable lead over our opponents. How wrong we were!

The history books will show the Hungarians won 4–0 and every single Celtic player was totally embarrassed. Devastated is probably a better word. We had thrown away a massive advantage and we had no one to blame but ourselves. The pitch was OK. The referee was fine. We were awful – naive in the extreme. We were lucky there wasn't the live coverage on television of European football that we have today. A few us might have thought it would be preferable to spend the rest of our lives in the Hungarian capital rather than face the wrath of our raging support after an appalling, wretched display.

Back then, though, all the TV audience in Scotland saw were some flickering black-and-white images that lasted only a matter of minutes. There were no panels of so-called experts poring over our every error, highlighting a blunder here and a clanger there. Believe me, this was one for those connoisseurs of calamity. You know those annoying videos that come out every

Christmas and poke fun at poor individuals who have floundered in front of thousands? There would have been no need for a compilation job of our efforts against the Hungarians. All they would have needed was to show the ninety minutes of the game and that would have been enough. We made every mistake possible. No one was singled out to take the blame – we were all culpable. MTK played well enough but we should never have lost 4–0. Tommy Gemmell, Billy McNeill, Jimmy Johnstone, Bobby Murdoch, Stevie Chalmers and I played that night. I say 'played' but I'm using the term loosely. We were all on the pitch but we hardly performed. Remarkably, all six of us would be in the side that conquered Europe three years later.

I am a great believer in learning from mistakes and, boy, did we make a few in Budapest. Turning up was probably the start of them! European football was relatively new to all of us at that time. In fact, we had only made our debut in that exclusive arena the previous year when we were toppled at the first round in the old Inter-Cities Fairs Cup. We lost 4–2 to Valencia in the first leg in Spain and scraped a 2–2 draw in front of our fans. I missed the first game but I made my bow in the second leg. There was nothing to prepare for us for what happened the following season as we beat Basle (11–1 on aggregate), Dinamo Zagreb (4–2) and Slovan Bratislava (2–0) and then we came up against MTK Budapest. The momentum that had got us all the way to Budapest suddenly vanished and, with it, our hopes of a first European final. We were well and truly derailed in Hungary and it hurt like hell. So I didn't have to look too far for inspiration or motivation as we prepared to take the field in Lisbon. That dark, awful evening in Budapest was still locked in my memory bank and I wasn't in the mood to suffer such abject failure on the European battlefield again. Inter Milan were going to pay for us getting a gubbing three years earlier!

I know Billy McNeill has already stated that he thought the Inter Milan game was the easiest we faced in the European Cup that season. Probably we didn't have to work as hard as we did in the goalless draw against Dukla Prague in Czechoslovakia, for instance, but I still thought it was a tough shift. We all knew about the Italians' attitude to football. They were superb on the counter-attack. They didn't waste time or energy coming forward in waves. They were cagey, would keep possession and then suddenly explode into action when they got anywhere near your penalty area. They obviously believed in the rapier thrust rather than the almighty bludgeon to get the job done. Thankfully, though, our guys in the middle of the field, Bobby Murdoch and Bertie Auld, and the lads up front kept the Inter back lot occupied throughout huge chunks of the game. Yes, I take on board what Big Billy says but I have to admit I feared Inter on the rare occasions they tried to get forward. It was a game where you knew that one lapse of concentration would bring about disaster.

I'll never forget that back-heel from Ronnie Simpson, for a start. I still break out in a sweat when I think about it. That came from just one long pass from the edge of their own penalty area. Ronnie, as he often did, saw it coming and was off his line swiftly. Their centre forward, Renato Cappellini, didn't give up the chase, however. He kept on going and, for me, there were danger signals flashing. Ronnie actually turned his back on the Italian and looked as though he was going to run towards his penalty area where he could have picked up the ball. Instead, for absolutely no fathomable reason, he decided to back-heel it to me. He told me he realised I was there all the time. I'll take his word for it. Anyway, if that had hit the Italian it would have been goodnight for us. They'd have gone 2–0 ahead and I genuinely don't think we would have got three to win in normal time. No one would have been talking about the Lisbon Lions four decades down the line. Or, possibly, I'm just not giving Ronnie the praise he deserves for a bit of off-the-cuff goalkeeping.

Mind you, Ronnie was prone to these sorts of things. I don't think he ever read *The Manual on Perfect Goalkeeping* but he was a great keeper – you can take that from me. Exceptional in so many ways. He was a very funny man, you know. He could split the tension with a one-liner and ease pressure. He could sense when it was the perfect time to inject a bit of humour into proceedings. I remember Scotland played Russia in a friendly international at Hampden in 1967 and it seemed to be a Celtic Select with a couple of guests. Anyway, it was goalless at one stage in the first half and both sides were enjoying just knocking the ball about – nothing too strenuous. I was playing left half that night and a ball ran through to Tommy Gemmell in his usual left-back berth. There wasn't a Russian in sight and I thought there was no threat.

Big Tommy, inexplicably, lofted the ball over the head of Ronnie as he ambled off his line to pick up the expected pass back. Ronnie looked aghast as the ball sailed high into the net. Tommy was so apologetic. 'I'm really sorry, Ronnie,' exclaimed Tommy. 'I got my elevation all wrong.' Now Ronnie could have been a bit upset – Can you imagine how a certain Peter Schmeichel might have reacted in a similar situation? – but he defused the situation by quickly saying, 'Oh, don't worry, Tam, you just looked up and saw an old bloke and thought I was Lev Yashin. It was just your natural instinct to score.' The legendary Lev Yashin was, indeed, in goal for the Russians at Hampden and, of course, he was one of the best in the world although, to be honest, he was past his prime when he played against us. We eventually lost 2–0 and that was the end of my international career!

Things, of course, went a lot better on the club front that year, thank goodness. It seems a bit of an understatement but it really was a fabulous experience from start to finish. Even getting to Lisbon was no mean feat – it was certainly something that hadn't been achieved by any other British club. And, as I'm sure the other Lions would insist, it was no easy trip to the European Cup Final. We encountered some first-class teams with so many fine players. The Yugoslavs of Vojvodina Novi Sad were probably the best actual team we played but Dukla Prague also impressed me. Whereas Vojvodina were more of a compact, controlled unit without any real star names, the Czechs had a wee bit of flair. We didn't know what to expect of them when they came to Celtic Park for the first leg of the semi-final on a fine evening on 12 April. It was a perfect setting for football and there would be no excuses for failure on our part. We were ready to go but imagine our surprise when Dukla started taking the game to us. Our thoughts of them retreating into a shell, as so many teams did when they arrived at Celtic Park, were immediately dispelled. In fact, if I remember correctly, they won a corner kick in the first minute. That wasn't in the script.

However, that didn't do us any harm. Of course, we realised it wouldn't be a walkover and we had a hard ninety minutes coming up. But their attitude underlined the fact that they were in Glasgow to do the business. We looked at one another. It was going to be a long evening in the east end of the city. A bumpy ride was ahead. They had so many good and gifted individuals. They had Josef Masopust, for a start. He had been the Czechoslovakian captain when they reached the World Cup Final only to lose to Brazil in Chile in 1962. OK, five years had passed since then but he was still top-notch. His control was excellent and he had a good eye for threading the ball through a packed defence. And, like any good midfielder, he had that extra special quality of finding space. There never seemed to be anyone within six yards of him when he got the ball.

I recall they also had a beanpole striker in the Peter Crouch mould – a guy called Stanislav Strunc. He was extremely dangerous and, a bit like the Liverpool and England lad, he had a splendid touch for one so tall. He was awkward and even Big Billy, who normally won everything in the air and left me to clean up the scraps, was toiling just a wee bit. No wonder! I think the bloke was about 6ft 8in and we hadn't come up against anything like him in Scottish football. We had big burly centre forwards but no one was built quite like Strunc. He was elusive on the deck and he proved that so capably on the stroke of half-time. We were leading with a goal from Jimmy Johnstone when we got into a terrible fankle on the edge of the box. It was one of those situations where you just couldn't dig the ball out. You would hit it and it would go three yards and bounce off someone and come back into the mix. We probably had about four chances to clear our lines and just didn't manage it. Then a Czech shoved it into the tracks of Strunc and he veered away from the defence and slid a neat effort wide of Ronnie Simpson. I talked earlier about Ronnie's sense of humour. He displayed none at that moment, let me tell you. We were all given a right rollicking – deservedly so, I may add.

Celtic Park was in total silence. The supporters, like ourselves, could hardly believe it. If there were any Dukla Prague fans there that night, I didn't hear them. There was the surreal sight of all those Czech players dancing around in delight and there was no sound, like someone had simply pushed the off button on the remote control. Big Jock was calm all the way through the half-time talk. He stressed the responsibility that was on all our shoulders. We were at home, we had almost 75,000 supporters there backing us all the way and, he reassured us, we were the better team. We just had to prove it by scoring a couple of goals. And that, of course, was exactly what we did.

Willie Wallace, signed from Hearts in December 1966, was forced to miss the earlier games against Vojvodina and you had better believe he was well up for this one – his European Cup debut in front of his new-found legion of supporters. To our surprise, Dukla did appear to back off in the second period. We weren't complaining, though, as we stormed forward. I recall they had a very good goalkeeper in Ivo Viktor, who was the Czech international No. 1. I think he would prove his class conclusively three years later in the World Cup Finals in Mexico. Come to think about it, we faced a few good keepers during that run and I can't recall us getting any gifts from any of them. However, Viktor, good as he may have been, was completely flummoxed when Wispy got our second goal with a neat little effort off the outside of his boot after a long ball downfield from Tommy Gemmell. It really was a straightforward pass but it opened their rearguard with surprising ease. Wispy was deadly in those situations and you rarely, if ever, saw him panic. If he was one-on-one with a goalkeeper, you would have put your house on him scoring. He got the third, too, with a rasping shot after a cute free kick from Bertie Auld. We were leading 3–1 and the Czechs were definitely rattled. The composure and poise that had been so evident in the opening forty-five minutes evaporated. We could have scored a couple more but, at the end of a fairly frantic evening, we were satisfied to take a 3–1 lead to Prague.

The Juliska Stadium has a nice ring to it, hasn't it? That was Dukla's ground and it was anything but pleasant. It was a fore-boding, grey old place that could have done with a lick of paint. It looked as though the construction outfit who were putting it together got fed up halfway through and went home. The atmosphere wasn't helped when it looked as though the entire Czechoslovakian Army was there too. It could have been a ter-rifying experience but, being only ninety minutes away from the European Cup Final, we were prepared for anything. Jock, of course, went against all his principles and philosophies that day to play defensively and those poor Czech fans never saw the real Celtic on that occasion. They must have been more than just a bit bemused when they saw us perform against Inter Mi-lan –they surely didn't believe they were witnessing the same players or the same team.

I think even Wee Jimmy Johnstone was given defensive duties against Dukla. Can you imagine the Wee Man as an auxiliary right back? Me neither but that's where he played for the entire ninety minutes. We were helped too by the presence and reassurance of the experienced Ronnie Simpson behind us. His was the fairytale to end all fairytales and he wasn't going to allow anyone to take it away from him. He talked us through that game as only he could. When the Czechs got through and, thankfully that wasn't too often, Ronnie was there to pull off the save. Dukla were gracious in defeat but I do remember Masopust being a bit grumpy. He had played in a World Cup Final and now, in his mid thirties, he must have been looking forward to an appearance in a European Cup Final. Sorry, Josef, we were in no mood to stage an action replay of our blundering performance in Budapest in 1964.

Yes, we did come up against some footballing thoroughbreds in the competition that year. I also remember Ladislav Kubala, the former Barcelona star, playing for FC Zurich in the second leg against us in Switzerland. He had been a truly magnificent player at the peak of his powers. He had been a key player in the superior Hungarian international team of the fifties and, in fact, had played in five championship-winning sides while at Barcelona. As player/coach of our opponents, he chose himself in an effort to overthrow our 2–0 first-leg lead. He was thirty-nine years old and searching for that last pot of gold at the end of the rainbow. That was one fairytale we were not interested in making come true. Tommy Gemmell netted twice, one a penalty kick, with the other coming from the ever-industrious Stevie Chalmers. Nantes, in the next round, were another exciting proposition. The French international side hadn't had the best of luck in the World Cup Finals in England the previous year but they were still a fine outfit and I liked the look of their captain Robert Herbin, who was also skipper of Nantes.

Herbin, with his shock of bright red hair, reminded me a little of Leeds United and Scotland's Billy Bremner and they both played in a similar role in midfield. Once again, we knew it was going to be a fairly open contest. Interestingly, it was the first time we had been drawn against a French club in European competition so we were all looking forward to breaking new ground. Nantes, in front of their own fans, started off brilliantly against us – they really knew how to knock the ball about and keep possession. Herbin seemed to be in the thick of the action and, to be honest, it was no surprise when they took the lead. We couldn't exactly say it was against the run of play. But we kept our nerve and, slowly but surely, we got back into the game. We started giving a lot more of the ball to Jinky and he was in one of his moods to show he was the real deal.

Basically, we started to break up their attacks and this gave us the chance to indulge ourselves a bit in their half of the field. The longer the game went on, the stronger Jinky seemed to get and the French simply capitulated. Our greater stamina had seen us take control and goals from Joe McBride, Stevie Chalmers and Bobby Lennox saw us rack up a 3–1 victory. It was not bad going – two away games in the European Champions Cup and six goals scored by a team playing in the tournament for the first time. Good things were around the corner, we were positive. The second leg saw us win 3–1 again and this time the French looked a fairly dispirited bunch. I believe they had given it their very best shot in their own stadium and had been found wanting. They made the usual noises before the game about not ruling them out but, even in that wonderful accent of theirs, it didn't quite ring true.

Next up, of course, were the Yugoslavs of Vojvodina Novi Sad. I used to keep up with European football back then. I read all the football magazines, weeklies and monthlies, and such like, but even I was struggling to come up with some inside information on them. I knew their manager, Vujadin Boskov, was extremely highly rated and their goalkeeper, Ilija Pantelic, was being hailed as the best in the world. Other than that, it was difficult to put faces to any of the names and I don't mean any disrespect by that. They might have said the same about us – who knows? What a hard time they gave us over the two legs. It took Big Billy's last-minute winner to see them off and, honestly, we were happy to see the back of them. It's strange how they disappeared off the big-time scene shortly afterwards. I know Boskov went to Real Madrid a year or so later and French clubs had the habit of picking up the cream of the Yugoslav talent. The team must have been taken apart but, if they had stuck together, I'm sure we would have heard a lot more about them.

I wonder, though, if you would have heard a lot more about me if I had signed for Birmingham City! Yes, it almost happened and the registration would have gone through if the Midlands club had shelled out a couple of quid to my junior side, Larkhall Thistle. I'll tell you a wee story. I was happily going through the routines with Larkhall when I heard Birmingham City, then in England's top division, had taken a liking to my style of play. They sent up a scout to take in a couple of junior games – I wonder what he thought of the rough and tumble in that particular set-up! – and he was impressed. I was told to pack my bags and head off for Birmingham for trials. 'This is it,' I thought. 'My big chance.' Again, they liked what they saw and I was informed they would, indeed, make an offer. Then it all went wrong – or right, as the case turned out later on. They wanted me but they weren't prepared to pay a transfer fee to Larkhall. It would probably have been something in the region of £200, but they refused to cough up. My junior side still held my registration and bluntly told the English side, 'If we don't get the money, you don't get the player.' And with that my great sojourn in English football came to an end. Thank God!

I returned to Larkhall Thistle, got my head down and worked at my game and that's when Celtic came on the scene. I think someone had tipped them off about the Birmingham City fiasco and they must have reasoned I had something to offer outwith the juniors. I signed for the team of my dreams on 8 October 1958 at the age of seventeen and you could say I was more than just a shade overjoyed that someone down in Birmingham was a wee bit tight with the purse strings. Whoever you are or wherever you are, I would like to say a big thank you from the bottom of my heart. You helped shape my career.

If you look at my statistics, you will see I was hardly a goal machine. In my 318 games for Celtic, I netted three goals in all – not bad for a guy who hardly ever crossed the halfway line!

Actually, there is one of that fabulous total that does stand out and, would you believe, I scored it against Ronnie Simpson! It came in a fairly tense Scottish Cup tie against Hibs at Easter Road on 16 March 1961. We had drawn 1–1 at Celtic Park on the Saturday with Bertie Peacock, a tremendous Northern Ireland international half-back, playing in the left-half berth. I got a chance in the second game and I could hardly believe it when I got the only goal of the game. It was a heavy night with a muddy surface but I came forward and just took a belt at the ball. It simply flew into the net with Ronnie just too late to get a hand to it. John Clark, Goalscorer Supreme! I ribbed Faither about it on the odd occasion afterwards but he would just shrug his shoulders and say, 'That was another Ronnie Simpson, Luggy – nothing to do with me.'

My debut for the club came against Arbroath at Gayfield on 3 October 1959 and it was the first time I have ever paired up with Billy McNeill. Being mainly defensively minded, I have to say I was fairly satisfied with my first game. We won 5–0 and the defence hadn't conceded. As I recall, Stevie Chalmers scored twice and Bertie Auld was on the left wing. Bertie, of course, left Celtic for a spell at Birmingham City before coming back. I should have told him to make sure the English club gave him the money upfront!

Talking of cash, I really rolled out the barrel with my European Cup bonus. I had just bought my first car, a Hillman Imp, six months before Lisbon. I put down a deposit and the rest would be paid in instalments over a period. My former Celtic team-mate Johnny Divers had opened up a car salesroom just opposite Bearsden Railway Station and I thought I would put a bit of business his way. He persuaded me to buy the Hillman Imp, despite the fact it was blue. What was I thinking of – a Celtic player driving a blue car? Anyway, I wasn't a flash bloke, unlike Tommy Gemmell. I think he was the first guy at the park to pay over £1,000 for a motor. That wasn't my style, though. I just wanted something to get me from A to B. I remember turning up at Johnny Divers' car lot shortly after we got back from Lisbon and paying off the rest of the car immediately. The remainder of my fortune? I took the family away for a good holiday and anything left after that would have gone into the bank.

I look back to those days and realise how lucky I was. Someone up there liked me. Johnny Divers, for instance, was a very good inside-forward who could chip in with a goal or two when needed. He had a good footballing brain too and, at times, formed a good partnership up front with the likes of Stevie Chalmers and John Hughes. He started off season 1965/66 as the man in possession of the No. 8 shorts but you got the impression that, for whatever reason, Big Jock wasn't convinced about him. Possibly, he lacked a wee bit of pace. Johnny played and scored in a 4–0 league win over Dundee United at Tannadice on 25 August, the opening day of the league campaign. He was in again for the next match, a 2–1 victory over Clyde at Celtic Park. Next up was Rangers at Ibrox on 18 September and we went down 2–1. Poor Johnny, I don't think he played another first-team game again. See what I mean about being lucky? Sometimes your face fits and sometimes it doesn't. The managers have got to stand or fall by their decisions and, in truth, you cannot say Big Jock called it wrong too often.

I often wonder how Big Jock would fare in today's football climate. Possibly not too well, I think, if I am being totally honest. The Big Man was always the boss. He made all your decisions for you and you had to abide by them. Let me tell you, he wouldn't have known what to do with football agents. Well, for a start, he wouldn't have allowed them to get their foot in the front door at Celtic Park. That would have created ructions and Big Jock was never happy in that sort of environment. Football has changed so much over the past forty years and there are things happening today that Jock simply wouldn't have tolerated.

However, back in 1967, The Boss could have gone for a stroll across the River Clyde if he so wished, according to our support. He deserved every bit of praise that came his way. He was so clued in. I remember an English television commentator coming up to The Boss shortly after our Lisbon triumph. 'We've done it, Jock,' exclaimed the excitable English chap. 'We've done it!' Jock glanced round, gave him one of his withering looks and said, 'What do you mean "we"?'

OK, what was Big Jock's secret? How did he fuse the Lisbon Lions together? What made him so good? For a start, he never asked anyone to carry out anything on the park he knew they weren't capable of. Tommy Gemmell would tell you that he thought I was terrible in the air. And, yes, he has got a fair point. I wasn't brilliant in that area but I would like to think I more than made up for that on the deck. Big Jock would say, 'Let Billy take the high balls, Luggy. Just you look out for what is going on all around you. Make sure everything is covered.' OK, not the most spectacular of roles in the team but someone had to do it and I was happy enough to carry out Big Jock's orders.

I left the sensational stuff to Big Tommy, Bobby Murdoch, Bertie Auld and Wee Jinky. They were the guys who caught the imagination with the way they played. Big Tommy's shooting was out of this world – sometimes out of the park, too! Bobby had range and vision. Wee Bertie had guile and touch. And Jinky had the ability to do anything he wanted with the ball, really. He loved that leather sphere – I'm sure he must have had one in his pram when he was a baby. So I'm sure our fans would be talking in the pubs afterwards about our flair players and the name John Clark would rarely, if ever, be mentioned. I can't imagine anyone saying: 'Did you see that intervention from Luggy?' or 'What about the way Luggy anticipated that forward pass?' Did I care? Not a jot!

I knew my role in the team and was content to get on with it. I was never one to go searching for headlines. Everyone had a part to play in Big Jock's formations and we never wavered from it. If you did, you would find someone else in your position the following week, doing exactly what Big Jock had ordered. One instance, to give a reasonable example of what I am saying, came in the 1965 Scottish Cup Final win over Dunfermline. Anyone who was there or who has witnessed that game on film will undoubtedly talk about Big Billy's brilliant headed winning goal. They'll also recall Bertie's two goals that brought us back into the game twice when the Fifers were leading. After all, those goals were the highlights in a match that was so important to us all. That encounter opened the door for all the good things that were to follow. It proved we could win silverware with Jock Stein as our manager. It was so crucial – absolutely vital – that we were not runners-up once again. We were all getting a bit fed up and frustrated with being second best.

Big Billy and I had played against the same opponents in the final of the same tournament four years earlier when Big Jock was in charge of Dunfermline. We were favourites in 1961 and should have taken the trophy in the first game which ended goalless, mainly thanks to some heroic goalkeeping from the Fifers' Eddie Connachan – not to be confused with Dennis Connaghan, note the different spelling, who joined us from St Mirren ten years later. But Connachan was superb that afternoon and we knew we deserved to win. The replay was the following Wednesday. Jock changed the shape of their team but we couldn't get into our stride and we lost 2–0. We were beginning to wonder if we would ever win anything again. It wasn't a particularly good time to be a Celtic player and I never thought I would hear myself say that.

That was why the Cup Final against the Fifers four years later was so important. We had to shake off the stigma of never being good enough to walk up those stairs at Hampden and hold aloft a trophy – any trophy. So, it is obviously understandable that the support still talks about Big Billy's wonder header and Wee Bertie's two efforts. How many remember a John Clark clearance off the line when the game was deadlocked at 2–2, though? One of their players – I think it was a bloke called John McLaughlin – beat John Fallon and the ball was heading goalwards until I managed to get a thigh in the way. The ball spun up into the air and there was a bit of a melee before someone thumped it clear. Not a headline-grabber, I agree, but critical to what was to come later. If that had gone in, it could – and, knowing our luck, probably would – have been an entirely different outcome.

People still ask me today if winning in Lisbon was the absolute pinnacle of my career. I think they are rather taken aback when I say no. My happiest-ever memory from all my days in football was actually signing for Celtic in the first place. Before the ink dried on that registration form, I knew had arrived. John Clark, of Celtic Football Club – now that really did have a good ring to it.

7

WILLIE WALLACE

I knew I had arrived on the big-time scene when a truly great world-class international star refused to shake my hand! That's exactly what happened at the end of our goalless draw against Dukla Prague in the Czechoslovakian capital – the game that sealed our date with destiny in Lisbon.

I turned to Josef Masopust, Dukla's captain and superb midfielder, and offered my hand as soon as the referee blew for time up. I had always admired Masopust and had watched him on the television as he skippered his country all the way to the World Cup Final in Chile in 1962 where they eventually lost 3–1 to Brazil. He had acted as a gentleman back then, even in defeat, but he wasn't acting like one after our semi-final. He looked at me and simply walked away – I'd been snubbed by Josef Masopust. I didn't blame him, really.

Jock Stein had changed our tactics for that fateful match in Prague. Whereas we had really got about the Czechs in Glasgow and had won 3–1 with yours truly scoring twice, Big Jock, for the first time, sent out a side to defend. Everyone knew that was not Celtic's style – we were a team happiest going forward – but, for that particular occasion, Big Jock changed everything. My role in the line-up was fairly basic – keep Masopust company for the entire ninety minutes and make sure he didn't do anything special. Thanks, Jock! I had played up front alongside Stevie Chalmers on my Celtic European debut a fortnight beforehand and now I had to adopt a man-marking role. Fair enough. I had played several roles in football since making my breakthrough at Stenhousemuir. I then moved on to Raith Rovers before landing at Hearts. Then, of course, it was off to Celtic in December

1966, the only one of the Lisbon Lions bought by Jock Stein. I had operated as a wing-half and as an outside right so shadowing a player for a whole game was alien to me.

I knew it made sense to try to nullify Masopust's presence. He was Dukla's engine and, without him, they would not have been as much of a threat. So, I stuck to him throughout and, when the end of the game arrived, I think he had had enough of Willie Wallace. He didn't want to shake hands but, being the true sport he was, he did search me out in the Celtic dressing room afterwards. He shook my hand then and apologised for his actions. Looking back, he must have been dreadfully upset. Really, that probably had been his last chance of doing something on the European scene. He had entered the veteran stage and you don't get too many opportunities in your mid thirties of conquering Europe – unless you are Ronnie Simpson, of course!

I'll let you into a little secret – Europe could not have been further from my mind when I joined Celtic. I didn't think about it at all. I had been in dispute with Hearts and just wanted a transfer. Newcastle United and Stoke City were showing an interest so it looked as though I would be packing my bags and crossing the border. Then Jock Stein came on the scene and he didn't have to try too hard to sell Celtic to me. As soon as I realised there was a chance of going to Celtic Park and working alongside Big Jock, there was no choice to make. Newcastle United and Stoke City, without any disrespect, had no chance of getting my signature on transfer forms. Let's try to clear up a few mysteries that have followed me about for forty years or so. I was not, and never had been, a Rangers supporter. The story goes that I was poised to sign for the Ibrox side until Big Jock made his move. There was a tale that the Celtic manager waited until Rangers were away from home and playing in a European tie before he quickly sealed the deal with Hearts. Sounds like a good yarn but it simply didn't happen that way. I don't know if Rangers were ever interested in me at all. OK, my whole family were Rangers fans and they would have loved for me to sign for them but I was overjoyed when I got the opportunity to move to Celtic.

Yes, some of my family didn't share my enthusiasm for all things Celtic back then. Actually, I admit I did see a lot of Rangers in the fifties because my Uncle Jim just happened to be President of the Kirkintilloch Rangers Supporters' Club! However, I spent more time watching Falkirk at Brockville which was just up the road from where I lived in Larbert. But I am a Celtic fan now, you can be certain of that. Once you have mixed in that company, you couldn't be anything else.

I live in Queensland in Australia these days but I still bump into hundreds of Celtic supporters. They are everywhere. I was always made welcome at Celtic. I was aware of the religious divide that existed in the West of Scotland at the time but it never bothered me and, anyway, Celtic had always signed Protestants. Big Jock – for a start. And there was me, Tommy Gemmell, Ronnie Simpson and Bertie Auld among the Lions. I may have gone to a Proddy school but, after they came knocking on my door and took me to Glasgow, I was Celtic through and through. I said Europe didn't mean an awful lot to me and that is true. Celtic winning the European Cup five months after I joined would have been a step too far in my imagination. I simply wanted to sign for them and who wouldn't want to play for Big Jock?

There is also speculation that I should have taken my European bow in the quarter-finals ties against Vojvodina Novi Sad. I have heard that, although I was registered to play in the domestic competitions, someone had been a little late in getting the forms to UEFA to allow me to play in European tournaments. I signed for Celtic on 10 December 1966 – I believe the transfer fee was £30,000 – and the first leg against the Yugoslavians was on 1 March 1967. That's a fair period between signing and that game and, to be completely honest, I don't know how long you had to be registered back then to allow you to play in Europe.

I am not complaining, though. You never know what might have happened if I had played against Vojvodina – maybe we wouldn't have got through! As it was, I was more than delighted to play against Dukla Prague in the following round. I had been sitting beside the injured Joe McBride in the stand at Celtic Park to witness that astounding quarter-final against the Slavs and I thought, 'Wispy, this is the place for you!' I wanted a slice of that, believe me. I know the other lads would all say the same thing but the atmosphere generated by our support in those European occasions was just breathtaking – quite staggering, really.

I was well up for the Dukla game. I had anticipated it for weeks and just hoped I would get the go-ahead from Big Jock to play. You never took anything for granted with The Boss – that would have been a huge mistake. I know of at least one instance when one of our players had been talking to a newspaper about a forthcoming game. Our guy was saying how much he was looking forward to it and what he was going to do. The player arrived at Celtic Park the following day to be greeted by Big Jock holding a pen and a piece of paper, 'Would you like to jot down the rest of the team?' asked our manager. The player got the message.

Everything went so well for me on my European debut for Celtic in that semi-final. I couldn't have scripted it better myself. A 3–1 victory and two goals from me. OK, it would have been nice to have claimed a hat-trick but I wasn't grumbling. I came close, you know. I actually hit the face of the crossbar near the end. Big Jock had told us beforehand, 'Get a two-goal advantage and I'm sure we'll get through.' My first goal came just before the hour mark when Big Tommy launched one downfield. It might have been a clearance but he has always assured me it was an inch-perfect pass! Anyway, suddenly I had a bit of freedom in the Dukla penalty area and managed to flick the ball with the outside of my foot and it carried past their keeper.

BRIGHT-EYED BHOY! A fresh-faced Billy McNeill prepares to embark upon his glorious career in the green-and-white hoops of the only team he wanted to play for. The captain made 790 appearances before retiring after the Scottish Cup Final triumph of 1975.

EUROPE, LOOK OUT! A young and grimly determined Tommy Gemmell poses for the camera. But, during play, Big Tommy managed to put a smile on the faces of the Celtic support with his cavalier style as he pioneered attacking play by fullbacks.

READY FOR ACTION! Jim Craig races from the Celtic tunnel as he prepares for another shift at right back. The dependable defender rarely made a mistake and contributed handsomely to the triumph in Lisbon when he set up the equalising goal for Tommy Gemmell.

HEADS I WIN! John Clark displays his aerial ability but the classy sweeper was more at home with the ball on the ground as he patrolled behind his defenders. John was one of the unsung heroes as he played in every one of Celtic's games en route to Lisbon.

HIGH-FLYER! Willie Wallace's career soared after he signed for Celtic from Hearts in December 1966 – the only player bought for the Lisbon Lions by Jock Stein. He made an instant impact on his European debut, netting two goals in the semi-final win over Dukla Prague.

THE MAN WITH THE GOLDEN TOUCH! Stevie Chalmers relaxes away from football but the energetic striker's lightning reflexes were evident in Lisbon when he crashed the winning goal past Inter Milan goalkeeper Giuliano Sarti with only five minutes remaining.

BRING 'EM ON! Super-confident Bertie Auld patrolled the Celtic midfield alongside Bobby Murdoch. His motto was, 'Let the other team worry about me!' Bertie started his career with Celtic but moved to Birmingham City and then returned just before Jock Stein arrived.

BUZZ-BOMB BOBBY! Celtic's fleet-footed frontman Bobby Lennox was one of the fastest men in football. Jock Stein utilised his pulverising acceleration when he moved him in from the wing where his sheer pace used to terrify defences at home and abroad.

THE WIZARD OF THE WING! No one ever had to ask why Jimmy Johnstone was nicknamed 'Jinky' – one glimpse of the little outside right in action told you immediately. Johnstone took severe punishment from defences over the years but never once flinched.

MIDFIELD MAESTRO! Bobby Murdoch helped to make Celtic tick as he surged forward. He was the possessor of an awesome shot that saw him score over 100 goals for the club and he was a key man all the way through the nine games that led to Europe's pinnacle.

SAFE HANDS! Ronnie Simpson made a football fairytale come true when he picked up a European Cup winners' medal at the age of thirty-six. The veteran goalkeeper also made his Scotland international debut at the same age – and helped beat England at Wembley.

THE MASTERMIND! Jock Stein was the motivating force that turned Celtic from a team that hadn't won a trophy in seven seasons to conquerors of Europe two years after his return. He was the man who gave the players the belief they were the best.

JOE McBRIDE just couldn't stop scoring goals at the start of the eventful 1966/67 season but, unfortunately for him, injury ruled him out after the turn of the year.

WILLIE O'NEILL played in the first four European Cup games at left back but missed out when Tommy Gemmell moved over from the right.

CHARLIE GALLAGHER was an underrated midfield player who was a more than capable understudy to the likes of Murdoch and Auld.

JOHN HUGHES played in five of the eight games that took Celtic to Lisbon but had to step down when Jock Stein named his historic line-up.

SIR ROBERT KELLY was the ambitious chairman of Celtic who always believed that football should be played in a flamboyant, attacking mode.

BACKROOM BHOYS Neilly Mochan (extreme left), Sean Fallon and Bob Rooney (extreme right) listen to some tactics advice from The Boss, Jock Stein.

GLORY HERE WE COME! The Celtic team group at the start of the memorable 1966/67 season – only Willie Wallace, yet to sign from Hearts, was missing from the squad that would become masters of all they surveyed.
Captain Billy McNeill (centre) has the Scottish Cup at his feet – more were to follow!

About five minutes or so later, Celtic Park just went crazy when I scored again. It was all down to the cunning antics of Bertie Auld. He stepped up to take a free kick, paused and looked as though he was about to re-centre it. I knew what was coming next, though. Bertie merely slipped the ball to the left and I was coming in behind him to hit it first time. The ball flew through their defensive wall and was in the net before Ivo Viktor could move. It looked like an impromptu bit of skill from Wee Bertie but, take my word for it, that little bit of trickery came straight off the training ground. We practised that move every day. It was an idea from Big Jock who was always looking at ways of developing free kicks and corner kicks. He always urged us to put variety into dead-ball situations and Wee Bertie seized the moment against Dukla Prague. The Czechs were startled. They started pointing at Stevie Chalmers and claiming offside. Stevie had followed my shot into the net but there was no way he was off. It was just his speed getting round the back of the wall that got him into that position. When I connected with the ball I can assure everyone that Stevie was well onside.

So, we got our two goals and it was off to Prague a fortnight later for the second leg. Big Jock had a dilemma before that confrontation. He didn't want to play defensively but he knew how close we were to Lisbon and he also rated the Czechs as a fine team. An early goal for them in front of their own support could have made all the difference. Big Jock wasn't prepared to give them that opportunity. Hence, he took me aside and had a word about my new role in the side. He assured me it was a complete one-off and I was happy to hear that. But I was also determined to get the job done properly.

Big Jock always did his homework and he knew Masopust was the key figure in the side. He had played well enough at Celtic Park, drawing a couple of gasps from our fans with his deft little touches. However, by the time the kick-off came round, I was ready for the challenge. I think I did fairly well, even if I do say so myself. Masopust had a quiet game with me at his side throughout. I could sense he was getting frustrated as the game wore on. To their credit, the Czechs put a lot into that encounter. We had surrendered possession as we picked up their forward players and, consequently, they had a lot of the ball. We were determined they weren't going to make good use of it.

Ronnie Simpson had a couple of super saves in the first half that helped settle the nerves. Faither was a top-class goalkeeper and I had known him for years – long before either of us turned up at Celtic. When I was Hearts and Ronnie was across the city at Hibs, we used to play in the same Edinburgh Select teams. English sides such as Spurs and Chelsea would come up for these specially arranged games and, more often than not, Ronnie and I found ourselves in the same line-up. Ronnie, in fact, was the epitome of a real gentleman. He was a likeable guy with a great sense of humour. In Prague, though, it was all about getting the job done. I recall him screaming at his defence after a lapse in concentration by someone. There was only about a minute to go but Faither wasn't having anyone switching off at any time.

I must give a special mention here to Stevie Chalmers. I know he is a modest chap who would never blow his own trumpet but he was quite outstanding in Prague. He covered every inch of ground inside Dukla's half for ninety minutes and never complained. He was our lone frontman and he must have found that strange. Normally, Stevie would have had me for company with Bobby Lennox and Wee Jinky not too far away. He would have been used to Bobby Murdoch and Bertie Auld coming up from behind him to add their weight to the attack. It didn't happen that way in Prague. He was on his own, a solitary green-and-white hooped shirt in enemy territory.

We got through and, after being involved in only three hours of the competition, I was in a European Cup Final! It all came so quickly for me. And I genuinely mean it when I say Europe wasn't on my mind when I joined the club. But there we were, in the European Cup Final where we were told later we would be playing Inter Milan in Lisbon. I had come an awful long way from making my debut for Stenhousemuir in front of a sparse crowd at Ochilview. It was all a dream, really. I was so delighted to be there. Maybe my Uncle Jim, back in Kirkintilloch, might even have been happy for me, too!

I'm fairly certain he wouldn't have been cheering me on when I made my Old Firm debut at Ibrox on 6 May, nineteen days before Lisbon. Celtic got a 2–2 draw and clinched their second successive title. Wee Jinky was great that day. He netted twice, the second being a left-foot long-range effort into the roof of the net, and, generally, turned in one of those performances that leave you with a smile on your face – unless, of course, you were a Rangers player. I don't suppose too many of my family were cheering from the rafters, either, when I made my first appearance against Rangers at Celtic Park on 30 August later that year. It was a League Cup tie and, with about fifteen minutes or so to go, we were trailing 1–0. It looked like curtains for us when Willie Henderson, their bag-of-tricks right-winger, was brought down in our box and the referee immediately pointed to the spot. We couldn't complain. Something extraordinary happened next, though. Kai Johansen, the Ibrox side's right back, took the kick and blasted it against the crossbar. With Ronnie out of position, Johansen actually got in front of a teammate to head the rebound goalwards – an immediate foul for us as he had touched the ball twice without an opponent getting a touch.

That was the wake-up call we needed that night. With time running out, we knew it would have been just about impossible to pull back two goals. We went into overdrive after that let-off and I scored, following a corner kick. I just threw myself at the ball and it bounced behind their goalkeeper, Erik Sorensen. Rangers were still trying to regroup when Bobby Murdoch flighted in one of those incredible lobs of his and Bobby Lennox raced clean through to tuck number three into the Rangers net.

It was absolutely enthralling stuff and we realised we had got out of jail with Johansen's miss. Celtic had played in the three pervious finals, beating Rangers twice, but we were only fifteen or so minutes away from ending that run until our remarkable comeback. Uncle Jim must have been getting a bit fed up with his nephew around this time!

I was on the score sheet again when we claimed the trophy, beating Dundee 5–3 at Hampden. Stevie, with two, Bobby Lennox and Big Yogi were our other scorers.

We left for Argentina right after that game to play Racing Club in what was officially called the Inter-Continental Championship, but was more commonly known as the World Club Championship. With the help of Big Billy's aerial ability and a soaring header, we had won the first leg at Hampden in front of 90,000 fans. Racing's players were a disgrace and we didn't know what exactly awaited us in Buenos Aires. We had a fair idea, though. However, we hadn't anticipated Ronnie Simpson coming close to being knocked out even before a ball had been kicked. Ronnie was doing his rounds, checking out his goal area and suchlike, when some thug threw a piece of metal at him. Unfortunately, his aim was true and it smacked our keeper on the head. Ronnie had to have instant medical treatment and there was no way he could continue. John Fallon was hastily prepared and thrown on for only his second first-team game of the season – the other coming in a 2–0 win over Ayr United in the League Cup.

We should have walked away when Ronnie got injured but the lure of conquering the world was just too much of a temptation. Tommy Gemmell actually gave us the lead via a penalty kick but Racing came back to win 2–1. If the away-goals rule had been activated back then, we would have returned to Scotland as world champions. Instead, we faced a third game play-off in Uruguay and that just descended into utter farce. It was mayhem and madness in Montevideo on 4 November, three days after the match in Argentina.

WILLIE WALLACE

Would you believe I was the only Celtic forward not to get sent off? Jimmy Johnstone, Bobby Lennox, John Hughes and Bertie Auld were all ordered off. Bertie, in fact, told the Paraguayan referee, a bloke called Rodolfo Osorio, that he wasn't going to leave the field. The match official, who had lost the plot and had also sent off two Argentinians, didn't know what to do. Wee Bertie just point-blank refused to go and the ref started the game with a free kick to Celtic. It was all getting completely out of hand. I'm still not sure why Wee Jinky and Bobby were sent off but Big Yogi went after clattering into their keeper. 'I didn't think anyone was watching,' said Yogi afterwards. Just the world!

Robert Kelly, the Celtic chairman, didn't want to play the third game. He was all for us getting on the next plane and coming home. Big Jock, though, thought Racing Club might behave better in a neutral country and we might be allowed to play. That was wishful thinking. Racing's players were brutal and they clearly would go to any lengths to win that trophy. I could always look after myself but you do get a bit frustrated with people trying to kick you, spit on you, nip you and, in general, abuse you. It wasn't football as I knew it. We lost that crazy confrontation 1–0 and it was immediately dubbed The Second Battle of the River Plate. We were all happy to get home. If Lisbon was a dream, then, plainly, Buenos Aires and Montevideo combined to become our worst nightmare. I'm glad to say the good thoughts of Lisbon by far outweigh the nonsense we encountered in South America.

Of course, all this was far removed from my early days in football. I had two interesting years at Raith Rovers while playing alongside an extravagantly gifted young guy who performed at left-half. You might know the name – Jim Baxter! Slim Jim would, of course, go on to join Rangers but, strangely enough, he needed a whole load of persuading to leave Stark's Park in the first place. As a Fifer, he was quite content with life at the Rovers and never had any ambitions to go elsewhere. If Jock

Stein had been at Celtic at the time there may have been a twist in the tale of Jim Baxter's career! Jim became a huge admirer of Jock after their stints together on the Scottish international front. Big Jock became caretaker manager of the team as they tried to qualify for the 1966 World Cup Finals in England. Jim liked Big Jock's style and his thoughts on how football should be played and there was no surprise there. Jim, it must be said, wasn't a great fan of defending. He is remembered for other things, though.

I enjoyed playing alongside Baxter – he really was one of football's great characters. He was all left foot but what a left foot it was. He used to call it The Glove. When he was playing and you were looking to pass the ball to someone, you would hear this Fife accent shouting, 'Just give it to The Glove.' There would be Jim strolling around, without a care in the world, completely at ease with his many skills. Rangers would eventually entice him out of Fife and on to a bigger stage where Slim Jim came into his own.

Raith Rovers didn't play in front of vast crowds back then but, on one of the odd occasions Jim and I were in the same line-up again, it was just a wee bit different – England v. Scotland at Wembley! That game came just days after our 3–1 victory over Dukla Prague and it was expected that Wee Jinky would play at outside right against the world champions. Unfortunately for the Wee Man, he picked up an injury against the Czechs and was ruled out. That left the way open for a certain Willie Wallace and I got the call to play against the English. Two goals in a European Cup semi-final and then a place in the team to face England at a packed Wembley – I knew my life would change when I joined Celtic but possibly not to this extent.

Jim Baxter was at his imperious best that day. We all remember him strutting his stuff and, in such an arrogant manner, putting England to the sword. 'World champions? England? Don't make me laugh!' he said often enough as we prepared for Wembley. It certainly wasn't a case of bravado either. It was the real thing and Jim knew he was going to have a great day out against Sir Alf Ramsey's side. I wasn't complaining either. Happily, I was involved in our first goal when I fired in a low shot from the right side of the penalty area. Gordon Banks went down and got a hand to it but couldn't hold the attempt. He spilled it and that was all Denis Law needed to swoop and put the ball away. Denis's reflexes in the box were like lightning. Make a mistake when he was around and you would get punished. Bobby Lennox and Jim McCalliog netted the others as we won 3–2 and I was celebrating once more. I was getting used to the high life! Denis Law said afterwards, 'Beating them on their own midden made it even more satisfying!'

Talking of Jim Baxter reminds me of George Connelly who was very similar in so many ways and, in fact, was also a native of Fife. Big Geordie had all the skill in the world – a lovely languid, flowing style with unerring vision. He really should have had a great career but, sadly, it never materialised. He could cope with anything on a football field but not so well off it. It was a real waste of God-given talent. He was quite a shy bloke and I remember rooming with him for three nights at our hideaway at Seamill before the Scottish Cup Final against Rangers in 1969. I'll never forget it because I got hardly any sleep the night before the big game.

Geordie had been told early by Big Jock that he would be playing because we would be without both Jimmy Johnstone and John Hughes. Geordie must have been fairly confident of emerging as a winner because he was already trying to figure out how to spend his bonus money. I was trying to get some shut-eye when Geordie stretched across from his bed and nudged me on the shoulder. 'Wispy, do you think I should get a new bathroom suite?' I was asked.

'Aye, goodnight,' I answered.

A few minutes later there was another nudge. 'Wispy, do you think I would be better off with a new kitchen?'

'Aye, goodnight.'

Another few minutes. 'Wispy, how about a conservatory?'

'Get some bloody sleep!'

'Wispy, how about an extension to our dining room?' It just went on throughout the night. I was knackered by the time we sat down for breakfast. And, no, I haven't a clue what he spent his bonus cash on. Probably a car!

Geordie played magnificently against Rangers at Hampden the following day. He oozed class. With the ball at his feet, anything was possible. He ambled through the game and even scored a superb solo goal to give us a 3–0 interval advantage. We went on to win 4–0 and, once again, I don't think Uncle Jim would have been too ecstatic! Me? I was just happy to get home for a good night's sleep.

Wee Jinky, of course, was another unbelievable character. I've always thought someone should write a Harry Potter-style book about a wee footballer who could do all these magical things as he grows up. You could base it on the life and times of Jimmy Johnstone, I suppose. People chat about the Wee Man and, inevitably, the talk gets round to the rowing-boat incident at Largs when he was fooling around late at night and, without oars, took off doon the watter while his Scottish team-mates looked on in horror. Someone managed to plunge into the freezing waters of the Firth of Clyde that evening and save Wee Jinky's bacon. The press got hold of the story and they had a field day. The Wee Man wasn't too pleased about figuring on the front pages. And it was hardly ideal preparation for the next game, which just happened to be against the Auld Enemy, England, themselves, at Hampden.

It was 1974 and manager Willie Ormond was putting the finishing touches to his squad for the World Cup Finals in West Germany that summer. Willie Morgan, then at Manchester United, was pushing for a place in the team in Jinky's position at outside right and Ormond was in a bit of a quandary. Should he stick with Jinky against England? Or leave him out and risk being accused of dropping him for a matter unrelated to football? Either way, Ormond wanted to put a team out on the pitch that would be good enough to beat the English – that was his main concern. Jinky played a stormer and Scotland won 2–0. I am told that Jinky made an interesting gesture in the general direction of the Hampden press box as he came off the pitch. Maybe he was informing them Scotland had scored two goals!

Jinky was a law unto himself, of course. Big Tommy and I had him at Dundee when Tommy was manager and I was a coach. His signing really excited our supporters and I can tell you Jinky was about to pick up some really good money. However, it was all related to him actually playing. That was back in 1977, two years after he had left Celtic. He had had a spell at Sheffield United but was now up for grabs again after they allowed him to move on. Jinky was only thirty-two at the time and Big Tommy and I reasoned he still had a lot to offer as a player. We offered him a two-year contract with, I believe, a very good signing-on fee spread over the length of the deal. There were all sorts of other add-ons – bonuses for points, where Dundee were in the league and the like. However, as I said, it was all totally dependent on Jinky being out there and playing. He wasn't going to earn a fortune sitting in the stand.

He kept the family home in Lanarkshire and solved the problem of travelling by staying at Big Tommy's hotel in Errol during the week. I was told to give him a doing in training some days by Tommy if he thought the Wee Man's fitness levels weren't quite what he expected. Jinky, it must be stated, was a great trainer. Hard work didn't frighten him. But he wasn't as dedicated off the park as we had hoped and, after a heart-to-heart among the three of us, it was decided to cancel his contract. He was at Dens Park for all of three months. It was all quite sad but you could never get upset at the Wee Man.

The whole of Europe would have wanted to sign Wee Jinky a decade before. He was a special player and Lisbon was an ideal setting for him. He told me and all the other Lions afterwards that he wished he could have contributed more that day. We told him to behave himself and stop looking for compliments. Inter Milan stuck a bloke called Tarcisio Burgnich on him that day and he was one of the best man-markers in the world – if not *the* best. But Jinky stuck at his task throughout the ninety minutes and he must have felt as frustrated as Masopust was with me in the semi-final. Burgnich never left his side and Jinky took him into areas that opened up the way for Bobby Murdoch and Wee Bertie to come through. It's not the stuff that is immediately noticeable, or even appreciated by some supporters, but players know what it is all about.

Anyway, I will always remember Wee Jinky coming so close that day with a header, which wasn't bad for a bloke who stood 5ft 4in. Cairney dinked one in from the right and, for once, Burgnich was nowhere to be seen. Jinky just took off and made perfect contact with his head. The ball was hurtling high into the net until Giuliano Sarti, who might have thought it was going over under its own steam, suddenly reacted to the danger and sprang high to get a hand to the effort and turn it over the crossbar. If he had hesitated, Wee Jinky would have scored – with a header!

Remarkable things happened around the Wee Man, of course. I recall a European Cup tie at Celtic Park in season 1968/69 when we were playing a very classy Yugoslav team, Red Star Belgrade. It was hard going and we got in at half-time, drawing 1–1 and finding it extremely difficult to prise open their defence. Big Jock then pulled off a masterstroke. He took the Wee Man aside and said, 'If we win this one by four clear goals you won't have to go to Belgrade for the next game.'

As everyone knew, Jinky hated flying. He looked at The Boss. 'Are you serious?' he asked.

'I'm not joking – four goals and you can stay at home.'

Jinky always gave 100 per cent, of course, but the thought of not having to step on to a plane and fly to Yugoslavia was an extra ingredient in him reaching new levels. He rolled up his sleeves and demanded the ball. Big Tommy could have had it over in the left-back position and Wee Jinky could have been on the right wing but he was still screaming for a pass! As I recall, the second half had hardly started when Jinky fired us into the lead with a strong shot that hit the roof of the net. Not long after that, he took off on one of those mind-boggling mazy runs of his. I swear he beat four Red Star defenders before slipping the ball across for Bobby Lennox to rattle into the net. Two down and two to go.

With about fifteen minutes to go, Jinky nodded the ball neatly into my path and I connected to drill a shot low past their goalkeeper.

'I still need another one,' exclaimed Jinky as he ran back to the halfway line.

It looked as though he would be out of luck, though, as the clock ticked down. Then, minutes from time, he picked up a loose ball about ten yards inside his own half. The Red Star defenders should have sensed danger. Jinky went into that wee crouch of his and started to make his way towards goal. One defender was dismissed with a swerve while another tackled fresh air. Another shimmy and Jinky was in on the keeper. He didn't even hesitate as he fired the ball low and true into the corner. All we could hear above the din was Wee Jinky shouting, 'I don't have to go! I don't have to go!'

I netted in the second leg as we got a 1–1 draw and advanced into the next round on a formidable 6–2 aggregate victory over a team who were no one's mugs. It was just their bad luck they were up against Wee Jinky in one of his moods. His performance against Inter Milan may not have been as eye-catching but it was just as effective.

I am glad to say I had a hand, quite literally, in Big Tommy's equaliser in Lisbon. I took the shy that moved the ball around the field before finishing behind the redoubtable Sarti! I recall I was going to throw it into the penalty box but their giant defender Giacinto Facchetti blocked my view. Big Jock used to hammer it into us to play the ball into the opposing team's box because you couldn't be offside at a throw-in. If you had a guy, for instance, standing right on the byeline, your opponents would be forced to cover him because he will be onside. By that reckoning, their defence would fall back and that would give someone else the opportunity to be played onside if there was a flick on or a rebound. So, in effect, I should have pitched the ball into the mix. But Facchetti prevented that and I actually threw it back to Big Tommy. I thought, if nothing else, it would be better for us to keep possession. And from that came our leveller.

Now, if big Facchetti had just minded his own business . . .

8

STEVIE CHALMERS

Jock Stein used to con me rotten. I can never thank him enough for that! He was a master manipulator, that's for sure, and Celtic would never have won the European Cup without him.

He really shook things up when he arrived at Celtic Park in March 1965. His eye for detail was simply amazing. He knew how to get the absolute best out of a player and I should know because he worked his psychology on me time after time. He would leave me out of the first team and take me aside to tell me, 'Look, I know you should be playing. You are better than that mug who's in your position but I've got to play him. You should be keeping him out of the side but he's in and you're not and it's up to you to do something about it. Force me to play you.' What I didn't know was the fact Big Jock would be saying the same to the other players. If I was playing, he would grab Joe McBride or whoever and say, 'You should be playing – you're better than that Chalmers.' It worked a treat too, didn't it? Everyone wanted into that first team and, even when you were dropped, you were geed up because The Boss thought you were better than the player in your position and you just had to work that wee bit harder to get your place back.

I must have done something right because I played in all nine games in our European Cup run in 1967 and that, for me, was fairly impressive. I might be the guy who got the winning goal in Lisbon, but, believe me, being involved all the way through is something that will live with me forever. Now, how did I feel when I netted against Inter Milan with only five minutes to go? Exhausted! Cramp was coming on but that evaporated as soon as that ball hit the back of the net. OK, it may not have been as spectacular as Big Tommy's effort but, for me, it was special because it was part of a routine we worked on day in, day out at training at Barrowfield. Big Jock would get Joe McBride, Willie Wallace, Bobby Lennox, John Hughes and me to line up around the six-yard line and he would get Big Tommy, Bobby Murdoch, Bertie Auld, Jim Craig and Charlie Gallagher to hammer over crosses from the left and, after that, the right. Then he would vary the routine with Big Tommy playing the ball back from the line to, say, Bobby to hit the ball diagonally across the face of the goal. He would then do the same on the right with Cairney laying the ball back for someone to hit a similar effort into the penalty box. This would go on for hours until you knew off by heart where you were expected to be in the penalty box whenever a move was developing. It was no fluke, believe me, that I was standing where I was when Big Tommy pulled the ball back to Bobby to thump in his shot from the edge of the box.

People have said they thought Bobby's effort might have found the net without my help but Bobby himself would tell anyone his shot was heading for a shy! I simply side-footed the ball past Giuliano Sarti, Inter's superb goalkeeper, and the European Cup was heading for the east end of Glasgow. You'll see pictures of Sarti appealing for offside – well, he would, wouldn't he? – but there was no way I was off. I was well onside when I got my touch to the ball. Big Jock always hammered into us the importance of being aware of where you were in the opposition's box. He didn't want a move breaking down because of a lapse of concentration on anyone's part.

The whole European Cup run was one great adventure and, like I said, I was just delighted to have played in every single minute of every single game. Ronnie Simpson, Tommy Gemmell, Bobby Murdoch, Billy McNeill, John Clark and Jimmy Johnstone were the others who achieved that feat. Obviously, scoring the most historic goal in Celtic's history is something I treasure but I would like to think I also played my part in beating Vojvodina Novi Sad in the quarter-final. And I am not talking about my goal that made it 1–1 on aggregate and set up the grand finale for Big Billy to head in the last-minute winner. Our skipper was accused of fouling their goalkeeper, Ilija Pantelic, but I can now confess he didn't come close to touching him . . . because I did! It wasn't a foul, though, I hasten to add. It was something that happened all the time in penalty boxes and I was blocked off a few times myself. However, on this occasion, I took a wee step in front of the keeper as he left his line in order to cut out Charlie Gallagher's right-wing corner kick.

It was only half a yard or so but it managed to put Pantelic off his stride. He couldn't get anywhere near the swirling ball and Big Billy, as he did so often, got his head to Charlie's cross to bullet an effort high into the net. Celtic Park erupted! The Yugoslavs were pointing fingers at everyone. They shouted at the referee but he was having none of it. The goal was good and he pointed to the centre circle. These things happen in football. I got knocked around a few times and, of course, I will always remember our semi-final against Dukla Prague in Czechoslovakia. That was the one and only time I was banned from entering my own team's half of the field. Big Jock laid it on the line. 'Keep busy, Stevie,' he said. 'Let them know you're out there.' OK, Boss! I was never afraid to put myself about and, as I recall, a few players bumped into my elbows that afternoon! It's a man's game, after all. I just kept going for the entire ninety minutes and the Dukla back lot weren't pleased. It was one of the hardest shifts I ever put in but we were ninety minutes away from the European Cup Final and, if that doesn't give you momentum, then nothing will.

Obviously, Dukla wanted to give me a hard time. They tried to get me to retreat into my own half beside my team-mates but I was having none of that. I had a job to do and that was to get about their defence and keep them stretched. Not the most glamorous role in the team, I'm sure you'll agree, but one that was vital in that game. The Czechs were a very good team and they liked to build from the back. They used their captain Josef

Masopust a lot, passing the ball through the midfield so that's where I came in. I was asked to harry them, chase them and make sure they didn't get the opportunity to dwell on the ball. If that's what Big Jock wanted, then that's what Big Jock would get – I was desperate to stay in his first team!

But Dukla did pin us back by their attacking play. They had scored that vital away goal and they must have thought a win against us was within their scope. They may even have been heartened to know that we had thrown away a three-goal advantage in Budapest against MTK only three years earlier. However, this was a different Celtic team with an entirely different attitude.

Looking back to 1964, our preparation for that European Cup-Winners' Cup semi-final second leg was a joke. I don't think we trained at all on the Tuesday prior to the match. We did a bit of sightseeing and then went to a bash at the British Embassy in Budapest. We should have got some ball work in and we could have done with a rest. We were told afterwards that the MTK players had been taken away to a retreat somewhere for a fortnight and told to do nothing but concentrate on beating Celtic and getting into that final. I had scored two goals in our 3–0 success in the first game and, naturally enough, everyone believed we had done enough to get through.

I recall the Celtic fans chanting for us to come out and do a lap of honour after that victory. We were already in the dressing room and were without boots when we were told to go out and take the applause from our support. They were refusing to budge and, like us, must have been fairly confident of playing in Brussels in the final. We came out, took a bow and everyone went home with a smile on their faces.

I don't think they were celebrating too much when they heard the second-leg score! So, Dukla maybe believed they were about to face a team that could collapse under pressure but, if so, they were to be sorely disappointed. They may even have noted that we had also lost in our previous away game

– the 1–0 defeat in Yugoslavia against Vojvodina Novi Sad. But we were learning all the time and we put our experience to a good use in Prague.

Ironically, Big Jock actually looked a bit disappointed at the end of that match against Dukla. Sure, he was delighted that Celtic had become the first British club to reach the final of the European Cup. However, he realised we hadn't done it in our normal fashion. The flair, the ambition, the adventure wasn't in evidence and those facets of our play were very important to him. He gathered us around him in the dressing room and said, 'We will never play like that again. I will never ask you to play all-out defence again.' He was as good as his word. If we were defending in games after that, it was because we were being pushed back and never as a pre-arranged tactic.

Lisbon was made all the sweeter because I had been at Celtic eight years before then, signing from junior club Ashfield, and life was fairly tough until Jock Stein walked back through those doors. He turned the whole place upside down and pointed us in the right direction. He went into everything in minute detail. He seemed to enjoy training sessions and he worked us hard – anyone caught slacking would find himself doing an extra few laps. I've got to laugh when I think back then about our training gear. We were expected to wear these horrible woolly polo necks that must have weighed a stone or two! I'm not sure they were ever washed. They just always seemed to be there, lying in a heap in the dressing room, and, of course, we didn't know any better as there were no alternatives. So, on would go these monstrosities and, if you were really lucky, it wouldn't rain. If it poured down from the heavens, these things doubled in weight.

Thankfully, that out-of-date gear vanished overnight when Big Jock arrived. Suddenly, we were handed training kits that actually looked like training kits. It was a small detail, perhaps, but just another instance of Big Jock's fine-tuning of the team.

He reasoned that, if we looked more professional, we would act and play in the same manner.

There was absolutely no way I could have ever believed Celtic would one day conquer Europe when I signed for the club on 6 February 1959. I made my debut just a month later, in an instantly forgettable 2–1 defeat by Airdrie at Celtic Park. Imagine that – one month, I was turning out for Ashfield in a junior game and the next I was playing for the famous Glasgow Celtic! Couldn't happen today, could it? Possibly not surprisingly, that was my only league appearance of that particular campaign. Now you see me, now you don't!

But I got a run in the top side at the start of the following season when I played in eleven out of twelve games, all at outside right. Could I show that Jimmy Johnstone a thing or two! I always had a fair turn of speed and Jimmy McGrory, the Celtic manager at the time, thought I would be better suited to life on the wing. I still wanted to get in among the goals, though, and I netted five in those eleven games. I was fortunate enough to also play in the Scottish Cup semi-final against Rangers that season and I scored in the 1–1 draw on 2 April 1960. To be honest, Rangers dominated us back then – it still hurts to admit that – and they beat us 4–1 in the replay four days later. Neilly Mochan, our trainer in Lisbon, was the Celtic goalscorer that evening. Billy McNeill played against the Ibrox men too and, if anyone had even mentioned to Big Billy, Neilly or me that we would rule Europe in seven years' time, I am pretty certain we would have had them locked up.

But, of course, things changed drastically and dramatically under Big Jock. Jimmy McGrory was a real gentleman, a lovely man in every way, but, if I am being honest, it seemed his main job was to read out the team. We were never too sure if he or Robert Kelly, our chairman, picked the side. There was always talk that McGrory would pin up the team sheet on a Thursday night after the weekly board meeting and Kelly would take it down and make a few changes as he saw fit. I mean this as absolutely no disrespect to Jimmy McGrory. That was just how it was in those days. The managers rarely took training, for a start. They had other things to do. I knew of one club where the manager used to make up the team's wages!

So, along came Big Jock and the revolution kicked in. I was selected in his very first team when I played outside right in the 6–0 win over Airdrie at Broomfield. In rapid succession, I played against St Johnstone, Dundee, Hibs (twice) and Third Lanark but Wee Jinky came in for the last three league matches of the season against Falkirk, Partick Thistle and Dunfermline. However, I got the nod ahead of the Wee Man for the Scottish Cup Final meeting with Dunfermline at Hampden on 24 April and, my goodness, am I delighted I did not miss out on that one! What a fabulous memory – I remember it being a rollicking encounter that ebbed and flowed and kept everyone on tenterhooks almost right to the end until Big Billy headed in our winner. People often say Celtic were like one big happy family back then and I think this result helped forge that special relationship. It was just great to be part of a Celtic team that had actually won something. I know the other players felt the same. Suddenly we were winners and, take it from me, it certainly beat the alternative.

The road to Lisbon kicked off on 28 September 1966 with a match against the Swiss champions Zurich at Celtic Park. As I recall, they were an excellent side and I believe Ronnie Simpson had to make a brilliant save while the game was still goalless. A Zurich player tried his luck from outside the penalty area and the ball took a severe swerve in mid-air. Ronnie was already moving to his right when he suddenly had to check his movement, throw up a left hand and punch the ball to safety. It was pure instinct but, of course, a lot of what Ronnie did was just that. His reflexes were still as sharp as they were when he made his debut for Queen's Park as a fourteen-year-old. So, if it hadn't been for some improvisation from Faither, we could have been in big trouble. We breathed a sigh of relief and kept chipping away at the Swiss defence.

The breakthrough goal came from a rather surprising source – our right back Tommy Gemmell. It was his first goal of the season and, boy, was his timing pretty good. If you thought his equaliser in Lisbon was sensational, you should have seen this one. He belted it from way out on the right and the keeper hadn't an earthly as it raged over his head into the net. Joe Mc-Bride grabbed a second and we were fairly confident we would be in the next round. And so it proved. Big Tommy thumped in two more, one a penalty kick, and I got the other – my first-ever goal in Europe's premier tournament. You could say it was a typical Chalmers finish from close-range.

I claimed another in the second round against Nantes in France as we won 3–1 and I was on the score sheet again in the second leg when we triumphed at Celtic Park by an identical score. Then it was on to Yugoslavia to face Vojvodina Novi Sad and, yes, like all the other Lisbon Lions, I really rated this team. You know, I couldn't name any of their outfield players although Pantelic was gathering a bit of a reputation throughout Europe as being a top goalkeeper. He was class all right although, to be fair, he wasn't exactly overworked in the opening game when they won 1–0.

It was an entirely different story in Glasgow, though, as you might expect. The atmosphere at Celtic Park was electrifying that night. The fans were in great voice and they did become our twelfth man. Again, I was fortunate enough to score and it was all down to Big Tommy belting down that left wing. Both Big Tommy and Cairney would run all day up and down their wings and they were way ahead of their time. On this occasion, Big Tommy, on the left, swung in an inviting cross and I tried to get between the goalkeeper and a defender. It was one of those crossed balls that just needed a touch to knock it over the line – any touch would have done. Pantelic threw himself at it but got caught up with his own defender – nothing to do with me this time, honest! – and the ball dropped right in front of me. I couldn't miss and I just fired it over the line.

That set up the big finish and Billy duly provided us with our semi-final passport with a little assistance from yours truly, of course. Dukla Prague was another stern test. They were a good side, too. I've already talked about Masopust and I think he is still one of the most famous Czechoslovakian names in football. OK, he wasn't in his prime when he played against us but he was still a very clever midfielder with the ability to hit superb passes. Dukla surprised us by taking the game to us at the start but normal service was soon resumed, especially when we got Wee Jinky on the ball. He set up a great chance for me and I nodded the ball past their goalkeeper but the referee ruled it out for an infringement by the Wee Man. The match official stated Jinky had his foot too high as he collected the ball but I couldn't see much wrong with it. Funnily enough, even the Czechs didn't appeal when I netted but the ref saw it differently and proved conclusively that he wasn't a homer. Wee Jinky did get one shortly afterwards, though, and that made us all a lot more happy. The frowns returned, however, when they levelled, on the stroke of half-time, with a bit of a scrappy goal. However, Willie Wallace, playing in his first European tie for the club, finished them off with two brilliant goals after the turnaround.

Wispy was my sort of guy. He was unselfish, would run all day, could put himself about and was always there with an encouraging word when it was needed. He wasn't bad at putting the ball in the net either, which was quite handy! We all knew Big Jock rated him even before he bought him from Hearts. When we were due to play the Edinburgh side, Big Jock would always make a special mention of Wispy. 'Keep your eye on him,' he would tell the defence. 'He's a danger.' We were all delighted to welcome him on board at Celtic, reckoning it was a lot better to have this guy in the team rather than lining up against us. I have to say he always gave us trouble. Folk have often said Jock moved swiftly for Wispy when he realised Joe McBride was going to be out for the remainder of the season. After forty years, I can now point out that is not the case. Joe, in fact, was injured on Christmas Eve 1966 in a 1–1 draw with Aberdeen at Pittodrie. And who was lining up alongside him in attack? A certain Willie Wallace. I know Big Jock was good at anticipating events in football but even he wasn't so exceptional that he could forecast the future. Wispy made his debut in a 4–2 win over Motherwell at Celtic Park at the start of December and he scored his first goals in a 6–2 triumph over Partick Thistle. Just thought I should clear that up!

I think, back then, Big Jock had it in his mind to play both Joe and Wispy as his main strikers with Bobby Lennox and me playing slightly wider but, after Joe was injured, I moved inside to play beside Wispy and Wee Jinky took over at outside right. We'll never know what the line-up in Lisbon would have been if Joe hadn't been stricken by injury. He had scored more than thirty goals before the turn of the year and was going like a bomb. Big Jock would have been hard pushed to leave him out of his first team. It was really unfortunate for Joe because he never got the chance to really cement his place in the top side again and, of course, left in 1968 for Hibs. Take a look at his record at Celtic Park, though – eighty-six goals in ninety-four appearances. Magnificent!

I was fortunate, as well, to get a few goals in my career although none, of course, would ever be more important than that one in Lisbon. I recall getting a hat-trick against Rangers on 3 January 1966 at Celtic Park and, after forty-one years, that record was still standing. Believe it or not, I was the last Celtic player to score three in a league game against the Ibrox side. Records are there to be broken – so get out there, someone, and do the business. There have been a few close calls, of course, since then. Kenny Dalglish, Charlie Nicholas, Brian McClair, Henrik Larsson and even Wispy have all claimed two but no one has hit a hat-trick. I well remember that game against

Rangers – because they scored in ninety seconds and led 1–0 at half-time! Davy Wilson was their goalscorer with a low shot that just eluded the diving Ronnie Simpson on a flint-hard surface. We came storming back but just couldn't get the ball past Billy Ritchie. That changed rather dramatically after the interval. I scored three and Bobby Murdoch and Charlie Gallagher pitched in with two thundering long-range efforts.

I had a quiet chuckle when I heard a Rangers fan talking to a Celtic supporter as I left the ground. 'Whit did ye think of that?' the Ibrox fan asked. Then he added, 'Two bad lots!' Slightly blinkered thinking there, I think!

I was fairly happy at knocking in three against our oldest rivals but you can imagine my surprise the following day when all the headlines were given to John Hughes! I score three and Yogi gets the praise – it's just not fair. Seriously, though, Yogi was unstoppable in the second half of that game and I think he actually set up all my goals after some fabulous runs down the left flank. He changed his boots at half-time and put on sandshoes. That was highly unusual in those days but Yogi was complaining about the slippery surface and decided to change his footwear, casting aside the more traditional boots. It worked a treat.

I was lucky enough to score a few more goals against Rangers and another that springs to mind came in our 4–0 win in the Scottish Cup Final in 1969 when I received an ear-bashing from one of my team-mates into the bargain! Rangers actually started that particular game as favourites as we were without our two natural wingers, Wee Jinky and Big Yogi. We had beaten Morton 4–1 in our semi-final but Rangers had dismantled a very good Aberdeen team 6–1 in their semi, which was played at Celtic Park. But we opened the scoring with a first-minute header from Big Billy and we didn't look back after that. Bobby Lennox drilled in the second and George Connelly, in for Wee Jinky, dispossessed John Greig, the Rangers skipper, walked the ball past Norrie Martin and rolled it into the empty net. He took it like he had been playing in Old Firm games all his life but, in fact, that was one of his rare first-team games that season.

So we were 3–0 up at half-time and we knew the game was over – the days of us surrendering three-goal leads were very much in the dark and distant past. Towards the end of the game, I picked up the ball wide on the left and just took off in the general direction of Norrie Martin. His team-mates had been caught upfield and I was allowed to keep on going. A colleague, I'm pretty sure it was Bobby Lennox, was racing into a good position for me to square the ball across goal. It would have been a simple tap-in but I was going for glory! I shaped to pass it but then hit it off the outside of my boot and it took the Rangers goalkeeper by surprise at his near post. As I celebrated, I heard a voice say, 'Greedy beggar!' Too right – I was a striker and I wanted my name on that score sheet.

I also remember scoring a goal for Scotland against the then world champions Brazil when they came to Hampden for a friendly back in 1966 as they prepared to defend their trophy in England later that year. The game had hardly started when Jim Baxter sent me away after conjuring up another of those wonderful through balls of his. He split the Brazilian defence and I raced on to it before slamming the ball high past the stranded Gilmar, their star goalkeeper. It ended 1–1 but I also recall what a great marking job John Clark did on the one and only Pelé that night. The Brazilian was, of course, rightly lauded as the best player in the world at the time and he could do things with a ball that we could only dream about. However, he met his match in a determined John Clark at Hampden and didn't threaten at all.

Another guy who was fairly adept at doing all sorts of things with a football was, of course, Wee Jinky. Where do you start with the accolades for the Wee Man? Like every other Lisbon Lion, I can only say it was a genuine pleasure to play with this character. He was always good fun, on and off the pitch. You know, Big Jock could have us all surrounding him as he talked tactics out on the training pitch. We would be standing there, arms folded and listening to The Boss. Jinky, though, would have the ball at his feet, juggling it from right to left and back again. He could never bear parting with that object. Maybe he overdid it sometimes on the pitch but he just couldn't help himself. He would beat a defender and then try to beat him a second time. The strikers would be running around the penalty box trying to make space and Jinky would be out there having a ball on the right wing. More often than not, though, he produced the goods.

He had a few run-ins with Big Jock but I believe The Boss genuinely liked the Wee Man. I think he realised he was just a bit different from the rest of us. If Jinky had a problem of some sort, Big Jock would want to hear about it. He always wanted his players to be 100 per cent concentrated on any forthcoming game. He didn't want anything cluttering up their thought processes. Nothing was to interfere on what they were about to produce out on the pitch.

Unfortunately, I didn't play against Leeds United in the European Cup semi-finals three years after Lisbon and, in fact, I left the club a year later for Morton. Naturally, though, I knew how much the two games against Don Revie's English champions meant to Big Jock. The English press had continually rammed it down everyone's throats that Leeds United were already the best team in the world, never mind Europe. It seemed they just had to turn up against Celtic to book their place in the final in Milan later that year.

Big Jock, as I have already said, was a master at getting the very best out of an individual. Anyway, as he prepared for the second Leeds game, he would go through his usual routines, working out systems and talking about formations on his favourite blackboard. He kept talking to the players, informing them of what he expected them to produce against the English side. Big Jock was never one to leave too much to chance. He rarely spoke to Jinky on this instance, though. He would talk to the other players but would simply point to the No. 7 marker, stop and say, 'This is the guy who is going to win this game for us. Give him the ball when you can – he'll be our ace.' Jinky would just sit there, beaming. The Boss was showing a lot of trust in him and he was loving it. Jock would continue talking, stop again and point once more to the No. 7 marker. 'Remember, this is the guy who is going to win this for us.' And so on and so on throughout his speech. By the time he had finished, Jinky was about 10ft tall and ready to take on the universe on his own.

Needless to say, Jinky did, indeed, go out there, pumped up to the heavens, and turn in a devastating display against Leeds United in the second leg at Hampden Park in front of a record European Cup attendance of 136,505. Celtic were already 1–0 ahead from the first game at Elland Road where George Connelly scored in the first minute.

My Scottish international team-mate Billy Bremner, whom I knew to be a lifelong Celtic fan, equalised with a long-range effort that left our goalkeeper Evan Williams standing. It was time for Jimmy Johnstone to stamp his authority on proceedings and he did so in that grand manner of his. Listen, Leeds were no ordinary team. They were packed with stars and had the English international left-sided defenders, Terry Cooper and Norman Hunter, in direct competition to Jinky. It didn't matter to the Wee Man, though, as he carved them open, time after time. I was beginning to feel sorry for Cooper and Hunter by the time it was almost over.

John Hughes put Celtic 2–1 ahead on aggregate and it was all over when Bobby Murdoch scored with a typical screamer, timed with awesome power from the edge of the penalty area. But it was Wee Jinky's game and trust him to do it when there was a record crowd watching his every move.

Bobby Lennox and I went to see Jinky during his illness. Even then the Wee Man displayed his great sense of humour. Bobby told his great friend that he was going to have a pacemaker fitted to his heart. Imagine the Buzz Bomb with a pacemaker!

Jinky looked at him and burst out laughing, 'Aw naw, Bobby, will I have to start calling you Gerry now?'

Bobby looked at me, 'Gerry?'

Jinky broke in, 'Come on, get with it – Gerry and the Pacemakers!'

That Wee Man cheered up so many people with that infectious humour of his. We all miss him.

I agree with Bobby, by the way, about the pre-season trip to America being a great thing for the club. Living with the same guys day and night for five weeks really did pull us together. You would have players who were friends with others, like Bobby and the Wee Man, for instance. I really liked Bobby Murdoch and Ronnie Simpson. There were no cliques, though. But the States did help us to get to know each other fairly well and I think that stood us in good stead for the rigours that were to come in the forthcoming year.

Lisbon capped it all and I wouldn't have minded playing in the next game, the Alfredo Di Stefano testimonial against Real Madrid at the Bernabeu. Big Jock, though, was adamant that the Lisbon Lions would never be beaten – that those eleven players would never taste defeat – so he rested Ronnie Simpson and me and brought in Willie O'Neill and John Fallon, our reserve goalkeeper. Actually, he should have rested everyone bar Wee Jinky because he was just out of this world that night in the Spanish capital. I told you he always saved his best for the big occasion. I've never seen a better individual performance.

After Lisbon, I came home to spend my bonus money. To be honest, I can't remember too much about my so-called spending spree. The wife, Sadie, would have got something, of course, and I probably spent the rest on things around the house. Not exactly Flash Harry, eh? But winning the European Cup was not all about money. It was about football and putting Celtic's name on the European map. We managed that and, of course, Big Jock was smiling afterwards because we did it in the Celtic manner.

Ach, I suppose we weren't a bad side.

9

BERTIE AULD

One major disappointment for yours truly on our big day in Lisbon was the fact that I did not get the opportunity to pit my wits against Inter Milan's Luis Suárez. Injury forced him out of their team and, in the aftermath of our triumph, the Italians immediately pointed out they would have picked up the trophy again if their much-vaunted Spanish midfielder had been playing. Believe me, that is utter nonsense. Suárez? They could have fielded Superman and they wouldn't have prevented us from winning that day!

The Italians, as ever, were just a bit too quick to delve into that well-thumbed tome, *The Big Book of Football Excuses*, although, to be fair, their manager Helenio Herrera and a few of their players were just as swift to congratulate us. They knew they had been outplayed, outfought and outwitted.

But I really would love to have squared up to Suárez. I was on the left-hand side of the Celtic midfield and his favoured position was the right-hand side of the Inter midline. It would have been very intriguing, to say the least, to see how we got on. These days, thanks to satellite television, you can get pictures of players and watch them in action at the flick of a button. Forty years ago, of course, that was not the case. You rarely saw up-to-date film of foreign players and all you had to go on was what your boss told you about so-and-so's strengths and weaknesses. They were all a bit mythical back then and you had to take someone else's word about their ability. Of course, you could catch up with reports in the newspapers but there's nothing quite like matching up with the guy in the flesh. Genuinely, I welcomed that opportunity in Suárez's case.

Suárez was one of the first football superstars. We all took a sharp intake of breath when we were told Inter Milan had paid a mind-boggling £214,000 to sign the player from Barcelona in 1961. That was massive money all those years ago – easily the world record transfer. Look at the Celtic team that took the field at the Estadio Nacionale six years later – it cost a total of £42,000, a mere fraction of what Suárez had been signed for. We were also informed the Spaniard had negotiated a signing-on fee of £60,000 for himself. I didn't think there had been that much money printed. The player was said to be picking up around £7,000 per year in wages. OK, I know an average player in the SPL can now command a figure like that on a weekly basis but, back in the sixties, that was massive dough. If I've got my sums right, the Celtic players were lifting something in the region of £1,300 a year in those heady financial days.

So, can anyone blame a wee chap from Maryhill for wanting to go toe-to-toe with this bloke? I would have loved it. I would have thrived on it. Apparently, Suárez was said to be suffering from a thigh strain in the run-in to Lisbon but we did hear other suggestions that, at the age of thirty-two, he might not fancy playing against Celtic. He would have known about our high energy levels. He would have heard about our fitness and our willingness to go flat out for ninety minutes. He was a cultured playmaker, of course, but this might not have been a setting for him to show those skills. I'm not saying he chickened out but what I will say is that it did not matter one jot whether or not he was on the field of play on Thursday, 25 May 1967 – we would have still won the European Cup.

Think about this, too. Suárez was not known for enjoying defensive duties. He did all his playing facing the opponents' goal from middle to front. Would he have chased Tommy Gemmell into corners? Would he have made runs to block off Bobby Lennox? Would he have trailed all over the place alongside yours truly? I doubt it. His replacement was a guy called Bilic and he was actually more of a defensively minded player and, naturally enough, Inter needed those sorts of performers the way that particular ninety minutes turned out. Maybe, if Suárez *had* turned out, we might have won a bit more comfortably than 2–1. I was also disappointed to read that the Italians were saying they had struggled for a replacement. They were having a laugh, weren't they? Inter Milan with their many millions, the most expensively structured line-up in the world could not find a suitable player to take over from Suárez? A team that had won the European Cup in two out of the previous three years and had also lifted the World Club Championship twice at the same time? Pull the other one!

So many fabulous memories come flooding back about that day. I'll tell you this, though – I'm totally convinced there was no need to kick-off in Lisbon. We won that game in the tunnel, believe me. I will always, always remember the horrified look on the faces of their players when I belted out 'The Celtic Song' and all my team-mates joined in. There was a fair distance to walk to the tunnel from the dressing room and we were all left standing there in this cramped space waiting for the go-ahead to come out and walk into that glorious sunshine en route to the lavish green grass of the pitch. The timing had to be absolutely right because, of course, the match was being beamed live throughout Europe and some networks would have timed it to start only five minutes or so before the kick-off, giving them time to list the teams, referee etc.

Anyway, we were in the tunnel and these guys from Inter Milan looked like gods, never mind footballers. I recall they were all immaculate, there wasn't a hair out of place anywhere. They oozed glamour. Their blue-and-black tops had been hand-pressed by an expert. A lot of us were standing there minus our false teeth. It didn't look like a fair fight. I looked at Giacinto Facchetti, their world-famous left back. At about 6ft 3in, he was such an imposing figure. He looked as though he had stepped straight out of a sportswear catalogue. He could have been the guy you would often see standing there in a perfect location pointing to something or other while posing away madly. I turned to Wee Jinky and motioned towards one of their players with my head. 'Hey, Wee Man, did I not see that bloke in that movie with Marcello Mastroianni? Did he not get off with Anita Ekberg in *La Dolce Vita*?' Wee Jinky looked back, puzzled. Indicating another of their players, I asked, 'Did he not used to go out with that Sophia Loren?' We were all having a good laugh and the Italians simply looked bemused. I heard mutterings of 'loco, loco' among their ranks. They really didn't know what they were up against. The sound of 'Hail! Hail! The Celts are here!' bounced around the walls of the tunnel. We kept it up all the way until, at last, we got the OK to emerge from the tunnel.

Big Billy, of course, was first out, chest proudly expanded to its maximum. In order, our captain was followed by Ronnie Simpson, Tommy Gemmell, John Clark, yours truly, Bobby Lennox, Stevie Chalmers, Jimmy Johnstone, Willie Wallace, Jim Craig and Bobby Murdoch. Reserve keeper John Fallon came next with his lucky teddy bear and then out strode Jock Stein alongside Neilly Mochan, our trainer, with assistant boss Sean Fallon and physiotherapist Bob Rooney following on. If you get the opportunity to watch footage of the teams strolling out on to the track and then on to the playing surface, have a look at the Italians. A lot of them are actually eyeing us up and down and shaking their heads. They were just a tad bemused. They were going to be a lot more bemused by time-up – that was certain!

A lot of people don't realise this but Lisbon was actually my second appearance in a European final, the first being for Birmingham City back in 1960 when we played Barcelona over two legs in the Inter-Cities Fairs Cup, which, of course, became the UEFA Cup in the seventies. It was a two-legged affair back then and we drew 0–0 at St Andrews but were well and truly put in our place at the Nou Camp, with the Spaniards triumphing 4–1. Strangely enough, I don't have too many memories of those games. Let's get back to Lisbon! I hit their crossbar with a run and shot as we swept down on them looking for a first-half equaliser. I've often been asked if I intended a cross but the ball took a strange swerve and ended up heading for goal. Take it from me, that was an attempt at goal. I put a little bend on the ball as I hared into their box and I thought it looked good. Well, it would have had to be good to beat their keeper Sarti who was unbelievable. However, the woodwork got in the way of me and glory and the ball bounced to safety. Thankfully, Tommy and Stevie had better fortune later on.

We weren't exactly a cosmopolitan bunch in 1967. For a start, we were all born within thirty miles of Celtic Park with me, Ronnie Simpson, Jim Craig and Stevie Chalmers being able to boast that we were, indeed, true Glaswegians! The others came from places such as Bellshill, Bothwell, and Kirkintilloch and, in Bobby Lennox's case, Saltcoats. I'd always thought that was just a place people went for their holidays – I had no idea people actually lived there. Anyway, the Glaswegians among the lads used to kid the others on about being hicks from the sticks. Big Billy, from Bellshill, was often fond of saying, 'Don't ask me, I'm just a lad from the country – you'd better ask Bertie.' But we were one big happy bunch, you can believe that. There is genuine camaraderie among us and nothing will ever split that up.

I met up with Big Billy and Tommy when we were doing a wee bit of 'research' for this book, jogging a memory or two, shaking loose a tale from the past. Research? That's got to be a euphemism for something. Anyway, we'd arranged to meet for a spot of lunch at the excellent Italian restaurant, O Sole Mio, in Bath Street, Glasgow. It just became one huge laugh-in. Time certainly lends enchantment, doesn't it? Goals I used to score from the edge of the box are now getting drilled in from the halfway line!

That afternoon became a bit of a football convention because Rangers' Nacho Novo came in and was on the receiving end of some good-natured banter. He was told he had, in fact, signed for the wrong Old Firm side. Thankfully, the little Spaniard took it all in good heart. We were delighted that he had heard of the Lisbon Lions as he was growing up in his homeland. We told him he might just have been about good enough to get in our third team in the sixties. Willie O'Neill, who played in the first four of Celtic's European Cup games in 1967 at left back, turned up, too. Alan Rough, my old goalkeeper at Partick Thistle, of course, also appeared and I wondered if Michael Aspel or someone was going to pop out with a big red book and give us the *This Is Your Life* treatment. I mention this because the Lisbon Lions are football people. The boots have been well hung up but there's nothing better than having a rare wee natter about the good old days.

Back then, Jock Stein used to taunt me about my 'useless' right foot. 'What a player you might have been, Bertie, if only you had two feet,' he was fond of saying. I would retort, 'When you've got a left foot like mine, boss, you don't need another one!' And, with that, he would just walk away shaking his head.

I know there are all sort of crazy and weird goal celebrations these days – although FIFA and UEFA want to ban them – where players will dance with corner flags, cavort around like acrobats, cradle invisible babies, pull their jerseys over their heads or generally just go slightly doolally once they have placed the ball in the opposition's net. I recall one from 14 September 1966 that baffled an enormous crowd at Celtic Park but Big Jock knew what it was all about all right. We were playing Dunfermline in a League Cup tie and I thumped one in from about twenty-five yards with my right foot. It was one of those shots that just took off and kept on going until it thudded against the net. Not bad, even if I do say so myself. But I raced over to the Celtic dugout and held up my right leg. I was waving it about and I was aware only myself, our players and Big Jock had a clue what this goal celebration was all about. The Boss had the good grace to have a hearty chuckle. It also helped that we won the game 6–3 in one of those astonishing high-scoring spectacles that became a bit of a trademark with Celtic in those days.

What was so special about the team? Well, the word team gives you a clue. We may have had some excellent individuals, such as Jimmy Johnstone, Tommy Gemmell and Bobby Murdoch, but we all fitted into a structure. We trusted each other and that was so important. It was comforting to go out on the field on match day and know you had so many good players around you. Take Ronnie Simpson, in goal, for a start. How reliable was he? You instinctively knew he would do a good job. He may not have looked like your typical goalkeeper but, to me, there was none better. Maybe he was on the small side but Ronnie always insisted he was close to 6ft. He must have been using a different measuring tape from everyone else in the world, that's all I can say! But he was a brilliant shot-stopper and was extremely agile.

Do you know, out of the team that faced Inter Milan, only Ronnie and I had played football outside Scotland – amazing. Ronnie, of course, won two FA Cup medals with Newcastle United while I had my stint at Birmingham City before I returned to Paradise. Jim Craig, Tommy Gemmell, Bobby Murdoch, Billy McNeill, Jimmy Johnstone, Stevie Chalmers and Bobby Lennox had all been brought up through the ranks at Celtic Park although I believe Clark may have been on the books at my old club at St Andrews very briefly. See what I mean about hardly being cosmopolitan!

Big Jock and I had a run-in or two – that's true – but I will never say a bad word about The Boss. He was the man who drove us all on to what we achieved, no argument about it. Apart from Willie Wallace, a superb buy at £30,000 from Hearts, we were all there before Big Jock arrived in 1965. I must have impressed him immediately. We were playing Airdrie at Broomfield on 10 March 1965 in The Boss's first game in charge since returning from Hibs. We won 6–0 and I was lucky enough to claim five. We didn't need strikers that evening! The old Broomfield was a strange wee ground, as I recall. They had a stand that contained the dressing rooms over at one of the corner flags and it looked as though it was straight out of Chad Valley. But I do remember a funny incident there during my first spell at Celtic.

Bobby Carroll, a much underrated player in my book, was struggling to make an impact that day. Anyway, he went over to take a corner kick on the right wing when suddenly a flying object hurtled in his general direction and landed at his feet. It was a huge pudding. 'That's two of you on the pitch now, Carroll!' bellowed some bloke from the crowd. We all fell about laughing but I'm not too sure Bobby saw the funny side.

When Jim Craig asked me something recently, I don't think he could make up his mind, either, whether or not I was joking when I gave him my reply. Jim asked me if there were any Celtic players since 1967 that I thought could have made it into the Lisbon Lions line-up and, if there were, who I would drop to make way for them.

It was an interesting question and I thought for a moment, before saying, 'Henrik Larsson.'

'OK,' said Jim, leaving himself wide open, 'where would you play him in the team?'

I said, 'Simpson, Larsson and Gemmell, Murdoch . . .'

Jim's face was a picture when he realised he had been given the chop to make way for the Swede. Only joking, Cairney!

I've already said Jock Stein is the man who deserves all the credit for what Celtic achieved and quite rightly so. He was way ahead of all the other managers of that era with his thinking and planning. He would develop wee things in training and, on the pitch during a match, opponents and supporters alike might have thought we were just improvising but, believe me, we had gone over these things meticulously in training at Barrowfield. Jock would keep hammering away at you and wouldn't let it rest until he was convinced you knew exactly what you had to do in any given set of circumstances that may emerge during ninety minutes. He was naturally a great believer in the old adage of 'fail to prepare, then prepare to fail'.

I'll give you an example. When we were playing Dukla Prague in the European Cup semi-final first leg at Celtic Park, we were awarded a free kick some thirty yards out. The Czech players, as usual, erected a wall in front of their goalkeeper, the excellent Ivo Viktor. They were covering all angles as I stepped up to take the kick. I strode forward, hesitated and went to touch the ball as though I was about to steady it. That might just have made them take their eye off the ball for a split second but that is a fairly lengthy period in football. I pulled my hand away at the last moment and nudged the ball sideways to Willie Wallace. Wispy knew what was coming, of course, and he was waiting to give the ball a good old skelp. He raced forward and thumped it first time. It flew past the wall, a startled Viktor didn't even move and the ball was in the net. We were 3–1 ahead and heading for Lisbon!

A little thing, maybe, but it is just another illustration of Big Jock's eye for detail. Yes, as I have said, he was meticulous to the point of being pernickety but we all realised it was for the good of the team. He would have us working, time and time again, on free kicks from all angles. I have a laugh these days when TV commentators go a bit overboard when a team goes through a free-kick routine and it pays off. They all say that it was a move that came straight from the training ground but Big Jock was doing these things decades ago. He was very much an innovator and not an imitator.

Of course, he put us through our paces but you also knew the defence would be working overtime if they conceded from a dead-ball effort. He would pull the move apart and show the players how they were expected to defend it if it cropped up again. They would go through it time after time, day after day, until he was satisfied. God help them all if they lost a goal in identical circumstances in the next game! It would be straight back to Barrowfield for another long, hard slog. But we all appreciated it because we knew it was making us better all-round players and we'd be so much more aware of the things that could develop during a game.

It is surely no surprise that so many of the Lisbon Lions went on to try management themselves: Ronnie Simpson had a short spell at Hamilton Accies; Jim Craig had a stint with Irish outfit Waterford; Tommy Gemmell was at Dundee – I'll tell you a story about that later – and Albion Rovers (twice); Bobby Murdoch was a coach and manager at Middlesbrough; Billy McNeill was at Clyde, Aberdeen, his beloved Celtic (two stints), Manchester City and Aston Villa; John Clark was assistant to Big Billy at Clyde, Aberdeen and Celtic; Willie Wallace was No. 2 to Big Tommy at Dens Park; Stevie Chalmers was a player/coach at Morton; and, of course, I was in charge at Hibs, Partick Thistle (twice), Hamilton Accies and Dumbarton. Obviously Wee Jinky and Lemon were the only two guys in the team with brains – they stayed away from football management! Actually, the Wee Man was player/coach at junior club Blantyre Celtic for about four months in 1980 but I don't think that counts.

I was delighted when Big Tommy got the Dundee job but I can now admit it was only because I turned it down. In fact, it was Tommy who put me in the frame for the position in the first place. Davie White, the former Clyde and Rangers manager, was sacked as boss of the Dens Park outfit after failing to get them back into the top division after relegation the previous year. As Big Tommy tells it, the Dundee chairman, Ian Gellatly, got in touch with him that summer to see if he would recommend anyone to take over. I was doing quite well with Partick Thistle at the time and my old Lisbon Lion team-mate put my name forward. I was in no rush to leave Firhill but, when Dundee made their approach, I thought it was only good manners to at least talk to them. Tommy phoned me to give me the details of the Dundee board and what I might expect in the interview. Everything went well but, at the end, I wasn't convinced that it was the job for me. I had the family to think of and, of course, we were well settled in the West of Scotland. It would have meant a fair old upheaval and, as I said, I was quite happy at Partick Thistle although some extra cash from chairman Miller Reid would have been well accepted!

Anyway, when the interview had come to an end, I told them I wouldn't take up their kind offer, thank you very much, gentlemen. Before I left, though, I said to them, 'You know you have a perfectly good manager on your own doorstep.'

They were slightly taken aback. 'Oh, who is that, then?' I was asked.

'Tommy Gemmell, your own club captain – I believe he is the man for the job, no doubt about it. He is ready for the step up.'

Thankfully, they agreed and, eventually, Tommy Gemmell did indeed make the transition from player to manager for the first time. So, all those grey hairs in the Gemmell thatch are down to yours truly. Actually, I was merely getting my own back on him for everything he put me through as a player. My God, the amount of chasing back I had to do when he went AWOL on one of those sorties down that left wing. Tommy would tell everyone I was a lazy so-and-so but I would like to think I contributed to the cause.

European nights at Celtic Park, to anyone who has witnessed these spectacles, are something else altogether – something extra special. The fans create a cauldron and turn Celtic Park into a fortress for visiting teams. If Celtic could take all of that superb support around Europe with them, they would win the Champions League every year! I know the fans talk about these evenings as being massive events and something to look forward to every time there is a European tie due at Celtic Park. However, you really have to play in them to realise what that atmosphere is all about. Genuinely, it's quite breathtaking to look around and see all those fans doing their level best to urge you to victory. How could you let them down?

I missed out on only one game during Celtic's run to Lisbon – the dramatic last-gasp 2–1 victory over Vojvodina Novi Sad.

I became a supporter that night after failing a late fitness test. Even I was left gasping for air at our truly wonderful support. I swear Celtic Park was rocking that night. Of course, I would have loved nothing more than to have been out there contributing but the next best thing was watching the action and roaring on the lads. What a game that was! Honestly, the hairs still stand on end at the recollection. It was one hell of an exciting rollercoaster ride of emotions. Everything that is good in football was on show that cold, grey, but truly unforgettable evening in the east end of Glasgow.

I was witnessing two football teams at the peak of their powers and it was all spellbinding stuff. Celtic would surge forward in wave after wave of attacks but the Slavs were an extremely accomplished unit and they looked fairly comfortable soaking up awesome pressure while always looking for the out-ball to turn defence very quickly into attack. They were a very polished side with a very good manager in Vujadin Boskov although you did get the impression that he and Big Jock wouldn't have been exchanging Christmas cards later that year! Charlie Gallagher took my place in midfield that night and let me tell you something about Charlie – he would have been a first-team regular in any other team in the land outside Celtic.

You've heard the old expression about a player being able to drop the ball on a sixpenny piece – these are the days before decimalisation, of course – from sixty yards. Charlie was that player. He had outstanding talent, a lovely first touch and top-class vision to pick out a colleague from long range. Charlie did eventually leave Celtic late in his career to have three years with Dumbarton before packing it in altogether. He may have been a direct rival for my midfield berth but that didn't stop me admiring him as a player and as a bloke. Why didn't he leave earlier in his career? The answer is quite straightforward – he didn't want to. He was a Celtic man and he was willing to take his chances. Certainly, he was always ready for action when he got the call from Big Jock.

I have to admit he was magnificent against Vojvodina. His distribution on a fairly tricky surface was marvellous and, of course, Charlie was the guy who set up the last-minute winner for Big Billy with a thoroughly well-taken corner kick from the right wing. Again, that is a memory that will live with me forever. What a remarkable end to a remarkable night. Afterwards, I sought out Charlie and told him, 'What a ball for Big Billy! I couldn't have done better myself!' We both had a good laugh.

Actually, I've got a lot to thank Charlie for as he was hugely instrumental in one of my most important goals for Celtic. I'm looking back to 24 April 1965 and the Scottish Cup Final against Dunfermline at a sell-out Hampden Park with the official crowd given as 108,800. The conditions were perfect for a good game of football and, of course, it was Big Jock's first chance of winning a trophy with Celtic since returning the previous month. To be fair, he didn't have a lot of time to shape us into a side that could claim silverware and it had been an awful long time since the Celtic support had anything to sing about – 19 October 1957, to be precise, when the club overwhelmed Rangers 7–1 to lift the League Cup. As the Parkhead legions went wild with delight at seeing their age-old rivals given a right doing, they wouldn't have believed that they would have nothing to cheer about for another eight years. Football, indeed, is full of surprises – and shocks, for that matter.

We knew it was going to be an extremely tough encounter against the Fifers – they were a smashing team with good, strong characters and, more importantly, they had a settled line-up. The only surprise I can recall in their manager's team announcement was the absence of a bloke called Alex Ferguson, who, to be honest, always seemed to revel in games against Celtic. I wonder where he is now! I remember Jock reading out our side – Fallon, Young, Gemmell; Murdoch, McNeill, Clark; Chalmers, Gallagher, Hughes, Lennox and . . . Auld. I was in! I hoped this was going to be the start of something good but even *my* vivid imagination could never have stretched to just how good!

Mind you, I wasn't too pleased when Dunfermline took the lead after only fifteen minutes but my big moment wasn't far away – sixteen minutes, in fact. Charlie gathered a ball about thirty yards out and looked as though he was about to pass it sideways. He thought better of it, though, and lashed a sensational effort at the Dunfermline goal. The ball sizzled past the leaping Jim Herriot, the Fifers' Scottish international goalkeeper, and clattered against the crossbar. I saw my chance. Herriot was on the ground and desperately trying to recover as the ball spiralled skywards. I was timing my run and I was aware the Dunfermline right back Willie Callaghan was in the vicinity. That ball seemed to levitate above me forever. From eternity to here. 'Come down, you bugger,' I thought – or words to that effect, anyway. I was poised, Herriot was getting back to his feet and Callaghan threw himself into a mid-air challenge. I didn't take my eye off the ball and, eventually, it decided to return to earth. I was waiting and I leapt high to get the first touch and head it into the net. What a feeling!

But the Fifers just wouldn't give up and they went back in front just before half-time with a long-range free kick. I wasn't too impressed when I saw that effort fly past John Fallon, I can tell you. During the break, Big Jock looked composed and confident. 'Keep moving the ball around. Use Yogi in the middle. Stevie, use your pace.' All that sort of stuff. It worked. We kept possession well, frustrated our opponents and I got on the end of a pass from Bobby Lennox to wallop our second equaliser beyond Jim Herriot. They might as well have given us the trophy there and then. It had our name on it, no doubt about it. Big Billy duly arrived on the scene to head in the winning goal near the end – after another inch-perfect corner kick from Charlie – and the cup was bedecked in green-and-white ribbons. A wonderful excursion into soccer dreamland was awaiting us. It's strange to look back and describe how happy we were with that win.

You would have thought each and every one of us had won the first dividend on the pools. Two years later, the celebrations would be even more splendid for seven of that team – Gemmell, Murdoch, McNeill, Clark, Chalmers, Lennox and yours truly.

I haven't a clue what we got as a bonus for winning the national trophy in 1965 and, to be honest, I can't remember how much we actually received for lifting the European Cup, either. Big Tommy assures me it was £1,500 per man and, as he is a financial consultant these days and presumably better with figures than me, I'll take his word for it. I do recall, though, carpeting Chez Auld, at that time situated in Giffnock, from just about top to bottom and I know that wasn't cheap. We had a fairly expansive living area and dining room. All that was carpeted and we did the hallway and the stairs, too. Doesn't seem too exciting, does it? I wonder what George Best did with his bonus for winning the European Cup with Manchester United a year later. Can't see him decorating his house, can you? Actually, we met George a fair bit when we on the road to celebrate the twenty-fifth anniversary of the Lisbon triumph. He would pop in at a few of our functions and I can tell you he really rated our team of 1967. He gave us great credit for knocking down barriers. He once told me, 'You made it easier for Manchester United to win it in 1968. You showed us it could be done.' Well said, Georgie!

The Lisbon Lions became a family. We grew up together and, like I said earlier, we are like a bunch of school kids when we meet up again. We hand out stick and we take it but it's all good fun. I'm sure we must astonish other people who are in the vicinity when we go for a walk down memory lane. It's great fun because there are so many special memories. Of course, Wee Jinky was a central figure in so many of our recollections. He was a real one-off but a genuine character who would give you his last. Celebrating forty years as a Lisbon Lion has been extraordinary but how I wish the Wee Man, Bobby Murdoch and Ronnie Simpson were here, too, to throw in their tuppence worth. They have all played major parts in the life of Bertie Auld.

As the other Lions have said, Wee Jinky was not satisfied with the way he performed against Inter Milan. Frankly, I know the Wee Man could be a humble bloke but I find it simply un-believable that he would genuinely believe this to be the case. I hope the other guys don't mind me saying this but he was my man of the match against the Italians. I heard not that long ago that my old team-mate Davie Hay has named me as Celtic's top performer that day. Thanks, Davie, but you've got the wrong man – Wee Jinky was streets ahead of anything I conjured up against Inter.

Aye, it was a fabulous day in Lisbon and one I obviously thoroughly enjoyed from start to finish. It's just a pity that a bloke called Luis Suárez wasn't around to witness it. I wouldn't have minded showing him a trick or two!

10

BOBBY LENNOX

I reckon Stevie Chalmers did Inter Milan's players a massive favour when he stuck that winning goal in their net with only five minutes remaining in Lisbon. Really, the Italians should have overtaken any Celtic player in the race to congratulate Stevie. If that game had gone to an extra thirty minutes, we would have hammered them, believe me. I am utterly convinced we would have notched up a scoreline that would have embarrassed the Italians. They were out on their feet towards the end of that wonderful game. They were shattered after chasing shadows for eighty-five minutes and they didn't look as though they were up for some of the same in a bout of extra time. It would only have been a matter of time before we scored again and, the way we were playing that day, I don't think we would have known how to take our foot off the gas. We wouldn't have had the inclination, either. We would just have kept on going, no matter what the score might have been.

Their goal had led a somewhat charmed life although, to be fair, their keeper, Giuliano Sarti, should have got some sort of individual medal for his bravery as he kept the scoreline respectable. But even he would have capitulated in the event of another half an hour. He simply couldn't have replicated his efforts in the regulation time. So, when Stevie side-footed that one in from six yards, it put Inter Milan out of their misery. That is not meant to sound big-headed or arrogant. Anyone who knows me will tell you that is certainly not my style. I'm just stating a fact. The Italians were on the verge of collapse. Meltdown was minutes away. I think the stretcher-bearers might have been working overtime during any extra-time period. Thankfully, we didn't need it.

Our fitness levels in Lisbon were awesome. We were primed and ready to go. The hard work, the preparation, the dedication and the resilience all came together at the right time and we were unstoppable. Jock Stein always demanded a lot from his players. He never asked anyone to do something he didn't believe was in their locker but, when he did order you to do something, he expected you to give it your undivided attention and 100 per cent commitment. Our tactics in Lisbon were basically quite simple. He looked at Willie Wallace, Stevie Chalmers and me and said, 'Keep on moving, make runs for the midfielders coming through. Take defenders with you, continue to make space for others.' He might have added, 'If you want to chuck in a goal or two, then fine!'

We were a very mobile team. There was a lot of pace about the place and another thing that was very important and must have worried Inter Milan manager Helenio Herrera when he watched us or had his spies looking at us was the fact that the goals were spread throughout the team. The side did not rely on me to score. Or Stevie. Or Wispy. With the exception of Ronnie Simpson in goal, of course, and John Clark, as our defensive rock, everyone else was capable of getting a goal or two. Tommy Gemmell, to my mind, was an exceptional left back. He revolutionised that position in our team. Funnily enough, for a guy who was principally a defender, he used to admit he couldn't tackle too well. He didn't have to as other teams used to fear him as he bombed forward, threatening to use that mighty right peg of his.

I could go through the team: Jim Craig might not have claimed many goals but he certainly set up his fair share; Bobby Murdoch could score goals from distance; Billy McNeill was known to get the odd headed goal or two; Bertie Auld knew where the opposition's net was; Jimmy Johnstone, Willie Wallace, Stevie Chalmers and I were always good for double figures during the season. If I had been Herrera, I would have wondered how to stop this side. The Italians were big fans of man-marking, of course, but how on earth do you man-mark an entire team? Running through that line-up, it is still fairly difficult to believe we had played so defensively against Dukla Prague in the Czechoslovakian capital to get to Lisbon in the first place.

I think, after four decades, I am about to become the first man to give Dukla huge credit for how they performed against us. Yes, Big Jock had come up with a strategy that was foreign to all of us and we were going to make sure the back door was bolted firmly shut. My pal, the Wee Man, just about played the entire game standing beside Cairney at right back. I spent an awful lot of my ninety minutes keeping Big Tommy company over on the left. That's not exactly how it was planned. Dukla, a fine team, pinned us back for lengthy periods of that game. They took control in front of their own fans and they made a real contest of it. They made it hectic for all of us and we were forced to defend to the very end. The only guy who wasn't given any defensive duties that day was Stevie Chalmers. I remember Big Jock telling him, 'Chase everything.' And, you know, he did. From start to finish, Stevie put himself about all over the place. The Czech defenders must have hated the sight of him. He never gave them a moment's rest. He was a one-man forward line. Somehow, it seemed so fitting that Stevie should get the winning goal against Inter. He earned it with his exhausting stint in Prague.

People often ask me what was my favourite goal in that European Cup run. Well, it wasn't one of mine! As it happens, I only scored two – in both legs of our 6–2 aggregate win over Nantes in the second round – and neither, I have to say, was particularly spectacular. However, Big Billy's winner against Vojvodina Novi Sad was something special altogether. What a thrilling climax to a truly eventful evening! Naturally, I was overjoyed for all the obvious reasons but I was also doubly pleased because we had stuck two past their goalkeeper, Ilija

Pantelic. I would like to believe I am a fairly easy-going type of bloke but I really hated that guy.

I know making a comment like that is way out of character for me so please let me explain why I disliked the Vojvodina No. 1 so much. In the first leg of our quarter-final in Yugoslavia, I made a challenge for a 50/50 ball as I was quite entitled to do. I did it every week in Scottish football and no one complained. Pantelic didn't like being disturbed, though. I slid in, my momentum took me forward and the goalkeeper collapsed on top of me as he collected the ball. It certainly wasn't a foul but Pantelic wasn't too happy. He got to his feet and motioned to help me get up too. It was all very sporting but, if anyone had bothered to take a closer look, they would have seen the Slav had a handful of my hair as he 'helped' me back up off the ground. I've got a sense of humour but that was no laughing matter. Mind you, I should get in touch with him just in case he still possesses clumps of my hair – I could do with it now!

I know all the other Lions rated Vojvodina and I did too. I wasn't a huge fan of the town of Novi Sad, though, that's for sure. It's pretty well-named . . . if you dropped the 'Novi'. The game was played on 1 March and I've got to say that particular part of Yugoslavia isn't heaven on earth at that time of the year. It was a dreich, dreary place and we were all happy to escape after the match and get home. It certainly made me appreciate Saltcoats a lot more!

We were also fairly satisfied with the result although, of course, it's never ideal to lose by any margin in Europe, even against first-rate opposition. However, as we travelled back, we were all convinced we would overturn their one-goal advantage. Me? I just wanted to stick one or two behind a certain Mr Pantelic to welcome him to Glasgow in no uncertain fashion. Alas, I didn't get my wish but we still beat them and that was the main objective all along. However, if you see footage of our first goal by Stevie Chalmers, have a look at what I'm getting up to. I'm right in the goalkeeper's face and giving it 'Yahoo!' Normally, I would run to the goalscorer to offer my congrats and give him a pat on the head but I just couldn't help myself and made a beeline to their crestfallen keeper to let him know exactly how I felt. I'm sorry – I just had to do it. If I was happy then, you can imagine my feeling of sheer elation when, a minute from time, Big Billy sauntered forward in that manner of his and got his head to Charlie Gallagher's beautifully flighted right-wing corner kick. My friend Pantelic was caught in no-man's-land as the ball soared high into the net. I kept away from him that time – I didn't want to push my luck! He was a big guy, after all, and his side had just been sent reeling out of Europe. I must say in his favour, though, that we shook hands at the end of the game and he wished me all the best for the rest of the competition. I appreciated that.

Another good sportsman I met on my travels through the 1966/67 season was Bobby Charlton who seemed to rate yours truly quite highly. I don't know why! I remember a piece in a football magazine back then where the Manchester United legend was asked to name his ideal team from the current crop of players in Europe. You could say I was just a tad surprised to see the name of Bobby Lennox in there. Does Bobby Charlton know quality or what? I must have impressed Bobby when he arrived at Celtic Park, with his United team, consisting of Denis Law, George Best, Pat Crerand and Co., for a pre-season friendly. Bobby and his Old Trafford colleague Nobby Stiles were fresh off the back of England's World Cup triumph a couple of months beforehand. They were certain to get a rousing reception in Scotland. And they did – Celtic hammered them 4–1. That more or less put down our marker for the rest of that campaign, I suppose. It's strange, when you look at it, but we kicked off that season with a victory over the team that would win the European Cup the year after us and we finished it with a triumph over the team, Real Madrid, who'd won it the year before us. And somewhere in there we overcame Inter Milan who had triumphed in the competition, of course, in 1964 and 1965. We were mixing in good company.

Talking of Bobby Charlton, we came up against each other again, of course, at Wembley in April 1967 and I got the chance to show him how good I was again when I scored in Scotland's 3–2 win. I must say I have always found him very pleasant company. I've met him a few times now and we have a wee chat about all sorts of things. By the way, back then, Bobby thought England's three-goal World Cup Final hero Geoff Hurst and I would make a great strike force. Sorry, Geoff, Stevie Chalmers got there first.

Stevie, like Big Billy, had endured some pretty grim times before Jock Stein came back. Take a look at Stevie's goalscoring record and you will see a player who would be in the multi-million-pound transfer bracket these days. Stevie notched up 228 goals in 405 appearances and you don't have to be a mathematical genius to work out that is a fantastic scoring rate. He was a totally unselfish guy to play alongside. He would make lung-bursting runs all day long, chasing balls into corners and continually putting pressure on defences. If you look back then, you will see we scored an awful lot of goals after the hour mark. That was testimony to our stamina as well as our hunger for success and never-say-die spirit. No defender got an easy ride against us. Some may have tried to mete out a little bit of 'extras' to try to keep us quiet but all they found was that we could give as good as we got.

There was a surprise or two along the road, of course, and I was on the receiving end of one very early in my career. I turned up for the reserves at Celtic Park to be told I would, indeed, be playing . . . at outside right. I thought there must be some mistake as I had never – not even at school – played in that position in my life. Not once. I was an old-fashioned inside right, playing beside the centre forward and I thought someone was pulling my leg. I checked the calendar but it wasn't April Fools' Day and I was handed the No. 7 shorts. Baffled? You bet. But I was happy to play anywhere for Celtic although I admit I might have struggled in goal! I did, in fact, make my first-team debut in my original position in a league game against Dundee at Dens Park on 3 March 1962 and we won 2–1 with goals from Big Billy and Frank Brogan, brother of Jim who would later play in the 1970 European Cup Final against Feyenoord when we lost 2–1 in extra time. We don't want to dwell on that one, do we? Actually, looking back on our line-up against Dundee that day, it is interesting to note that only Big Billy and I were involved in Lisbon. John Hughes, who played in five out of the eight games en route to the European Cup Final, was at centre forward that day. The others, Frank Haffey, Dunky Mackay, Jim Kennedy, Pat Crerand, Billy Price, Johnny Divers, Bobby Carroll and Brogan had all moved on by the time we made history.

I was hardly a regular back then but I wasn't complaining. I would get, maybe, six games and then go back into the reserves. I would get called up again, have a few games and then go back to the second team. This went on for about four years and you could say I served a proper apprenticeship at Celtic. I was getting a fair run in the side before we received the news that Jock Stein was about to become our manager. I played in six successive league games from the end of January into March and I was lucky enough to score in a 3–2 Scottish Cup Third Round victory over Kilmarnock at Celtic Park on 6 March. Big Jock's first game in charge was four days later when we beat Airdrie 6–0 at Broomfield, with Bertie Auld scoring five. But you can't help wondering if the new manager rates you or likes your style. He may have other players in mind for your position and suddenly you are heading out the door. To be fair to Big Jock, he sat down with all the players shortly after he arrived and told us we were all starting on equal footing. 'You'll get your chance,' he told us, individually and collectively. 'Do the business and you will be in.' That sounded OK to me.

Before he arrived, I had played a few games wide on the left but he brought me in from the wing and I could never thank him enough for that. I much preferred to play alongside the centre forward in an effort to try to poach a goal or two. A lot was made of my pace and Big Jock realised I could utilise it more through the middle. I have to admit I did work on my speed levels and I was a regular visitor to the beach at Saltcoats where I would run up and down the sand. Bertie Auld once told me, 'See you, Lennox, you would chase paper on a windy day!' I'm not sure if that was a compliment or a complaint. Anyway, I worked on the theory, if you could handle running on sand, you could certainly cope with performing on grass. Have you ever tried to race in sand? It's not easy, believe me. So, when you were asked to go out and play on a lush, level playing surface, it was heaven. Getting out there and getting into your stride on that thoroughly superior pitch of the Estadio Nacionale in perfect conditions in Lisbon was just a wee bit different from the sand dunes of the Ayrshire coast.

I scored a few good goals in my career – 273 in 571 games, in fact – and, naturally enough, one of the questions I am often asked is which one is my favourite. That's a difficult one. They were all welcome in their own way but, searching my memory banks, there are a few that come to mind as being that little bit extra special. I recall a goal against Aberdeen where I hit my shot with such force that the ball stuck up in the stanchion in the roof of the net. Another that means something to me came against Rangers in a Glasgow Cup tie at Ibrox in 1966. The tournament might not have been the most prestigious in world football but that didn't matter and we were all aching to get at our old rivals to make up for our Scottish Cup Final defeat against them two months earlier. That loss was a massive disappointment, to say the least. I played in the 2–0 semi-final triumph over Dunfermline but was injured when the final came round on 23 April. With or without me, Celtic were the bookies' favourites to clinch a league and cup double. I watched from the stand as we outplayed Rangers in the first game but they held out for a goalless draw. It was a replay the following Wednesday and, once again, not too many people gave Rangers a chance. Our name just wasn't on the trophy that year, however, and a second-half goal from their right back Kai Johansen took the cup to Ibrox.

That was one of those games that comes along every now and again where you just know fate it is against you. I could never be called a defeatist but I have to admit there are occasions when you instinctively know things will not run your way. I remember Celtic storming straight back at Rangers in that replay after Johansen's goal. If I recall correctly, big John Hughes ran down the left wing and pitched over a peach of a cross. In the busy penalty area, Joe McBride was first to react and thumped in a ferocious header. Their goalkeeper, Billy Ritchie, hadn't a clue where the ball was. As it happens, it struck him on the shoulder, flew upwards, came down, gently nudged the top of the crossbar and, with what looked like half the Celtic team queuing up on the goal line to knock it in, came back down again to settle on the top of the net and, as far as Rangers were concerned, out of harm's way.

So, when the Glasgow Cup First Round tie came around, we were well up for it. Big Billy scored the opening goal with a low shot from an angle after Rangers failed to clear a corner kick. That set the tone for the evening and I was fortunate enough to score three in an emphatic, one-sided 4–0 triumph. The one I can vividly recall, though, was our second goal – my first-ever against the Ibrox side. That would have been memorable enough but I am glad to say it was a real belter. I got the ball about thirty-five yards out on the inside-right position. I just took off, got away from John Greig and hit a left-foot effort from the edge of the box. Billy Ritchie had the good grace not to bother even going for it as it rattled high into the roof of the net. That was a sweet goal.

Another encounter that will live with me forever wasn't quite in the classic category but it was much, much more important as it virtually guaranteed us the League Championship for the third successive year.

We were drawing 1–1 with Morton at Celtic Park in the second-last game of the league season and it looked as though we were about to hand the initiative to Rangers. As everyone had come to expect from this Celtic team, it was never over until the referee blew for full-time. We had left ourselves in a bit of a predicament after Willie Wallace had put us ahead. Morton's Tony Taylor, who had been on Celtic's books as a youngster, equalised completely against the run of play and that was the way it was deadlocked with about thirty seconds to go. Suddenly there was a chance. A ball was floated in, the Morton defence didn't clear it properly and it dropped perfectly right at my feet. I didn't hesitate as I lunged forward to stab the ball beyond Andy Crawford from about six yards out. Game over. Job complete. Title No. 3 in the bag. Happy days.

Winning became a good habit back then. I was really enjoying my football and Wee Bertie and I struck up quite a good partnership. With Bertie and Bobby Murdoch feeding me with defence-splitting passes, it would have been criminal not to score so many goals. Both those guys were quality. I liked to run on to the ball and Bertie and Bobby realised that. I always wanted to use my pace. Danny McGrain once said I was born quick – I think I know what he meant. Anyway, there was little point in dropping a pass short to me that would have had me coming out to accept it and then about-turn and head back for goal. Put the ball in front of me and I was off. I knew that the first couple of yards were crucial. If I could get away from a defender, there was little chance of him catching me. So, I suppose, I got my fair share of the goals but, like I said, an awful lot of that was down to the quality service I got from Bertie and Bobby. It was an absolute pleasure to be in the same side as these guys. Bertie was super confident. I know he meant it when he declared he didn't care at all about who he was facing in any game. 'Let them worry about me,' was Bertie's message and I don't suppose that is a bad outlook. Bertie was deceptively fast, you know. He had started his career as an outside left and speed was a prerequisite to play in that position back then. You might not have noticed how fast Bertie was moving until you realised the defender was going at full pelt beside him and getting left behind.

As all the players who played in the 3–2 Scottish Cup Final success over Dunfermline in 1965 would emphasise, that really was the turning point for Celtic and Bertie, of course, played a major role in that triumph. The Fifers led twice that afternoon, only for Bertie to net two equalisers – the second of which combined his quickness and alertness. He made up something like thirty yards in double-quick time after passing the ball out to me on the left. I headed for the byeline before putting in a low cross and there was Bertie, not being picked up by the Dunfermline defence, racing in to thump the ball behind goalkeeper Jim Herriot. That was a right-foot effort, by the way, which would have been fairly enjoyable for a player who used to take a lot of stick about being all left-sided. Bertie had a great footballing brain and always wanted to be at the hub of things. He never hid in a game. In fact, none of the Lions could ever be accused of that.

Bobby Murdoch wasn't blessed with natural pace but he made sure the ball did all the work. 'Who needs all that running about?' he would ask. 'A sixty-yard pass can do all the damage you want.' Bobby was another super player who went about his work quietly and effectively. Every team would welcome a Bobby Murdoch in their engine room. For such a powerful guy, he possessed a lot of dainty touches. Big Jock deserves the utmost credit for changing Bobby's role in the team. When Bobby first came into the side, he played at inside right, often in front of guys such as Pat Crerand and John McNamee. His natural position, though, was at wing-half. It took Big Jock to spot that. It wasn't long before Bobby was moved behind the front line and his career soared after that.

I may have been scoring regularly for the champions, but someone once pointed out that I was 'scandalously misused and underused by the Scotland international team'. I only won ten Scotland caps in a career that spanned almost two decades so you might wonder about that statistic. Why the lack of appearances from Scotland? I haven't a clue. I suppose you would have to ask the Scotland managers back then but I wasn't grumbling. As long as Jock Stein thought I was good enough to play in his Celtic first team, that was fair enough by me. I backed his judgement above others.

My mate Jimmy Johnstone was selected only twenty-three times to play for his country and that, too, will always remain a mystery. He would have walked into any other nation's line-up, that's for sure. Do you know I never once called Jimmy by his popular nickname of Jinky? To me, he was simply the Wee Man. Well, I towered a good two inches above him, didn't I? What can I say about the greatest-ever Celtic player? Just that – he was the best. No one who witnessed his display against Real Madrid at a sell-out Bernabeu Stadium a fortnight or so after Lisbon will forget it. It was Jimmy Johnstone at his wonderful peak. He ran the show that evening and the Real Madrid support, who had turned out in their thousands to say farewell to Alfredo Di Stefano, ended by applauding every move made by the Wee Man. Those fans certainly knew a good thing when they saw it.

I got the only goal of the game against Real and you won't be surprised to hear that it came via another bit of mesmerising play from Jimmy. He picked up a ball from Tommy Gemmell on the left wing, deep in our own half. He looked up, controlling the pass instantly as usual, and scampered off in the general direction of our opponents' goal. He skipped nonchalantly past three tackles before rolling it in front of me. I was coming in at the inside-right angle. I hit it first time with my right foot and the ball went in at the far post. What an eerie feeling, though, when hardly a voice greeted my effort. I held my hands aloft in normal fashion and, of course, was used to the din that would come from our great support. There was silence in the Bernabeu and then, out of nowhere, in an unmistakeable Glaswegian accent, came the shout, 'Goal!' Just one word but it was enough.

I loved playing alongside the Wee Man. Really – he had it all – and he was first-class company off the pitch too. I'm sure people used to think we were joined at the hip. We always roomed together and that was unusual because Big Jock liked to chop and change to freshen up things but he never once separated the Wee Man and me. We were seen as a double-act and we were both happy with that. I miss him. Of course, Jimmy put in a thoroughly professional ninety minutes in Lisbon – we all did. As I said right at the start, the Inter Milan players must have been happy to see the back of us that evening.

How did I spend my bonus? Very quickly! I came home to get married to Catherine so, by the time we had a honeymoon and bought some bits and bobs for the new Lennox household, that was that. Money well spent, I think you'll agree.

I have often stated that Celtic really gelled and came together months before we even thought about playing in Lisbon. I am talking about our American tour in 1966 and it was a masterstroke by someone at Celtic to take us away for about five weeks. The players got to know one another even better than is possible when you are just turning up for training and, of course, playing on match day. We all enjoyed the experience but we also knew we were there to work. This was no holiday and Jock Stein was still getting to know the squad of players he had inherited. We all wanted to impress him and I think I did well enough – I managed to score nineteen goals in eleven games! OK, we did play a few select teams from Bermuda, New Jersey and St Louis but we also took on Spurs three times.

The London side were a really top outfit at the time and they went on to win the FA Cup in 1967, beating Chelsea 2–1 in the final. Of course, they had also won the European Cup-Winners' Cup in 1963 when they walloped Atletico Madrid 5–1 in Rotterdam. But I think they were a bit annoyed that they couldn't put one over on us. We beat them 1–0 and then 2–1 before we played them for a third time and they managed to get a 1–1 draw. These were important games for us. They were taking us to another level and it didn't do our confidence any harm either. Big Tommy Gemmell pestered Big Jock into letting him play at centre forward in one of our games – I think it was against the Hamilton Select – and The Boss eventually let him lead the attack. As I recall, Big Tommy did well enough, netting a hat-trick in an 11–0 triumph. Thankfully, though, he accepted that left back was his best position and the 'experiment' was never tried again!

I scored four goals in our first game, a 10–1 success against the Bermuda Select. I followed that up with a hat-trick in a 7–0 win over the wonderfully named Young Men of Bermuda. We beat New Jersey All Stars 6–0 and I claimed another treble. Next up, it was Spurs in Toronto and we won again and I scored the only goal of the game. We travelled on to Ontario and cantered past the Hamilton Select 11–0 and I netted four. John Clark got all the plaudits after that game, though, because he, too, scored with the help of a penalty kick. John didn't score an awful lot so the players made a fuss of him afterwards!

We went back to New York for the next thrilling encounter on our tour and we were held 0–0 by Bologna. The Italians played in much the same manner as Inter Milan would do, ten months later. They were so defensively minded, even in a friendly, but it was great experience. We moved base camp to St Louis where we won 6–1 against the All Stars and I had to settle for one. San Francisco was next and again Spurs were the opposition. They were determined to get revenge for losing in Toronto but we triumphed again, this time 2–1, and I got the winner. Actually, I was beginning to feel a wee bit sorry for the Spurs lads by this time. Whenever we were in town, the Scottish and Irish exiles would abandon the London team and start following us everywhere. Dave Mackay and the White Hart Lane outfit were the opposition again in Vancouver and this time they at least got a 1–1 draw.

We returned to San Francisco and Bayern Munich were waiting for us. They had just won the German Cup and had not been in America long. They were fit and fresh and ready to go. They also had some brilliant performers such as Franz Beckenbauer and Gerd Müller. They were beating us 2–0 with twenty minutes to go but, by displaying the fighting qualities that would stand us in good stead throughout the following season, we came back to get a 2–2 draw with Joe McBride and yours truly scoring.

Our last game was in Los Angeles against Mexican champions Atlas. The heat was almost unbearable and obviously our opponents were a bit more used to those sorts of temperatures. I recall they were a good side but we eventually wore them down and Charlie Gallagher got the only goal of the game late on. We were so happy to return home undefeated.

It's hard to believe that American trip was so long ago. When the Lions meet up nowadays, we talk about events like they were yesterday. Do you remember that game? Do you remember that goal? Do you remember that player? Honestly, it is all so special. The memories just come flooding back. But the preseason tour of the States should never be underestimated in what it meant to the club. There was a real sense of camaraderie among the players and I still believe that's what made 1967 such a memorable year. I used to look around our dressing room at the time and see Big Billy preparing for a game. Then I would look at the Wee Man. Then Big Tommy. Then Bobby Murdoch. Then Wee Bertie. I just looked around the entire dressing room and thought, 'Who can beat us?' We only lost three games that entire season – two, amazingly enough, to Dundee United in the league – but we were afraid of no one. We went out on to that pitch expecting to win. It was a great attitude. We really were a good team.

We deserved to win in Lisbon. After I scored against Motherwell to make sure we won the 1966 league title, our first in twelve years, I recall Big Jock saying, 'We mustn't look to the past, at the legends who have gone before us – we must build our own legends.' How prophetic were those words?

Yes, it was great to make history in Lisbon. Nothing will ever top that feeling. I will always remember the referee blowing that final whistle and I just turned round to see who was the nearest team-mate. It was John Clark and we just threw ourselves at each other. Honestly, we were like a couple of school kids. 'We've won! We've won!' We yelled our heads off as Inter Milan players walked disconsolately past us, heads bowed in defeat. Then I remembered my false teeth were in Ronnie Simpson's cap in the back of his net. I saw all those supporters racing onto the pitch and I suddenly thought, 'I'd better get my teeth!' I ran to Ronnie, picked up my gnashers and the Lennox smile was ready for the cameras.

I do like a happy ending.

11

JOCK STEIN: THE TRIBUTES

Jock Stein had his back turned to the pitch when West German referee Kurt Tschenscher put the whistle to his lips and blew for full-time to bring a halt to the most epic encounter in Celtic's history. Celtic were triumphant. Celtic had conquered Europe – the first British club to do so. Stein turned slowly and brought up his fist in acclaim. 'Yes!' he shouted to no one in particular.

The Celtic bench, thirty yards away, had already joined the cavorting players on the field of the Estadio Nacionale and were whooping it up with the best of them. There is a famous photograph of the Celtic bench leaping around on the touchline seconds after full-time. There is assistant manager Sean Fallon, substitute goalkeeper John Fallon and backroom boys Neilly Mochan, Bob Rooney and Jimmy Steele catapulting to their feet in salute. There is no sign of the man who masterminded it all, though.

With time ticking down, Jock Stein had decided to go walk-about. He strolled down the touchline while the action took place only yards away. Celtic were on the brink of a historic breakthrough, minutes away from becoming only the fifth team to win the European Cup. But Jock Stein, for once, couldn't bear to look. Those last remaining seconds must have been agonising for the Celtic gaffer. His hard work, toil, graft and genius were all fully rewarded as soon as that whistle sounded.

Back in Glasgow the following evening, the Celtic manager was cornered live on television as his beaming players paraded the newly won European Cup in front of the adoring thousands at Celtic Park who turned out to welcome back their heroes. The commentator pushed the microphone towards Stein and said,

'I am told the secret is that Celtic are one big happy family and you keep it that way.'

Stein thought for a moment and replied, 'Actually, there is a better secret than that – we are a good football team.'

Surely the manager was playing down the achievements of a team that now ruled Europe. Celtic weren't merely a good football team – they were a magnificent football team who echoed the thoughts, methods and ambitions of their equally outstanding manager.

When Stein swept into Celtic Park in March 1965, he was paid the highest compliment by Hal Stewart, the flamboyant chairman of Morton. He told Big Jock, 'You're a real upstart. There we were, going about our business and getting away with it. Now you are at Celtic and we all have to buck up our ideas and start working at the game.' Tongue in cheek? Possibly but you just knew Stein was the phenomenon who drove not only Celtic but also Scottish football forward – forward into a new era and achieving things that would have seemed to be simply outrageous possibilities in earlier times. The enthusiasm of the man was staggering. He would often be found at obscure junior grounds on a night off, watching Cambuslang Rangers, Johnstone Burgh or Baillieston. A few days later he could be taking in Manchester United v. Benfica. Football was football in its many shapes and forms for Big Jock. His hunger for knowledge was insatiable.

Sir Matt Busby, the Manchester United legend who was a close friend of Stein, once recalled, 'There were a few of us talking about a game we had just seen and some of us were discussing a goal that had been scored. To say we were dumbfounded when Big Jock had his say was to put it mildly. He took the play back about a minute or so. He told us of how some player had chosen the wrong option and had given the ball away and how it was moved around before it found its way into the opponent's net. He had a remarkable eye for detail and a memory bank that bordered on the impossible. As history shows, he put it all to a good use.'

Billy McNeill was his on-field general and he knew the man better than most. OK, what was his secret? McNeill would reply, 'He would always tell you to play to your strengths and disguise your weaknesses. He insisted you helped out a colleague who may not have been having the best of days. He told you it may be your turn in the next game to need assistance. He kept it simple. Big Jock never asked anyone to do something he didn't believe they had the skills to cope with. We had a real mixture of players at Celtic Park and he was the man who fused all those talents together.'

The mercurial Jimmy Johnstone was on the receiving end of a tongue-lashing from Big Jock on more than one occasion but, in truth, as one Lisbon Lion confided, 'Jock Stein loved the Wee Man. He always had a soft spot for him.'

Wee Jinky may not have thought that was the case after one particular game, a league encounter with Dundee United at Celtic Park. Johnstone remembered it like this: 'I wasn't having the best of games and I admit I was struggling for form. Big Jock would have been better off leaving me out but he kept playing me. Anyway, I wasn't too happy when I got the shout that I was coming off in this game. I didn't think as I raced off the pitch, frustrated and angry, and I threw my shirt at the dugout. I was running up the tunnel when I heard this growl behind me, "Johnstone – I want a word with you!" I didn't know what to do. I could either run into the dressing room or try to hide or just keep running out of the main door in the general direction of Parkhead Cross. I was convinced the Big Man was going to do me! He didn't, I'm glad to say, but he did fine me. I had no complaints.'

Stein's history has been well chronicled. He started as an awkward centre half with Blantyre Victoria before moving to Albion Rovers in 1942 and then on to Welsh club Llanelli. He returned to Scotland and Celtic in a £1,200 deal in December

1951. Many thought he was there as mainly a back-up defender and to help with the reserves. They didn't reckon on the desire and ambition of this man. He swiftly won a place in the first team and led the club to their Coronation Cup success in 1953 and the league and cup double the following season. He also skippered the side to victories in the Charity Cup (1953) and the Glasgow Cup (1955).

An ankle injury forced him out of the playing side of the game in 1956 and he was appointed coach of the reserve team. Celtic overlooked what he was achieving at this level and they allowed him to move on to relegation-threatened Dunfermline. He saved them from the drop and guided them to a Scottish Cup triumph in 1961, beating, of all clubs, Celtic 2–0 in a replay. He took over as Hibs manager in April 1964 before Celtic, in disarray, sent out the SOS in 1965. He answered that call and things were never to be the same again at Celtic Park.

The European Cup, ten league championships, eight Scottish Cups and six League Cups were to cascade through the front door at Celtic Park as Big Jock revolutionised the game in this country.

Victory in Lisbon in 1967 was of paramount importance for Stein as he pointed out immediately afterwards: 'Even some of the Italian press have been congratulating us. They were delighted we won. It is the trend for clubs to follow successful teams, who are winning things by playing defensive football. We hope our success will make the game better throughout Europe. We would like to think people will now follow our example.'

He left his beloved Celtic in 1978. After a short spell at Leeds United, he became manager of the Scotland international side. Jock Stein died on 10 September 1985, following a 1–1 World Cup qualifying draw with Wales at Ninian Park in Cardiff. He suffered a massive heart attack and died thirty minutes after the game.

In the words of the Tartan Army's adopted national anthem, 'When will we see his likes again?'

Billy McNeill

Jock Stein was the reason I spent my entire playing career with Celtic. Without him, there would have been every likelihood I would have been off. Everyone knows I am Celtic through and through, always have been and always will be, and it would have been a wrench to leave the club but I would be lying if I said that wasn't a possibility before Big Jock arrived in 1965.

It wasn't about money – although the wages in England were far superior to anything on offer in Scotland. It was all about winning. I had a burning desire to win medals, to be successful, and, to be honest, that didn't look like happening at Celtic for an awful long time. I was told Spurs were interested and Manchester United too but it was mainly the London side who seemed the more persistent. I took that as a compliment. Of course, they had my Scottish international team-mates Dave Mackay and Alan Gilzean in their team back then. I knew they were enjoying life in England. My old pal Denis Law would fill my head with tales about Manchester United and how much he loved it at Old Trafford. And another of my great mates, Pat Crerand, had joined up with Law at United in 1963.

I recall the Scottish Cup Final against Rangers that same year. We forced a 1–1 draw in the first game at Hampden and our fans were delirious. They celebrated like we had won the actual trophy. I could well understand why. Our old rivals had beaten us twice in the league that season, 1–0 and 4–0, and, in general, they were just too good for us. I played in both those defeats and they were never easy to swallow.

Rangers beat us 3–0 in the Cup Final replay on 15 May with Jim Baxter turning in an outstanding, peerless display. He may have been an Ibrox idol but he was still one of my best mates.

THREE CHEERS! As Bobby Lennox slides in to net for the third goal against Nantes at Celtic Park, goalkeeper Castel is left helpless. Celtic won 6–2 on aggregate.

HAPPINESS IS . . . a place in the European Cup Final. A beaming Jock Stein with Bertie Auld after the goalless draw against Dukla Prague ensured a place in Lisbon.

PRICELESS! Or, at least, worth £2.38p back in 1967. It's a ticket for the European Cup Final at Lisbon's Estadio Nacionale where Celtic had a date with destiny.

NINETY MINUTES FROM HISTORY! Celtic's line-up for the final – back row (left to right): Jim Craig, Tommy Gemmell, Ronnie Simpson, Billy McNeill, Bobby Murdoch and John Clark; front row: Stevie Chalmers, Willie Wallace, Jimmy Johnstone, Bobby Lennox and Bertie Auld.

INTER'S HERO! Goalkeeper Giuliano Sarti was the man between the Italians and a landslide defeat and he demonstrates his ability once again by pushing away a low drive from Tommy Gemmell (not in picture).

GOOD CROSS! Tommy Gemmell crosses over from the left wing as Inter Milan defender Armando Picchi tries to block the ball. Big Tommy had better luck with his shooting boots later on with the leveller.

SPOT OF BOTHER! Inter Milan's Sandro Mazzola turns away in triumph after netting with his seventh-minute penalty kick. Tommy Gemmell, Bertie Auld and John Clark can only look on in dismay.

GEMMELL'S GLORY GOAL! Tommy Gemmell is just out of the picture at the left-hand side of the 18-yard box but his unstoppable right-foot shot is already flying high past the helpless Giuliano Sarti for the leveller.

UNBELIEVABLE! Inter keeper Sarti throws himself acrobatically at the ball to hold a Tommy Gemmell effort on the goal line as Stevie Chalmers and defender Gianfranco Bedin get a close-up view.

THE WINNER! Stevie Chalmers is smack in front of goal as he turns a Bobby Murdoch effort wide of the helpless Giuliano Sarti and the European Cup is on its way to Celtic Park making Celtic the first British club to conquer Europe.

HAIL! HAIL! Celtic fans throw a green party in Lisbon as they celebrate the incredible feat of their heroes taking on and overwhelming the best Europe had to offer in an unforgettable season.

WE'VE WON! Skipper supreme Billy McNeill is mobbed by celebrating Celtic fans as he tries to make his way through to pick up the most glittering prize European football had to offer.

HAIL CAESAR! Billy McNeill holds aloft the European Cup after the most remarkable result in the history of Celtic Football Club – Celtic 2, Inter Milan 1 on 25 May 1967.

READ ALL ABOUT IT! An overjoyed Celtic fan holds up a Portuguese newspaper that tells the world that the Glasgow side have beaten Inter Milan and are now the European masters.

CHEERS! Celtic supporters in Glasgow's George Square celebrate after watching the events on television as their heroes made history.

HAPPY DAZE! The Celtic players proudly display the European Cup at the after-match banquet. Trainer Neilly Mochan is right behind the trophy.

CUP OF DREAMS! A clearly delighted Joc Stein keeps a close watch on the trophy as h reads the telegrams of congratulations from over the world.

He was rubbing our noses in it a bit that night and I sidled up to him at one point and said, 'Stanley, it's bad enough out here. Cut out the party tricks.' We named him Stanley, of course, after the Scottish comedian Stanley Baxter.

Celtic seemed to be going nowhere. If that hurt our support, can you imagine what it did to me as a young player desperate to get out there and win things? Yes, it would have been easy to move on and Celtic, as they had proved in the case of Paddy Crerand, would happily accept a big transfer fee for one of their players. They got £56,000 for Paddy and that was a heck of a lot of cash in those days. Somehow, though, I managed to hang in there. I kept hoping things would change. Then along came Jock Stein and, my goodness, did things change? With a vengeance! I never gave England a second thought after that.

Jim Craig

As we were all aware, Big Jock was the possessor of a fairly ferocious temper. He could let fly with the best of them if he wasn't happy with what you were contributing or what he was witnessing. I recall one game when I was on the substitutes' bench and sitting directly behind Big Jock in the dugout.

It would be fair to say he wasn't too enamoured with what was going on out on the pitch. In fact, he was going ballistic. He was shouting and yelling at everyone and, clearly, it was going to be an interesting half-time tactics talk. I sat there and thought, 'Thank God I'm not going to be on the receiving end of a Big Jock rant.'

It was goalless at half-time and the manager couldn't wait to get into the dressing room. John Fitzsimmons, the club doctor, came in too, as he always did. There would be the usual knock or two for him to work on. Not this day, though. Jock simply turned to him and ordered him out. The doctor hesitated and

Jock, by this time working up a good head of steam, roared, 'Get out!' I didn't realise our club doctor could move so fast!

What Jock had to say to the players was going to be done in private. The players were all lined up in numerical order: No. 1 goalkeeper Ronnie Simpson; No. 2 the right back; and so on. Jock looked at Ronnie: 'Call yourself a goalkeeper?' Then he moved on to the right back. 'What on earth are you playing at?' Left back: 'Did you just take up football today?' He went right through the line-up, pulling their performances apart.

I sat there in the background with my cup of tea, minding my own business. Jock finished with whoever was playing outside left that day. Then there was a silence. A minute passed and I was aware he was looking at me. There is just so long you can keep your head down and avoid eye contact. Slowly, I looked up and wondered what withering blast was coming my way.

'And you, Cairney,' he said, 'just how bad are you that you can't even get in this team?'

Tommy Gemmell

Without warning, Big Jock dropped me from the line-up for the League Cup Final against St Johnstone back in 1969. My crime? I had been ordered off playing for Scotland in West Germany in midweek and Celtic always frowned on anyone getting into trouble with authority, especially, I believe, while representing their country. I'll never know if it was Jock who made the decision or whether it came from higher up but I was raging at how I discovered I wasn't playing.

I had been outside Hampden Park that day, passing on tickets and chatting to some friends. As it got closer to the kick-off time at 3 p.m., I decided it would be a good idea to go up and get changed into my playing gear. I headed for the dressing room but was stopped at the door by Jim Kennedy, the club's former left back and now a general handyman. He gave me two tickets for the stand.

'What are these for, Jim?' I asked.

'You're not playing today,' he answered and I could hardly believe my ears.

No one had bothered to tell me. We had travelled up from Troon and Big Jock must have known his team but didn't say a word. A young Davie Hay, nowadays a very good friend, took my place at left back and I was left totally embarrassed. I believe my team-mates were, too. There must be a better way of letting someone know they are not in the line-up.

Celtic won 1–0 with an early goal from my wee pal Bertie Auld but I was out of Hampden and off home before the celebrations began. The following day I marched into Celtic Park to have a meeting with Big Jock. I was still very unhappy and, after saying my piece, I slapped in a transfer request.

'If you're sure that's what you want, Tommy,' said Jock.

'I'm sure,' I replied.

Do you know, I was on that transfer list for two years! Every now and again I would pop my head round the door of Big Jock's office and ask, 'Any offers, Boss?'

He would hardly look up as he shuffled papers around, 'Nope, no one's come in for you. I'll keep you informed.'

Listen, I knew for a fact Barcelona were more than interested. They were managed by an Englishman called Vic Buckingham back then and a newspaper contact told me he wanted me for the Spanish side. I couldn't march in and tell Jock I knew of Barcelona's interest as that would have smacked of me having been tapped by them, which was highly illegal, of course, and that would have created all sort of ructions. So, I had to play dumb.

'Anyone interested, Boss?'

'Nope, no one's come in for you. I'll keep you informed.'

It became a weekly routine and there was nothing I could do about it. Back then, there were no Bosman deals and the club held on to your registration. They had all the aces – changed days now, though.

I learned an awful lot from Big Jock. He made me the player I had become. I know he gave me a lot of credit for the way I developed and how hard I worked in training but his encouragement was immense. I will always appreciate what he did for me. If only he had played me that day against St Johnstone!

John Clark

I got to know Big Jock a lot better when he put me on the coaching staff in 1973. We used to travel up and down Britain, taking in all sorts of games. I remember realising just how famous he was one night when we were travelling to Anfield to watch Liverpool in action. Big Jock was driving and we were running a bit late. Anyway, he jumped a red light. There was no chance of an accident or anything like that, we could see all around us, and he took a wee chance. Suddenly, the sirens were going behind us and a motorcycle cop rode up beside us and motioned us into the side. This big English inspector appeared, looked in and said matter-of-factly, 'Mr Stein, how good to see you. Down for the game?'

'Aye,' said Big Jock and, with that, the inspector called over the motorcycle cop and told him to give us an escort right to the front door at Anfield. Only Big Jock could have swung that. It was just another illustration of how famous the Big Man was. Everyone knew him and his high profile never did Celtic any harm.

Willie Wallace

Big Jock knew a thing or two about a good player – he bought me, didn't he? We may have had a few run-ins during our time but I always respected him. Funnily enough, I knew the Celtic trainer Neilly Mochan fairly well even before I joined from Hearts. I used to pick up Neilly's brother Denis in Falkirk on our way through to Stenhousemuir when we were both at Ochilview. So I knew a few of the stories that were going around Celtic at the time.

That was before Big Jock's arrival, of course, and everything changed when he took over. Naturally, I was delighted to sign for the club. As you may expect, I was fairly pleased with myself at being rated by the Celtic manager.

Coaches seemed to be set in their ways back then, but Big Jock always believed in giving you some freedom to express yourself. His tactics were normally spot on and he had the honours to prove it. He also had the ability to make you feel super-confident. It got to the stage where you didn't expect to lose – and, of course, we didn't lose many.

Stevie Chalmers

I was an outside right going through the motions until Big Jock took over. I remained out on the wing for a few games at the end of the 1964/65 season but I was moved into a more central role after that and that is when my career really took off.

The Boss saw me more as a striker and encouraged me to use my pace through the middle. I think he would normally favour big John Hughes in the really heavy weather and, of course, Big Yogi could alternate between centre forward and outside left because he was so versatile.

Jock just had that ability to get the best out of everyone. He always managed to get you playing at your peak. As far as team formations went, he tweaked things every now and again to keep you on your toes. The defence didn't change much but Big Jock liked to manoeuvre his forward line around every now and again. When you look at the men he had at his disposal back then, it is entirely understandable. He was the man who pulled it altogether.

Bertie Auld

Jock Stein revolutionised things at Celtic Park and I was lucky enough to get in on the ground floor. I was seventeen years old when I signed for Celtic back in April 1955 – just around the time Big Jock had picked up the injury that would end his playing career. He would have been in his early thirties when he was forced to give up but, thankfully, someone at the club had the foresight to appoint him coach to the reserve team. And that's where it all started.

I loved being in his company when he talked football. Other first-team guys, such as Bobby Evans, Bertie Peacock and Bobby Collins, would meet at a place called Ferraris in Glasgow's Sauchiehall Street and would chat about all things football. Jock would hold court and, even back then, it was obvious he knew what he was talking about. It was great being involved in the inner sanctum and, remember, Evans, Peacock and Collins were international players. When they talked, you listened. But no one made a bigger impression than Jock Stein. I remember you had to chip in a shilling – five pence these days – as a tip but sometimes I had to try to sneak out because I was skint!

But Jock changed so many things with the reserves. Before he took over, we would turn about at 9.45 in the morning and then be told to go out and do laps for two hours! Then someone would appear and throw a ball at us and tell us to organise a bounce game. There would be about thirty of us at the time and we were all scrambling for a kick at the thing. Jock wasn't impressed and suddenly the chaos came to an end.

He put the emphasis on pushing yourself to the absolute limit of your capabilities. He wanted to discover exactly what you could cope with. Mainly, though, he encouraged us to entertain.

He wanted to win but he wanted to win in a certain style. I left for Birmingham City and Big Jock was allowed to move to Dunfermline where he won the Scottish Cup in 1961, beating Celtic, of course.

In 1965, around the turn of the year, I received a telephone call from someone asking, 'Would you like to come back to Celtic?'

'When? Tonight?' I replied. Honestly, I did not know that Big Jock was returning a couple of months later but I would still have been there. It was just such a massive boost when I did discover that The Boss was taking over. I dropped £5 per week in wages to go back. That was a lot of money back then, especially as I had a young family. I also had to find a house in Glasgow because I had been living in a Birmingham City club house in Solihull. The wife might not have been exactly overjoyed at the time but the upheaval was well worthwhile when Big Jock walked back in those front doors of Celtic Park.

He should never have been allowed to leave in the first place.

Bobby Lennox

I didn't know whether to be happy or sad when I heard the news that Big Jock was coming back to Celtic. I was having a run in the first team at the time and, of course, a new manager could have completely different ideas from the bloke who was in the dugout before him.

I needn't have worried – Big Jock worked wonders with me. From when I was a school kid, I had always played up beside the centre forward but Celtic started fielding me on the wings. I did as I was told, of course, and contributed as much as I could to the cause.

But it was Jock who brought me inside and everything took off after that. I could never thank him enough.

12

RONNIE SIMPSON: THE TRIBUTES

Ronnie Simpson should have finished season 1966/67 playing for Berwick Rangers in the old Scottish Second Division where they finished tenth in a league of twenty. Instead, as the history books show, he picked up a European Cup medal, played his first game for the Scotland international side and was voted the Football Writers' Player of the Year. Take into consideration the fact he also won medals in the league, the Scottish Cup, the League Cup and the Glasgow Cup. Not bad for someone whose next birthday would see him turn thirty-seven.

Yet things could have developed so differently for the Lisbon Lion, known affectionately to his team-mates as 'Faither' because of his advancing years. He had dropped out of the Hibs first team with Willie Wilson taking over the No. 1 spot. His Easter Road career looked as good as obliterated and Berwick Rangers were searching for a new goalkeeper. They turned their attention to Simpson and they were confident of landing the experienced professional. Hibs would hardly prove difficult to deal with as far as the transfer fee was concerned.

That was when fate stepped in to so rudely interrupt Berwick Rangers' progress in their pursuit of Simpson. Celtic, too, were in the market for another keeper. John Fallon was the man in possession of the keeper's jersey but they did not have reliable cover. The unpredictable Frank Haffey, who conceded nine goals to England at Wembley in 1961, had just been sold to Swindon Town for £8,000 in 1964. That opened the door for Simpson and he decided it was 'worth a chance'.

However, he couldn't have been best pleased when he was told, a year later in March 1965, that Jock Stein was about to take over as manager of Celtic. After hearing the news about the impending arrival of Stein, Simpson is reported to have gone straight home and informed his wife that she should get ready to pack. 'We're on the move again,' he was alleged to have said. It was Stein, of course, as Hibs boss, who had sold Simpson to Celtic for a transfer fee described by the then Celtic boss Jimmy McGrory as being in the region of 'sweeties'. Most assuredly, glory, medals and international honours did not figure in the wildest dreams of Simpson at that stage of his career.

There had been talk of a fall-out between the player and the manager nearing the end of his days at Hibs. Neither Simpson nor Stein was ever eager to talk about any friction between the pair. Luckily for Celtic, if there had been any ill-feeling between them, it never surfaced in their six years together in Glasgow. Naturally, their finest moment came in the Portuguese capital against Inter Milan and, quite remarkably, that historic game came almost twenty-two years after Simpson made his debut, at the age of fourteen years and eight months, for Queen's Park in a Summer Cup tie against Clyde at Hampden in June 1945.

Remember, too, this was the goalkeeper who had represented Great Britain four times as an amateur and played twice in the 1948 Olympic Games. He had also earned two English FA Cup medals in 1952 and 1955 with Newcastle United. Those not-inconsiderable achievements might have been more than enough for most individuals. Simpson had also served Third Lanark in his distinguished career before eventually landing at Celtic.

Jock Stein, in fact, did keep faith with John Fallon when he took over in 1965. And it was Fallon who was in goal a month later when Celtic defeated Dunfermline 3–2 in a dramatic Scottish Cup Final with Billy McNeill claiming the winner with a trademark header from a Charlie Gallagher left-wing corner kick. But, a year later, it was Simpson who was in charge when Celtic again made their way to Hampden for another Scottish Cup climax against Rangers. Unfortunately, for Ronnie and his team-mates, it wasn't to be a happy conclusion on this occasion as Rangers won 1–0 in a tension-laden replay after a goalless draw in the first confrontation. Simpson, as usual, was blameless as a thumping first-time effort from the Ibrox side's right back Kai Johansen almost burst the net.

Better times were ahead, of course. And everyone who can remember the Lisbon encounter with the stylish Italians still talks about Simpson's cheeky back-heel to team-mate John Clark when he was out of his penalty area with Inter Milan centre forward Renato Cappellini charging down on him. That was typical Simpson, though. A marvellous piece of improvisation from a goalkeeper who often said, 'I don't care how I keep the ball out of the net. It can hit my elbow, my knee, my backside – just so long as it doesn't cross the line. That's my only concern.'

Ronnie Simpson was a one-off. He thoroughly deserves his place in Celtic legend.

Billy McNeill

Faither was quite magnificent, as simple as that. You always felt safe when he was behind you. He talked you through a game and, by full-time, must have been exhausted even though he might have had very little to do.

Being a Celtic keeper back then was either the best job in football – or the worst. Because we had the ball in our opponents' half most of the time, Ronnie would be virtually unemployed. I know some keepers much prefer to be in the thick of it. Obviously, if you are busy it helps you keep your eye in. You're on the go all the time and that is no bad thing.

In Ronnie's case it was all about concentration. And, my goodness, did he possess that much-needed commodity in plentiful supplies. He could have been asked to do nothing for eighty-nine minutes and then produce a wonder save in the last minute. It really was a gift and he put every ounce of his vast experience to a good use.

Although fans say he was an unspectacular goalkeeper, relying solely on anticipation and positioning, I can tell you he still managed to pull off some breathtaking saves on the odd occasion when the situation demanded it. I can recall a save he made from Rangers' Orjan Persson in a game at Celtic Park that defied belief. I still don't know how he managed it. Persson volleyed an effort at goal, low, hard and accurate, to Ronnie's left. It was from about eight yards and Rangers' Swedish forward packed quite a wallop. It looked a certain goal but my moan was immediately stifled when Ronnie sprang to his left and not only got to the ball but held it.

If Ronnie had made that save in a World Cup Final or a European Cup Final you would still be watching it on television replays today. Yes, it was that good. Ronnie did, of course, make a very good stop against Inter Milan but, because of everything that happened that day, it, too, seems to have been swept away in the mists of time.

Even before the Italians got their early penalty kick, Sandro Mazzola snapped in a wicked close-range header from a left-wing cross. There was a lot of power in it but Ronnie, as ever, was alert and threw himself to his left to parry the effort and the danger was cleared. If Faither had made that save at the end of the game and kept the score at 2–1 for us everyone would have been raving about it.

It was a pleasure to play in front of Ronnie Simpson. He was the best.

Jim Craig

Ronnie may have been the oldest guy in the team but he was also one of the most agile. Age hadn't robbed him of his flexibility. He was good fun, too. I'll tell you this, though – he was a bit of a cheat. I well remember our team photographs back then when you had the likes of Billy McNeill, Tommy Gemmell and me standing in the back row alongside Ronnie. Now Ronnie used to tell people he was around 5ft 10in or so. But, when he stood alongside us – and we were all 6ft plus – he would get up on his tiptoes to appear taller. What height was he? I never found out but I still think he was maybe just a wee bit more than two inches short of 6ft!

Mind you, it didn't really matter because Ronnie had all the ability in the world. His experience was invaluable to Celtic. It was always kind of difficult to believe that our goalkeeper was making his debut for Queen's Park when most of the Lisbon Lions were still in nappies!

Tommy Gemmell

Ronnie's presence in goal undoubtedly had a calming effect on our back four, including me. He always looked in charge although, of course, he was not the most imposing of figures. Big Jock had a thing about goalkeepers and I'm not too sure he trusted any of them. They were a necessary evil in a team where all the other performers used their feet. Maybe Big Jock had played in front of a few accident-prone keepers during his time as a centre half and that had a bearing on his thinking later in life.

Critics have often said that the ability to spot a good goalkeeper was Jock's Achilles heel and they may have had a point – although he certainly brought plenty to the club during his time there. I can recall playing three games inside ten days back in 1965 when Jock selected three different goalkeepers for each match! John Fallon was the man in charge when we beat Raith Rovers 8–1 in a League Cup quarter-final tie on 15 September. A week later, an Irishman named Jack Kennedy was between the sticks for the second leg and we won that one 4–0. Three days after that, Ronnie was in for a league game against Aberdeen which turned into a 7–1 rout for us.

Jock had seen all three in action but still couldn't quite make up his mind. He recalled Fallon for a league match against Falkirk at Brockville. We escaped with a 4–3 victory but Jock wasn't too convinced with the form of his goalkeeper. The penny dropped, in came Ronnie and he was there until the end of the season. By the way, I don't think that bloke Jack Kennedy ever got near the first team again. However, he didn't lose a single goal throughout his Celtic career. There are not many who can say that!

Ronnie was brilliant to play alongside but I also recall he lumbered me once when he had to go off with a shoulder injury in a Scottish Cup tie against Clyde at Shawfield. That was on 12 February 1969 and, ironically, he sustained the knock going down on the flint-hard surface at the feet of Jimmy Quinn, who was on loan at Clyde from Celtic at the time! You didn't have substitute goalkeepers for domestic games in those days and yours truly was given the No. 1 jersey. Bertie Auld was our sub that day and he came on and went into his usual midfield berth. And, just like that Kennedy chap, I kept a clean sheet, we got a goalless draw and won 3–0 in the replay. Celtic lifted the trophy that year, beating Rangers 4–0 in the final with John Fallon back in goal with Ronnie sidelined. Thankfully, I was left back that day and feeling much more comfortable.

Unfortunately, that was the beginning of the end for Ronnie and, just before he turned forty, he hung up his gloves. I, for one, missed his presence in the team, as well as in the dressing room. He didn't say an awful lot but when he had something to air it was always well worth listening to. What memories he left us with, though. A magnificent professional and a great bloke.

John Clark

Ronnie Simpson got everything he deserved in football. It would have been a travesty if his career had just drifted away into oblivion – another of football's forgotten performers. Of course, that came so close to being the situation before he joined up at Celtic Park.

We all know of his qualities and he was a genuinely funny man. He could be every bit as droll as the great Chic Murray, a unique Scottish comedian in his day. There was no chance of anyone getting big-headed when Faither was around. His one-liners would soon put someone in their place if he thought they needed it.

Like Big Billy mentions, Ronnie was a real treasure to play in front of simply because of his steady stream of advice through-out the ninety minutes. I hadn't encountered that before and it did make life that little bit easier. He would spot someone making a run and let you know right away. 'Luggy, watch your left!' or 'Luggy, jockey him, keep him on his right.' It was all appreciated and he was spot-on every time.

The consistency of the man was quite incredible, too. Like any goalkeeper, he may have let in one or two you thought he might have done better with but I can't think of too many. There must be one out there somewhere but it doesn't come easily to mind. That merely emphasises just how good Ronnie was. Op-posing forwards had to work hard for anything they got from Celtic back then.

Willie Wallace

How many times did you see Ronnie racing from his goal and plucking the ball off the toe of an advancing forward? I know he did it to me often enough when he was at Hibs and Celtic while I was at Hearts. His timing was nothing short of immaculate.

I reckon his eye-to-ball co-ordination was all down to golf as much as anything else. Ronnie was an excellent golfer and his putting was one of his strengths. He would take his time lining up the shot and then roll it with ease towards that little hole. If you didn't know it was Ronnie out there and someone had told you that you were, in fact, watching a top pro you wouldn't have argued.

Of course, he took that timing into football and I couldn't even start to count the many occasions he made a late dash from his goal line to snatch the ball away from an opponent. If he does it once, you might think he was fortunate. If he does it twice, you might think Dame Fortune is still smiling on him. However, Ronnie did it time after time and you knew he never left anything to chance.

Like the other Lisbon Lions, Tommy Gemmell and Bobby Lennox, it was a real pleasure to be at Wembley a month before Lisbon in 1967 when Ronnie, belatedly, but quite rightly, won his first international cap. If England thought our thirty-six-year-old goalkeeper was a weak link they were swiftly put right. Wembley against the world champions was an extraordinary setting for an extraordinary character. And, once again, Ronnie emerged victorious. You can't get better than that.

Stevie Chalmers

Ronnie and I missed our vocation, of course. The world of golf was robbed of two top performers when we took up football. I suppose as footballers we were good golfers and as golfers we were good footballers. Ronnie's sense of humour would unravel that comment.

I liked the guy a lot. Bit of an understatement there, I can assure you. Celtic used Seamill as a training HQ before big games and Ronnie and I always had our golf clubs packed in with the football stuff to make sure we enjoyed the facilities to the full. It was a smashing way to relax and, take my word for it, Ronnie could have been a top-class golfer if he had chosen that profession. I should know what I'm talking about. I'm not too bad with the sticks either, even if I do say so myself, but I never beat him.

And he was difficult to beat, too, as a goalkeeper. Again, I am speaking from experience. I played against him a few times when he was at Hibs in the late fifties and early sixties and I don't recall ever getting too much joy out of our meetings. I had to laugh – and I'm sure Ronnie would have seen the funny side, too – when I was reading an old football book not so long ago. There is a sentence that went along the lines of, 'Hibs have signed Ronnie Simpson, the thirty-year-old goalkeeper of Newcastle United, who is thought to be past his best.' Is that the same Ronnie Simpson who would win a European Cup medal and everything else six years later?

Of course, he made his international debut in 1967, too, when Scotland beat world champions England 3–2 at Wembley. Jim Baxter took most of the headlines with his mickey-taking and keepy-uppy routines against Bobby Moore and Co. but Ronnie, in my opinion, was a genuine stand-out that afternoon. If you get a chance, have a look at that game again – Ronnie made some superb saves against the English. And his distribution, as ever, was exemplary. No one could turn defence into attack quicker than Ronnie.

He was a great all-rounder and he brought stability to a defence that may not have enjoyed that luxury too often beforehand. Big Jock may have changed his forward line around quite a bit to keep us all sharp and on our toes but our fans got used to the first six names that were read over the tannoy on match day – Simpson; Craig and Gemmell, Murdoch, McNeill and Clark. They came as a unit and Ronnie was in with the bricks. He thoroughly deserved to be, too.

Bertie Auld

Ronnie came in at just the right time to solve our No. 1 problem. Absolutely no disrespect to anyone who was there before him but we never really attained consistency in that position and Ronnie, with all his experience and vast knowledge, brought that with him. Before Ronnie, most of the Celtic goalkeepers thought the net behind them was for stopping the ball!

I know he really helped settle the defence because he was a shouter. Possibly, they hadn't been used to that before but Ronnie would fire out instructions left, right and centre throughout a game and tell them what was happening on their blindsides. John Clark, of course, was the sweeper who did some great work behind Jim Craig, Billy McNeill and Tommy Gemmell. However, Ronnie was a bit of a sweeper, too, who covered for Luggy! He just read the game so well.

He may have been a bit unorthodox but he didn't give a monkey's how he kept the ball out of the net, as he often said. I remember our Scottish Cup Final against Aberdeen at Hampden in 1967, only a few days after Faither had put up the shutters in the European Cup semi-final against Dukla Prague in Czechoslovakia. I think we were leading 2–0 through two goals from Willie Wallace at the time but the Dons were determined to get something back to stage a grand finale. They weren't going to give up without a fight.

One of their guys, I believe it was a Danish player called Jens Petersen, got a chance close in after a cross had come over from the right. Ronnie was at his near post and the Aberdeen guy was all smiles when he saw he had an empty net smack in front of him, about ten yards away. He rolled the ball forward and was startled to see our keeper race across his line and kick it to safety. Ronnie didn't have time to re-adjust his shape to dive at the effort so he simply improvised and booted the ball away. It may not have been the way Lev Yashin would have dealt with it but it was effective and Ronnie had kept another clean sheet. 'That's what it's all about, son,' he would say.

Who could argue?

Bobby Lennox

Ronnie was the wittiest, coolest guy I knew. He could cut you in two with his remarks. I remember a few years ago when I was invited along to a Supporters' Association function when they unveiled the eleven players who were named as Celtic's Greatest-Ever Team.

I was lucky enough to win the No. 11 place in that formidable line-up. As I stepped up to receive my award, I was handed the microphone to address the guests. I started, 'I'm really surprised to be given this honour . . .'

From behind me I could hear the unmistakable drone of my old colleague, 'Aye and so are we!'

On another occasion, Ronnie and I were in Ireland and we decided to take in some Gaelic football – you know, the game where they have the nets and the rugby goalposts. I believe you get a point for the ball going over the bar and through the posts and three for actually hitting the net. Most of the efforts seemed to be flying over the bar and Ronnie turned to me and said, 'Lennox, you would have been a star at this game.'

I was so happy to play at Wembley in 1967 when Ronnie made his debut at the grand old age of thirty-six. Imagine taking your international bow at that age. Ronnie was as calm and collected as ever, though. We came out to have a look at the pitch before the game and the Scottish fans were everywhere. Wembley already looked packed and there was still about an hour or so to go to kick-off. Lion Rampant flags were flying everywhere, the Scottish fans were singing their heads off and Ronnie turned round and said. 'Hey, Lennox, is there a game on today?'

I scored that day, of course, as did Denis Law and Jim McCal-liog, who like, Ronnie, was also making his debut. Mind you, there was the little matter of a seventeen-year age difference between Ronnie and our young goalscorer!

13

BOBBY MURDOCH: THE TRIBUTES

Bobby Murdoch went through all sorts of agonies as Celtic gatecrashed the European big-time in Lisbon. Murdoch, thoughtful with a delightful touch as well as possessing a shot of sledgehammer proportions, had his right foot stamped on by a desperate Inter Milan defender early in the game.

The midfielder would later say, 'The pain shot right through me. It was probably an accident but it was a dull one. If there had been outfield substitutes available back then, I might have had to go off. However, as it was, we only had substitute goalkeeper John Fallon on the bench that day. Big Jock told me, "Run it off, Bobby, you'll be fine." As the game progressed towards half-time, I looked down and my right ankle seemed to be twice the size it was at the kick-off. People must have wondered why I was favouring my left foot that day. Fortunately, I was two-footed but my right was undoubtedly the stronger of the two. I even managed to get a couple of left-footed shots on target that day but both were saved.'

Murdoch's midfield ally Bertie Auld, remembering that incident too, said, 'I saw Bobby grimace at one point and I asked him what was the matter. He pointed to his right foot and I could clearly see that his ankle was beginning to swell up. I said, "I don't like the look of that, Bobby." "I'm no' too chuffed myself, Bertie!" came the reply. What a performance he put in that day on one foot. The Italians got lucky – could you even start to imagine what he would have done to them if he could have used both feet?'

Jim Craig backs up the story, 'The fans will always remember that I was the guy who pulled the ball back for Tommy Gemmell to thump in our equaliser. However, I had an even better run and cross before that and this time picked out Bobby. I had seen him leather those sort of balls past the keeper before they had a chance to move. On this occasion, though, he allowed the ball to run across him on to his left foot. That gave an Inter Milan defender the opportunity to get at him and, in that split-second, the chance was gone. That was most unlike Bobby but it does illustrate how uncomfortable he was with his right foot. His display against the Italians was as brave as any I have ever witnessed. Thankfully, he and the rest of us got our reward at the end.'

Billy McNeill recalls, 'As Bobby said at the time, we didn't have a substitute to cover for him if he had gone off. Listen, there was no way Bobby was going off that day. No chance. He would have played on with his leg hanging off if need be!'

Murdoch's Celtic career got off to a rather bizarre start when, as a seventeen-year-old who had just returned after being farmed out to local junior side Cambuslang Rangers, he was told he was making his debut courtesy of an absent-minded team-mate. The teenager didn't expect to get the nod from the then manager Jimmy McGrory for the first game of the 1961/62 season. Remarkably, a Celtic player had turned up at the ground *without* his football boots. Suitable replacements couldn't be found and McGrory was forced to pitchfork the young Murdoch into the side. Operating at inside right, Bobby went out, scored the opening goal in a 3–1 win over Hearts and hardly looked back after that. Goodness only knows what happened to the colleague who forgot his footwear!

Murdoch was one of the most unassuming men you could have ever wished to meet. He played down his phenomenal ability and preferred praise to go the way of others. 'I'm not one for fuss,' he would often say. But Bobby was a key man with Celtic and rivals noted this – none more so than a representative of Racing Club of Argentina before the ill-fated and bad-tempered World Club Championship Final in 1967. The

South American observed Celtic over a number of games and was clearly impressed by the dynamic and powerful midfielder. When asked about what he thought of the European Cup holders, he said simply, 'Murdoch – he is Celtic.'

No one was unduly surprised when Racing Club had a two-man shadow squad on Murdoch throughout the three games. Nor was anyone shocked when they saw Murdoch being kicked very early in the first game at Hampden. Sadly, it was probably seen as some sort of backhanded compliment by the South Americans. Murdoch, though, still managed to shine in those torrid encounters and Boca Juniors, one of the biggest clubs in the world at that time, were reported to be getting ready to make a massive bid for his services. In typical Murdoch fashion, he responded, 'Ach, I'm no' interested – no way. I'm staying with the club I love. I'm only interested in playing for Celtic.' And you just knew that he meant every word of it.

On 25 May 1967 Bobby Murdoch realised a dream. He strode the immaculate surface of the Estadio Nacionale in Lisbon with a grace and guile that bewildered Inter Milan. He was in the thick of everything. Adding his powerful frame to defensive duties, making himself available for passes from the defence, patrolling the middle of the park with Bertie Auld, spraying the ball around with unbelievable accuracy and plunging into attack to bombard the overworked Sarti in the Italians' goal. All with one good foot!

It was a truly memorable performance from the masterful Murdoch. Inter Milan, doyens of their defensive craft, had no answer to the gifted linkman. Inevitably, he was involved in both goals that brought the European Cup to Celtic Park. No surprise, really.

Murdoch, never gifted with electrifying pace, was playing in the old inside-right position when Stein arrived in 1965. His ability to hit devastating, defence-shredding passes wasn't being utilised as much as might have been. His talent for hitting screaming shots at goal wasn't being seen at its best either as he often played in packed penalty areas as support to the centre forward, usually Stevie Chalmers or John Hughes.

Stein, much against the wishes of the then chairman, Sir Robert Kelly, had the courage of his own convictions to push Murdoch back into a deeper midfield role.

'He is not a wing-half,' said Kelly.

'You will soon see that he is,' countered Stein.

The move clicked from day one as Murdoch went on to become one of the Greatest-Ever Celts and a genuine world-class player. Alas, this wonderful personality was taken from us far too early. However, he left each and every one of us with so many joyous moments to savour and behold.

But, if you ever want to witness a midfield player in his absolute prime and doing everything with breathtaking precision, just look again at the European Cup Final of 1967. Bobby Murdoch, with one good foot, was on the greatest platform in football and, to everyone's delight, this wonderful and self-deprecating character played a pivotal role in the club's most famous triumph.

Billy McNeill

Bobby signed for Celtic in 1959, two years after me, and we knew the rough times before Jock Stein arrived. A cup run was about the best we could manage back then and I don't think we ever made much of an impact in the league. But, like me, Bobby was Celtic through and through. They were the only club for him.

He was the embodiment of quality and talent – he was pedigree material all right. Bobby was a first-class team man, too. I recall Jock Stein trying something different before we played a European Cup tie against AC Milan at Celtic Park in 1969. The first leg had ended goalless in the San Siro Stadium and, naturally, we were in with a smashing chance of reaching the next stage.

Big Jock had noticed, even in their home game, that the AC Milan manager Nereo Rocco, who always reminded me of a character straight out of *The Godfather*, had stuck a man-marker on Bobby. If they were going to carry out that tactic at home, you could be absolutely certain they would repeat it in Glasgow.

Now, the Italians had a marvellous player in their midfield in those days called Gianni Rivera. Like Bobby, he was quality. He ran the show for AC Milan – everything seemed to go through him. In actual fact, he was right up there among the best players I have ever faced. Big Jock thought it would be interesting to see how AC Milan reacted to Rivera being marked – by Bobby! Now that was a role Bobby had never previously been asked to carry out but he was more than willing to go along with the experiment. Jock wondered if the guy who was supposed to be sitting on Bobby would still follow him around even if Bobby was refusing to leave the side of Rivera!

So, for about fifteen minutes or so, we had the fairly comical sight of Murdoch, his marker and Rivera all situated within yards of each other as the action unfolded. The AC Milan players and their team-mates must have wondered what on earth was going on with this trio. The point is, though, the position was totally alien to Bobby but he went out and did it to the very best of his ability. Big Jock had reasoned we would nullify their best player while our player was also being nullified, if you see what I mean. Technically, that should mean we are a player up on the deal. Sadly, like a lot of theories, it didn't work in practice and they snatched a 1–0 win. Bobby was later released from his chains but we never got a break that night.

I'm not going to talk about Bobby as a loser, though. No way. Like I said earlier, we had come through the hard times at Celtic so, when we started to win, it was paradise, no pun intended. Leagues, cups, medals – that's what it was all about. It's what Bobby and I used to talk about after training in the late fifties and early sixties. It was only a dream but there was no harm in letting your imagination go for a wander every now and again.

The jigsaw came together in Lisbon. No one played a bigger part in our historic day than Bobby Murdoch.

Jim Craig

Bobby was known as Chopper for most of his career but he was also called Sam for a spell – and he didn't like it one little bit!

We were down at our usual HQ at Seamill on the Ayrshire coast preparing for an important game and Jock Stein set up a training exercise that saw us dribbling round paint pots. Bobby clattered into a few of these obstacles and sent paint flying all over the place. I recall there was a van parked nearby with the name Sam B. Allison emblazoned on its side. He appeared to be the local painter and decorator. Big Jock laughed. 'Hey, Bobby,' he said, 'you've spilled more paint than Sam has in a lifetime.' So, Bobby instantly became Sam and the nickname stuck for a while.

He may not have been able to skip round inanimate objects but Bobby knew how to get past more orthodox opponents. He had a very graceful, artistic touch. You would sometimes see him going up on his tiptoes, having a wee look around and then arcing a pass about fifty yards or so with uncanny precision. His shooting power was fairly devastating, too. He had it all. But there's something you might not know about Bobby and that is that he was a very emotional character. He would cry if we won. He would cry if we lost. He would even cry if we drew. We just cried when he wasn't in the team!

Tommy Gemmell

If Bobby had played in English football around the same time as, say, Billy Bremner at Leeds United, I am sure he would have been hailed as a superstar. As well as being incredibly strong in the tackle, Bobby could repeatedly bring the ball through to set up and score goals.

However, when Scottish international squads were being put together, the Leeds United skipper, a superb player in his day it must be said, invariably got the nod over Bobby. Yet my old mate was a lot more creative than Wee Billy. I am still of the mind that Bobby never received the recognition he certainly deserved. How many full caps did he win? Twelve! That's a paltry amount for a player who scored over 100 goals for Celtic while playing in midfield. You would have expected a guy with his talent to have won 100 caps never mind score a century of goals.

But it was so typical of the man that he never once complained. Let me say that all the players at Celtic back then appreciated Bobby Murdoch even if some other people didn't. We were all fortunate to play alongside him.

John Clark

I remember Bobby being quite a quiet, even reserved, sort of character. What a transformation when he got out on that football field, though. That was his stage and he revelled in that setting. If you asked me to list his strengths, I would say you might as well cut to the chase and try to detect a flaw. If there were any, I didn't see them and I played alongside him often enough.

Bobby was good with either foot, could shoot from range with equal power and accuracy, could tackle with the best of them and wasn't bad in the air either. He wasn't the fleetest of foot but he more than made up for that by his reading of the play. It was actually a pleasure to be on the same pitch as Bobby – especially as he was wearing the same strip as you.

A lot of teams paid him the compliment of sticking markers on him but they would simply be undone if Bobby spotted an opening and zapped one of his precision passes through it to a lurking colleague. And, if they weren't sticking the ball in the net, he wasn't adverse to coming forward and rectifying the situation himself.

A truly wonderful player and an all-round good guy.

Willie Wallace

Bobby and Tommy Gemmell were known as the Big Shots in the Lisbon Lions line-up and they both liked to have a crack at goal when they got the opportunity. Big Tommy was electronically judged to have had the hardest shot back then when he clocked 71 mph in some radar test set up by a newspaper. Bobby wouldn't have been far off that figure, either.

The thing about Chopper, though, was his ability to flight the ball into top corners. He would shape as if to blast the ball from the edge of the box and defenders would be throwing themselves in the way. At the last moment, though, he would relax, sell them a dummy and then almost nonchalantly flick a ball goalwards. I recall him doing that exact thing in a league match against Rangers at Celtic Park on 17 September 1966. I was a Hearts player at the time but I saw the game later that night on television, not realising, of course, that I would soon be lining up alongside Bobby.

If memory serves correctly, Bertie Auld slammed in the first goal in the opening minute and only a matter of a couple of minutes later, Bobby was about twenty-five yards out. Again, he took control of the ball, drew back his right foot in his usual manner and then, without breaking stride or taking a second look, simply floated an unsaveable effort high into the top left-hand corner. That was typical of the man, though. Sheer class.

Stevie Chalmers

Folk have often asked how I celebrated our European Cup triumph. They always look a wee bit disappointed when I tell them I spent it in a deserted hotel with Bobby! Let me hastily explain.

I roomed with Bobby at our rather splendid hotel in Estoril and, after the game, we both went back and got ready for the specially prepared banquet with all the UEFA delegates and so on. The beaten Inter Milan players were there too but they really looked as though they would have preferred to be somewhere else. Can't blame them.

Anyway, our wives had travelled over to Lisbon and were staying in a different hotel from the players. They were scheduled to travel back that night and Celtic were due to fly into Glasgow the following day. Anyway, after the banquet, Bobby and I saw our wives, said our farewells, wished them a safe journey home and then made our way back to our hotel. After a wee while, we decided to get some shut-eye. It had been a long and fairly exhausting day and we knew something special would be waiting for us at home. How special we couldn't possibly have known at the time.

So, we decided to get tucked up in our beds and no sooner had we put our heads on the pillows than there was a banging at our hotel room door. 'Hurry up, get up,' ordered Jock Stein. 'There's been a problem with your wives' plane. The flight's been cancelled. The girls have nowhere to stay. You'll have to give them your beds!'

So, a bleary-eyed Bobby and I dutifully gave up our accommodation for our wives, only to find there was no room at the inn for us. And the guys with whom we had made history that same day weren't at all interested in letting us bunk up with them. So, there you have it. Bobby and I were booted out and we spent the night rattling round the downstairs of the hotel on our own – mind you, if you have to spend a night doing that, I couldn't think of better company to be in.

Bertie Auld

I loved playing alongside this boy. He could do everything – he could tackle, he could shoot and he could pass. Everything Bobby Murdoch did was stamped with class and authority. His vision was phenomenal and you would have had to go far to actually meet a nicer bloke.

Bobby's career really took off when Jock Stein came back to the club. He gave the players the licence to go out and tackle, to go for 50/50 balls when, beforehand, the management never used to encourage that. From my own experience, I can tell you that you were inclined to be dropped from the team if you got involved in a bit of needle or suchlike. There seemed to be a puritanical presence about the place at the time. Jock, though, believed the game was a contact sport and the ball was there to be won.

The Boss would take his players aside and continually tell us, 'Win the battle and you'll win the game.' Simple enough words but the previous management just about frowned on these sorts of things. Look, the Lisbon Lions were all good guys but we knew how to look after ourselves.

Jock gave Bobby the confidence to go into challenges without thinking he might be dropped the following week if he possibly collided with his opponent. Can you imagine that? Big Jock, of course, actively encouraged you to play with adventure but you're not likely to achieve too much if you haven't got the ball, are you?

Jock Stein gave Bobby Murdoch the freedom to express himself and I don't think the player let anyone down – ever.

Bobby Lennox

I thought Bobby was Celtic's best player in Lisbon. I can't give him a higher tribute than that, can I? Of course, he had plenty of competition for that honour with my wee pal Jimmy Johnstone,

Bertie Auld, Tommy Gemmell and anyone else you care to mention really turning it on that day. But it was Bobby for me – a real ten out of ten performance.

He had all the talent in the world and he could also be very aggressive when necessary – I mean in a sporting manner. Bobby was never interested in an opponent trying to boss him around out on the field. That was his domain and he didn't invite anyone in there.

We all know what he contributed against Inter Milan. That, I swear, was one the most selfless displays I have ever seen. He was carrying that injury but he was still all over the place, trying to galvanise the rest of the team – just ask Big Billy or John Clark. When they got the ball, he wanted it immediately. Luggy seemed to have a lot of the ball that day, as I recall. He would do his sweeping up as Inter's rare attacks came to nothing and he would look around for someone to pass to. Bobby was always there.

I am sure Bobby was as happy for me as I was for him when we lifted that European Cup. We had grown up together at Celtic Park. I signed two years after him but, even as a young man, you could see he was going to go all the way to the top. You can't disguise that sort of quality.

14

JIMMY JOHNSTONE: THE TRIBUTES

When Jimmy Johnstone had his dander up he was just about unstoppable. Those truly astounding, spectacular serpentine-weaving runs had to be seen to be believed. England and Liverpool captain Emlyn Hughes once complained of having 'twisted blood' after facing the Wee Man in an international at Hampden Park in 1974. He was lucky – he wasn't even Jinky's direct opponent that day. Mike Pejic, of Stoke City, was the England left back who had that dubious distinction. That was to be Pejic's fourth and final appearance for his country after being torn apart by Johnstone as Scotland won 2–0.

Jinky, as his team-mates were only too well aware, was a highly temperamental bloke and you upset him at your peril. Scotland trainer Walter McCrae couldn't have been too aware of that side of the Wee Man as he prepared the international squad for an important game against England in 1968, the year after the Scots had overcome the world champions 3–2 at Wembley. The Home Championship back then was being utilised as a qualifying section for the European Nations Cup Finals – now the European Championships – to be held later that year in Italy. Scotland, in typical fashion, had carelessly thrown away their advantage after securing two points against Sir Alf Ramsey's side. A victory was a must at Hampden for the Scots but it was going to be achieved without the help of Scotland's most skilful player, Jimmy Johnstone. Injury had prevented him from playing at Wembley in 1967 and, on this occasion, the international manager, Bobby Brown, had made up his mind to go with Chelsea's Charlie Cooke in preference to the Celt.

The blissfully unaware McCrae then conjured up his outstanding faux pas as Scotland trained at their HQ at Largs. As luck would have it, Celtic were along the Ayrshire coast at their usual haunt at Seamill at the same time. The SFA asked for permission to play Celtic in a bounce game against the international line-up as a special training session. The Parkhead powers that be agreed but Jimmy was far from happy. 'I'm no' interested,' he said. 'I'm no' playing.' However, the Wee Man dutifully turned up to watch the session and McCrae then, unintentionally, made one of football's great blunders – he asked Jinky to be a linesman!

Tommy Gemmell, with the Scottish squad, recalled, 'I think you could say Jimmy let Walter know he was not interested in running the line, in any shape or form. For a start, two of his best pals at Celtic at the time were Bobby Lennox and Willie O'Neill. They would have been taking part in the game and Jinky would have been running up and down the touchline with his wee flag. You couldn't make it up. Lemon and Pumper would have made his life unbearable when they got back to Parkhead. Footballers, in the main, are terrible mickey-takers and Jinky must have realised he would be on the receiving end for some considerable time. Jimmy Johnstone? A linesman? Oh, dear!

'Quite apart from anything else, I suspect any world-class player would rebel, as Jimmy certainly did, at the idea of being used as a linesman. Would someone at the English FA have asked Bobby Charlton to run the line? Would anyone at the Irish FA have been daft enough to ask George Best to act as a linesman? Of course, not. Walter McCrae put his foot in it big-style and a week later would pay a terrible price.

'The international game, which ended in a 1–1 draw and effectively ended Scotland's interest in Europe, by the way, was played in late February to make sure all the qualifiers would be known by the time the summer finals were played. So, on 2 March 1968 Celtic turned up for a league match at Rugby Park to play Kilmarnock, where Walter McCrae doubled up as the club's trainer. Celtic hammered them 6–0 with, as I recall, Willie Wallace scoring four goals and others from Bobby Lennox and young substitute Jimmy Quinn. But everyone's man of the match was, without question, Wee Jinky. He tore their defence to shreds. He played like a man possessed. We all knew the capabilities of our wee genius, of course, but that afternoon he went into overdrive and only an elephant gun could have stopped him from running amok. He twisted, teased and tortured the Killie back lot and I knew what was going on in his mind – he was going to make Walter McCrae suffer.

'The Wee Man looked fairly pleased with himself as we came off at the end. I was walking beside him when he spotted McCrae in the home dugout. "No' bad for an effin' linesman, eh, Walter?" asked a beaming Jinky.'

Stories of Jimmy Johnstone are the stuff of legend. One of the greatest accolades Jinky earned, however, wasn't at his beloved Paradise or even from someone on these shores. On 7 June 1967, Celtic, still basking in the glory of their excellent European Cup triumph, took the team to the Bernabeu Stadium to provide the opposition for the legendary Alfredo Di Stefano's testimonial game. Just to be invited to play in such exalted company in a game for one of the world's greatest-ever footballers was an honour. To go to their fortress and win 1–0 while pulverising the opposition was quite unbelievable. Even the normally hostile Spanish fans had to applaud Celtic that balmy evening.

'Olé! Olé!' was the cry that rang round the stadium but it wasn't a Real Madrid performer being showered with praise. The standing ovations that night were for Jimmy Johnstone. He was unstoppable – a 5ft 4in bundle of mischief and magic that bewildered a Spanish rearguard that wasn't too used to being taken apart, especially in front of their own support. However, Johnstone never embraced a great respect for reputations and he simply dismantled the line of defenders who were put in front of him that evening. It was a virtuoso performance that would have been more than fit to grace a World Cup Final. If Pelé or Maradona or Cruyff or Best or even Di Stefano had delivered such flamboyant entertainment it would have been hailed as the most outstanding individual display ever witnessed. 'It really was that good,' added Gemmell.

Forget that this was labelled a testimonial match. Real Madrid had won the European Cup the previous year, beating Partizan Belgrade 2–1. They wanted to let everyone know they were still the true rulers of all they surveyed. In their minds, they – not a bunch of upstarts from Glasgow – were still the best in Europe. Real gave it their best shot but Johnstone and Co. were not to be denied another moment of glory. They, too, were at the Bernabeu to win and they did just that when Bobby Lennox flashed a low drive into the net from twelve yards after a sublime pass from, you've guessed, Jimmy Johnstone. Game, set and match to Celtic. The accolades went to a swivel-hipped little redhead who thrilled fans everywhere he went.

Another soccer great who admired Johnstone's style was Eusebio, the former Benfica superstar. 'I was privileged to call Jimmy Johnstone my friend,' said the Portuguese legend. 'He always played football with a smile on his face. When Celtic reached the European Cup Final in my country in 1967 I supported them against Inter Milan. They were a great attacking force and, of course, they had that special little genius on the right wing. But Jimmy Johnstone was not just a great player in Scotland. He was known throughout the world.'

Rangers' Willie Henderson, who was Johnstone's main rival for the outside-right berth in the Scotland team in the sixties, recalled, 'I was on top of my game at the time and I had quite a few caps under my belt before Jimmy actually came on the scene. He was a wee bit later in coming into the Celtic first team. I was definitely dislodged from my Scotland position after that. Billy Bremner, I believe, went to one of the Scotland managers and asked if there was a way he could fit both Jimmy and me into his team. "No chance," Billy was informed. "We can only play with one ball!"'

Bertie Auld is convinced his team-mate should have won more than his meagre haul of twenty-three caps for his country. Auld offered this angle: 'He didn't make as many international appearances for one simple reason – he was a Celtic player. If he played for any other club he would have won 100 caps for his nation. I am convinced of that. However, to be fair to Jimmy, he never grumbled. You knew he was only interested in playing for one club and that was Celtic. That was all he needed and that kept him happy.'

Auld, in fact, remembers one of the first times he clapped eyes on Johnstone. 'This wee lad with the big red curls turned up one day for training,' said Bertie. 'I thought he might be a fan. There wasn't an awful lot of him at the time – a wee, frail figure. He would sit in the dressing room and say nothing. He actually looked to be somewhat embarrassed to be mixing with some of the players. Well, that was until he got out onto the pitch and then we all knew who Jimmy Johnstone was. What a talent. He was like a rubber ball. Defenders would bowl him over and he would just keep bouncing back to his feet. You could see the fear in the eyes of our opponents when they looked at the Wee Man when he started to make a name for himself. They were frightened of what he could do to them. That fear was a real compliment to Jimmy. There was no disguising it, either. Those opponents knew they were in for a torrid time.'

Celtic fans probably won't recognise the title La Puce Volante, but that was another nickname that came Johnstone's way on his travels. This time it was conjured up by the appreciative French supporters of Nantes back in 1966 in the second round of the historic European Cup run. Nantes were an excellent team and, among a host of other exciting individuals, boasted the national captain Robert Herbin, who had led France in the World Cup Finals in England the previous summer. It would be fair to say they thought they would take care of Celtic, who were, after all, playing in the premier European competition for the first time in their history. Johnstone, once again, wasn't interested in being a bit-part player.

He shredded a frantic defence and set up chance after chance after some dazzling touchline trickery and goals from Joe Mc-Bride, Bobby Lennox and Stevie Chalmers eased Celtic to a 3–1 victory which they emulated at Parkhead in the second leg to go through to the quarter-finals. La Puce Volante – or The Flying Flea – was born that evening and it was a tag that followed Johnstone around Europe.

One title remains above them all – The Greatest-Ever Celtic Player. The inimitable Jimmy Johnstone is worthy of that immense honour. He paid his own tribute to the fans who encouraged him through his fourteen remarkable years at Celtic, enjoying his 'great job', as he often described it. Years after retiring, he took the microphone before one game, gave his usual cheery wave to the thousands and uttered twelve little words – 'You will always be in my heart. I will never forget you.'

The Celtic support will never forget him, either.

Billy McNeill

We are very fortunate there is so much wonderful footage of the Wee Man in action during his playing days. Film has captured all those marvellous images of Jinky doing what he did best – entertaining the fans. Those supporters were always so important to him.

He loved it when they sang, 'Jimmy Johnstone on the wing' and he would just keep playing away, ensuring they didn't stop! When people who haven't been fortunate enough to witness the Wee Man in the flesh see film of him playing they will understand why so many folk raved about him. Jinky was a Celtic man – that's the beginning and the end of the story. He was a genuine working-class hero and I don't think for a second he would mind me saying that. He was a Celtic fan who played for Celtic. He was one of the lads and success and adulation never went to the Wee Man's head.

Jinky played in an era where there were an awful lot of skilful players, talented individuals and colourful characters. But Jimmy Johnstone was the king of them all.

Jim Craig

I still laugh at the memory of Jinky the morning after we had played Real Madrid at the Bernabeu Stadium in the testimonial match for Alfredo Di Stefano.

Jinky could do no wrong that night and I well remember a Real Madrid defender, Grosso, I think, came racing out of defence in an effort to clatter the Wee Man. He had had enough of Jinky's one-man show and he was going to sort him out. Yes, he did wallop Jimmy but, if he thought that was the end of Jinky's meanderings that night, he was so wrong. I recall him trotting back into defence, probably thinking to himself, 'That takes care of that.' His face was a picture, though, when he looked over his shoulder to see the Wee Man bouncing back to his feet to take the free kick. I suppose he thought his opponent would fold under such treatment but he didn't know our Jimmy Johnstone.

Jinky had arranged to go on holiday with his wife Agnes right after that game. The following day, he was in good form as he prepared to go on holiday. I helped him down with the suitcases and he and Agnes jumped into the waiting taxi. I had assumed he was going to the airport but I heard him say, 'Benidorm, driver!'

The taxi driver almost fainted. Possibly geography wasn't one of Jinky's strong points but from Madrid to the holiday resort it was about 300 miles as the crow flies. Some hire!

I also recall a time when we were invited to play in some charity match in Iceland. There were two planes at the airport for the journey – the big one was an eight-seater! The other was a six-seater. Now, we all know Jinky wasn't a big fan of flying. Anyway, we headed for these diminutive aircraft and Jinky was sitting up front in the six-seater. He didn't look too comfortable and it didn't get any better when the door to the cabin opened and out stepped the pilot.

Jinky looked up. 'Are you the pilot?' he almost shrieked.

'Yes,' came the reply.

'Where's the other pilot?'

'There isn't one.'

Jinky looked aghast. 'That's all we bloody need. You're the only pilot? What happens if you have a heart attack?'

The pilot nonchalantly produced a booklet, handed it to Jinky and said, 'There are the flying instructions – they'll tell you all you need to know about flying a plane!'

I'm sure I heard the Wee Man praying all the way home.

Tommy Gemmell

As Cairney says, it was well known that Jinky had a fear of flying and I know why. He was travelling back early from the States during the club's summer tour in 1966 with right back Ian Young. They were both due to get married and the club had allowed them to go ahead of the rest of the party.

Now, Wee Jinky may have been afraid of nothing on a football park, where he often took some terrible punishment, but he really didn't like getting up among the clouds. The journey back from the States seemed to have been fairly uneventful with everything going according to plan. I think they had already been flying for about an hour. Jinky and Ian were discussing where they would be going on honeymoon and so on. And then the plane lurched as it hit an air pocket.

Jinky would look you straight in the eye and say, 'Tam, it must have fallen for about two minutes!' It must be said that the Wee Man was prone to a bit of exaggeration every now and again. 'All I could see were all these dinners suspended about two feet above the heads of the other passengers.' There was no point in confiding in Jinky that if the plane had, indeed, dropped for about two minutes he may not have been around to tell the tale!

A smashing lad and missed by all.

John Clark

I got to know Jinky fairly well during the early days because I was his unpaid chauffeur! I used to pick up Davie Hay in the mornings at Uddingston Cross and then we would make the short drive to Jinky's place. The Wee Man could keep you waiting about fifteen minutes while he got ready. I would be looking at my watch and wondering if he was going to make us late and earn us a rebuke from Big Jock.

Then out would step the bold lad and he'd jump into the passenger seat beside me, with Davie sitting in the back. The first thing the Wee Man did when he got into the car was immediately switch off the radio! The next day I would turn up with Davie and say, 'Watch this – the radio's going off.' Sure enough, Jinky would come in and immediately turn off the music. He never ever explained why he went through that routine, day after day. I guess he just wasn't a morning person!

But what a player. He had the heart of a lion and it was a pleasure to play in the same team as him. I wouldn't have fancied facing him, that's for sure.

Willie Wallace

Jinky always said his heart was broken when he left Celtic in 1975. He didn't see it coming but changes had to be made and he moved on. He was never the same player after that. Celtic Park was, indeed, his spiritual home. That's where he believed he belonged.

Tommy Gemmell and I had him for all of three months at Dundee. We threw him a lifeline because we thought he still had a lot to offer but, for a variety of reasons, it didn't work out. That was a great pity when you realise Jinky was only thirty-two at the time. He still had all the touches and trained exceptionally hard but he struggled with the reality of no longer being Celtic's No. 7.

He was a very modest guy and I know he was surprised when the supporters voted him The Greatest-Ever Celtic Player. His family revealed he was convinced it would go to Henrik Larsson! That sums up the Wee Man.

Stevie Chalmers

One of Jinky's many great strengths was his ability to take the ball for a walk. He was invaluable when you were under pressure. You could give him the ball and he would simply hold on to it.

There was no way our opponents had a clue what he was going to do next because I'm pretty sure the Wee Man didn't know either! However, once he had that ball, no one was going to get another touch until he was good and ready to part with it.

We could all step back and take a breather while Jinky went through his many routines. He was a marvellous guy to have in your team. He would have graced any side in the world.

Bertie Auld

Wee Jinky was so incredibly strong that he rarely sustained any kind of serious injury and, when you consider the amount of kickings he took, it speaks volumes. Yes, the Wee Man enjoyed life, as we all did, but he never abused his body. He looked after himself, trained hard and I always thought he resembled the build of a light-middleweight boxer.

People often compared Jimmy to George Best as both were so skilful and they were born entertainers. But George had his injury problems while Jinky soldiered on. The Wee Man, Bestie and Denis Law were the type of players back then who played with flair and invited tackles from the opposition. Denis, too, had injuries and, of course, missed the European Cup Final in 1968 after undergoing a cartilage operation.

So, no matter what you might hear about Jimmy Johnstone, believe me he never cheated on the football pitch. I used to marvel at him later in his career. He actually developed into a different sort of player. Maybe he had lost a bit of his pace or trickery to get down that wing but he became a lot more aware of what was happening all around the pitch. He was pinging long-range passes all over the place and, once again, he under-lined what a fine player he was.

He may only have been 5ft 4in but he had a superb leap on him, too. He scored a few with his head from balls that would have left 6ft-plus defenders wondering where on earth he had materialised from. In a word, the Wee Man was majestic.

Bobby Lennox

Jinks was the man. He had a special gift and he worked on that gift. He had all the talents in the world, but he also trained hard to make sure his fitness levels were high.

Stanley Matthews, the legendary Stoke City and England outside right, and Real Madrid's Alfredo Di Stefano were two of his particular favourite players as he grew up. He bought a book by Matthews on how to play on the wing. He must have absorbed everything and added a few chapters of his own unique skills.

And it gave him great pleasure to be with the Celtic team that played in Di Stefano's testimonial match shortly after we won the European Cup. The Wee Man was unbelievable that night. He always knew how to rise to the occasion.

15

THE NEARLY MEN

John Fallon was involved in all nine of Celtic's European Cup games during season 1966/67 – and didn't touch the ball once! In those days the only substitute allowed by UEFA was the goalkeeper and Fallon was back-up to the outstanding Ronnie Simpson. It must have been frustrating for the keeper who was brought to Celtic from Blantyre Vics and he was one of five squad members who weren't directly involved in the extraordinary, engrossing and, ultimately, enjoyable excursion into Europe – the others being **David Cattanach**, **Ian Young**, **John Cushley** and **Jim Brogan**. Unlike these four, though, Fallon *did* receive a winner's medal.

Willie O'Neill, **Joe McBride** and **John Hughes** fared a little better – at least they did participate on the way to Lisbon. The versatile **O'Neill** filled in at left back for Tommy Gemmell in the first two rounds against Zurich and Nantes. Solid and reliable, O'Neill was excellent as Celtic won all four games with an aggregate of eleven goals for and only two against. But Jock Stein switched Gemmell from right back to the left side to accommodate Jim Craig and O'Neill's glory run was over.

Joe McBride could also count himself dreadfully unlucky. The burly striker was on fire in 1966 and was heading for a record amount of goals at home and abroad. He played two games – against Zurich at home and Nantes away – and scored in both. However, injury was to strike him down just before the turn of the year and he was sidelined for the remainder of the programme. The nearest he got to being involved again was a seat in the stand.

John Hughes, a battering ram of a forward who possessed a curiously neat touch for one of his bulk, went one better than O'Neill and turned out in five of the eight games en route to Lisbon. His disappointment at missing out on the final must have been overwhelming. He played in the opening two triumphs over FC Zurich and missed the next two against Nantes before getting the call-up for the double test against Vojvodina Novi Sad. Jock Stein knew Hughes was invaluable in heavy going where he could power through the adverse conditions. Both matches against the talented Slavs were played in March and Big Yogi, as he was affectionately known to team-mates and fans alike, was in.

He kept his position for the first semi-final match against Dukla Prague but dropped out for the second leg. Stein reckoned the pace of Bobby Lennox, in a defensive role, may be of more value against the Czechs. That formation did the business and Jock agonised over his team selection for Lisbon before saying, 'Same again.' No one, though, should overlook Hughes's immense contribution throughout the campaign. He may not have claimed any of the eighteen goals scored during that run but he certainly made a few. He took the weight off the defence with his surging forays through the middle and on the left – a handy man to have around.

Charlie Gallagher also participated in two games and looked the part in the home encounters against Nantes and Vojovodina. Jock Stein used to juggle Gallagher and Bertie Auld but, although Charlie was an extremely gifted player, he didn't possess that extra bit of menace that was evident in Bertie. Auld thrived on the big stage where Gallagher looked as though he was satisfied in performing in the wings. However, the role he played in the vital match against Vojvodina Novi Sad should never be forgotten.

Stein rated the Yugoslavs as the best team Celtic had encountered on their way to winning the European Cup and Gallagher put in a magnificent shift that night at Parkhead. And, of course, it was the Gorbals-born Celtic fan who set up the winner for Billy McNeill with an inch-perfect corner kick in the last minute.

With football being the strange game that it often is, that was Gallagher's last kick of the ball in the remaining campaign. At least, he could always say he went out on a high!

16

SEAN FALLON: A PROFILE

Celtic's players of the sixties realised the true value of Sean Fallon, the gruff Irishman who was more than just Jock Stein's right-hand man. He was also the manager's confidante and a professional who was quite content to stand in his immediate superior's giant shadow. Sean Fallon and the limelight would, indeed, have made unusual companions.

The players knew Celtic's assistant manager might have been undervalued and underrated by some but not by those who worked closely with him. He carried out the duties Jock Stein overlooked and, along with Neilly Mochan, he worked the lads hard in training. What many may not realise, if reports from the past are accurate, is that Fallon could have been the manager at Celtic – he was the man who had been groomed to succeed Jimmy McGrory when the time was right.

Sir Robert Kelly had been giving Fallon, two months older than Stein, increasing responsibility at the club as regards playing matters. There is the belief that Fallon was just waiting for the nod to take over. If that was the case, he must have been taken more than just slightly aback when Celtic unveiled Jock Stein as their new team boss on the last day of January 1965. An agreement with Hibs meant Stein had to remain with the Edinburgh club until they found a successor – a process that took five weeks. Kelly would then make one final move to reward Fallon for his resolute loyalty. He asked Stein to accept the Irishman as his joint manager. This request surprised Stein somewhat. He had always been his own man and he wasn't about to change that outlook at this crucial juncture. Word from within the Celtic boardroom reassured Jock that he would get the post on his own terms. A game of bluff was about to be played and Stein was willing to wait it out. Sir Robert Kelly was known to be stubborn and a man who very much liked to get his own way. Not on this occasion, though. Stein would not relent but he did, without hesitation, accept Fallon, a former Celtic team-mate, as his assistant.

Both Stein and Fallon knew exactly where they stood with one another and it was a union that worked splendidly well. If Fallon had been upset at not getting the top job, he handled his disappointment well. One thing most certainly emerged all those years ago – Sean Fallon was a man of great integrity and overwhelming professionalism. He always stood up to be counted and he was the perfect foil for Stein.

Big Jock concentrated completely and solely on football matters; Sean took care of everything else that had to be done. Fallon had always been a Celtic man and was credited with bringing some of the most promising youngsters, such as Kenny Dalglish and Davie Hay, through the Celtic ranks. He earned the nickname of 'The Iron Man' when he played against Falkirk at Brockville in severe pain after breaking an arm in the first half. In those days, there were no substitutes and Fallon refused to come off.

He signed from Glenavon and made his debut at the end of the 1949/50 season. It wasn't the most auspicious of starts as a Celt – he scored an own goal in the 2–2 draw with Clyde at Shawfield. Unfortunately, the broken limb at Brockville was not an isolated incident in his days as a player and, after another run of injuries, his career ended in 1958 when he couldn't overcome a knee problem. He was thirty-six at the time. Stein had been forced into retirement two years previously at the age of thirty-four with the ankle injury that would leave him with a limp for the rest of his life. Fallon's great claim to fame was scoring the winning goal in the Scottish Cup Final against Aberdeen in 1954. He also played a vital part in Celtic winning the league that year. His captain? Jock Stein.

As the years passed, Jock and Sean, who lived close to each other on the south side of Glasgow, would often be seen in the Beechwood Restaurant, just beside Hampden Park, with their wives – Jean was the name of Jock's wife and Myra was Sean's wife's name. A young footballer would also join their company on occasion and remember the friendly banter and the excellent advice. Sir Alex Ferguson was that young man. He listened and learned.

Both Stein and Fallon had seen a fair bit of action by the time they paced the touchline in Lisbon as they prepared for their most demanding and daunting task yet in their eventful careers. They didn't fail. No one was surprised. Jock and Sean had answered the call to arms once again.

17

THE BACKROOM TEAM

Neilly Mochan, one of the Lions' trainers, found himself pitchforked into Celtic folklore in 1953 – without kicking a ball at Celtic Park. Smiler, as Mochan was known, walloped in a glorious thirty-yard effort that screamed past the Hibs goalkeeper Tommy Younger for the club's first goal in the Coronation Cup Final in front of 117,000 fans at Hampden Park. Celtic went on to lift the trophy with a second-half goal from Jimmy Walsh. Mochan had signed for Celtic in May of that year from Middlesbrough and played his first game in the Charity Cup Final against Queen's Park.

In the space of a few weeks, then, Mochan had played in two cups finals for his new side as well as helping them to two victories on their way to the encounter with Hibs. He was included in the team to face English champions Arsenal and the Highbury men were firm favourites. Celtic won 1–0 with a goal direct from a corner kick by Bobby Collins. Manchester United were next up and, once more. Smiler was celebrating. Celtic won 2–1 and he scored alongside Bertie Peacock. Mochan had played four games for the club – all at Hampden.

Tommy Gemmell recalls: 'Neilly was a great character and he used to walk me all over the pitch at Celtic Park. He would point to a spot about thirty yards out and say: "This is where I scored a goal against Dundee." Then he would point out another area: "I netted against Aberdeen from here." I don't think there was a spot on that Celtic pitch where Neilly hadn't scored from! You couldn't take anything away from him, though. He trained us well. Just look at all the goals we scored late in a game. That was no fluke. He made sure we were in peak condition at all times.'

Bob Rooney was another trainer, who, like Mochan and physiotherapist Jimmy Steele, was great for team morale when the club were on their European trips. On one such sojourn early on, the players had complained to Jock Stein about the quality of the food they had been served at their hotel. On the next trip, Big Jock had made sure there were Scottish steaks and the like in the hamper. And Rooney and Steele were despatched to the kitchen to watch over the foreign chefs and make absolutely certain everything was prepared properly.

These were small instances but, together, they helped to ensure that the team was in the right frame of mind when it took to that pitch in Lisbon. No detail was overlooked. Everything had to be perfect to make sure it turned out all right on the night. And it did.

18

PEN PIX

Ronnie Simpson

Born: 11.10.1930, Glasgow
Died: 20.04.2004
Position: Goalkeeper

Signed for Celtic: 03.09.1964
Previous clubs: Queen's Park, Third Lanark, Newcastle United, Hibs
Debut: 18.11.1964 (against Barcelona)
Retired: 07.05.1970
Celtic appearances: 188
Shutouts: 91
Honours: 5 Scotland caps

Jim Craig

Born: 07.05.1943, Glasgow
Position: Right back

Signed: 07.01.1965
Previous clubs: Glasgow University
Debut: 07.10.1965 (against Go-Ahead Deventer, Holland)
Left Celtic: 06.05.1972 (Hellenic, South Africa)
Appearances: 231
Goals: 6
Honours: 1 Scotland cap

Tommy Gemmell

Born: 16.10.1943, Craigneuk
Position: Left back

Signed: 25.10.1961
Previous clubs: Coltness United
Debut: 05.01.1963 (against Aberdeen)
Left Celtic: 12.12.1971 (for Nottingham Forest)
Appearances: 418
Goals: 64
Honours: 18 Scotland caps, 5 Scottish League caps

Bobby Murdoch

Born: 17.08.1944, Bothwell
Died: 15.05.2001
Position: Right midfielder

Signed: 23.10.1959
Previous clubs: None
Debut: 11.08.1962 (against Hearts)
Left Celtic: 17.09.1973 (for Middlesbrough)
Appearances: 484
Goals: 105
Honours: 12 Scotland caps, 5 Scottish League caps, 1 Scotland Under-23 cap

Billy McNeill

Born: 02.03.1940, Bellshill
Position: Centre half

Signed: 20.08.1957
Previous clubs: Blantyre Vics
Debut: 23.08.1958 (against Clyde)
Retired: 03.05.1975
Appearances: 790
Goals: 34
Honours: 29 Scotland caps, 9 Scottish League caps,
5 Scotland Under-23 caps

John Clark

Born: 13.03.1941, Bellshill
Position: Left-sided defender

Signed: 08.10.1958
Previous clubs: Larkhall Thistle, Birmingham City, Larkhall Thistle
Debut: 03.10.1959 (against Arbroath)
Left Celtic: 12.06.1971 (for Morton)
Appearances: 318
Goals: 3
Honours: 4 Scotland caps, 2 Scottish League caps

Jimmy Johnstone

Born: 30.09.1944, Uddingston
Died: 13.03.2006
Position: Outside right

Signed: 08.11.1961
Previous clubs: Blantyre Vics
Debut: 27.03.1963 (against Kilmarnock)
Left Celtic: 09.06.1975 (for Hamilton Accies)
Appearances: 515
Goals: 129
Honours: 23 Scotland caps, 4 Scottish League caps

Willie Wallace

Born: 23.06.1940, Kirkintilloch
Position: Striker

Signed: 06.12.1966
Previous clubs: Kilsyth Rangers, Stenhousemuir, Raith Rovers, Hearts
Debut: 10.12.1966 (against Motherwell)
Left Celtic: 19.10.1971 (for Crystal Palace)
Appearances: 234
Goals: 135
Honours: 4 Scotland caps, 4 Scottish League caps

Stevie Chalmers

Born: 26.12.1936, Glasgow
Position: Striker

Signed: 06.02.1959

Previous clubs: Kirkintilloch Rob Roy, Newmarket Town, Ashfield

Debut: 10.03.1959 (against Airdrie)

Left Celtic: 09.09.1971 (for Morton)

Appearances: 405

Goals: 228

Honours: 5 Scotland caps, 4 Scottish League caps

Bertie Auld

Born: 03.03.1938, Bellshill
Position: Left-sided midfielder

Signed: 02.04.1955

Previous clubs: Panmure Thistle, Maryhill Harp, Birmingham City

Debut: 01.05.1957 (against Rangers)

Left Celtic (first time): 01.05.1961 (for Birmingham City)

Re-signed: 14.01.1965

Left Celtic (second time): 06.05.1971 (for Hibs)

Appearances: 279

Goals: 85

Honours: 3 Scotland caps, 2 Scottish League caps

Bobby Lennox

Born: 30.08.1943, Saltcoats, Ayrshire
Position: Striker/outside left

Signed: 05.09.1961
Previous clubs: Ardeer Recreation
Debut: 03.03.1962 (against Dundee)
Retired: 08.11.1980
Appearances: 571
Goals: 273
Honours: 10 Scotland caps, 3 Scottish League caps

Squad Members

John Fallon

Born: 16.08.1940, Blantyre
Position: Goalkeeper

Signed: 11.12.1958
Previous clubs: Fauldhouse United
Debut: 26.09.1959 (against Clyde)
Left Celtic: 29.02.1972 (for Motherwell)
Appearances: 184
Shutouts: 61
Honours: None

Ian Young

Born: 21.05.1943, Glasgow
Position: Right back

Signed: 28.06.1961
Previous clubs: Neilston Waverley
Debut: 05.05.1962 (against Third Lanark)
Left Celtic: 01.05.1968 (for St Mirren)
Appearances: 164
Goals: 3
Honours: None

David Cattanach

Born: 27.06.1946, Falkirk
Position: Left-sided defender

Signed: 19.08.1963
Previous clubs: Stirling Albion
Debut: 09.04.1966 (against St Mirren)
Left Celtic: 20.01.1972 (for Falkirk)
Appearances: 19
Goals: 1
Honours: None

Willie O'Neill

Born: 30.12.1940, Glasgow
Position: Left back

Signed: 12.10.1959
Previous clubs: St Anthony's
Debut: 26.04.1961 (against Dunfermline)
Left Celtic: 13.05.1969 (for Carlisle)
Appearances: 86
Goals: 0
Honours: None

Jim Brogan

Born: 05.06.1944, Glasgow
Position: Left-sided defender

Signed: 11.09.1962
Previous clubs: St Roch's
Debut: 21.09.1963 (against Falkirk)
Left Celtic: 04.06.1975 (for Coventry City)
Appearances: 339
Goals: 9
Honours: 4 Scotland caps, 1 Scottish League cap

John Cushley

Born: 21.01.1943, Hamilton
Position: Centre half

Signed: 07.07.1960
Previous clubs: Blantyre Celtic
Debut: 27.03.1963 (against Kilmarnock)
Left Celtic: 17.07.1967 (for West Ham)
Appearances: 41
Goals: 0
Honours: None

Charlie Gallagher

Born: 03.11.1940, Glasgow
Position: Midfielder

Signed: 20.09.1958
Previous clubs: Kilmarnock Amateurs, Yoker Athletic
Debut: 22.08.1959 (against Raith Rovers)
Left Celtic: 01.05.1970 (for Dumbarton)
Appearances: 171
Goals: 32
Honours: 2 Republic of Ireland caps

Joe McBride

Born: 10.06.1938, Glasgow
Position: Striker

Signed: 05.06.1965
Previous clubs: Kilmarnock Amateurs, Shettleston Town, Kirkintilloch Rob Roy, Kilmarnock, Wolves, Luton Town, Partick Thistle, Motherwell
Debut: 21.08.1965 (against Dundee)
Left Celtic: 05.11.1968 (for Hibs)
Appearances: 94
Goals: 86
Honours: 2 Scotland caps, 4 Scottish League caps

John Hughes

Born: 03.04.1943, Coatbridge
Position: Striker/outside left

Signed: 03.10.1959
Previous clubs: Shotts Bon Accord
Debut: 13.08.1960 (against Third Lanark)
Left Celtic: 19.10.1971 (for Crystal Palace)
Appearances: 416
Goals: 189
Honours: 8 Scotland caps, 6 Scottish League caps

19

WHAT HAPPENED NEXT

Ronnie Simpson

A shoulder injury forced the keeper to retire on 7 May 1970. He briefly managed Hamilton Accies between October 1971 and September 1972. Also owned a travel agency in Edinburgh. Trained young goalkeepers for a spell at Partick Thistle and Hamilton Accies. Died of a heart attack in 2004.

Jim Craig

The right back spent six months in South African football with Hellenic before returning to Britain with Sheffield Wednesday. He played at Hillsborough for eighteen months before retiring as a player in May 1974. He became the manager of Irish club Waterford for a brief spell later that year. A dentist by profession, he also works in the media.

Tommy Gemmell

Joined Nottingham Forest for £40,000 in December 1971. The flamboyant left back later played for Miami Toros and then Dundee. He then managed the Dens Park side, with fellow Lisbon Lion Willie Wallace as his assistant, and also had two stints as manager of Albion Rovers. Now a financial consultant in Glasgow.

Bobby Murdoch

The gifted midfielder was allowed to join Middlesbrough on a free transfer in September 1973 as a reward for his services to the club. He quit playing to become club coach at Ayresome Park and took over as manager between May 1981 and September 1982. Was an early influence on a young Graeme Souness at Boro. Later owned a pub in Rutherglen. Died in 2001 of heart failure.

Billy McNeill

The popular skipper became manager of Clyde in 1977. He then moved swiftly on to Aberdeen to replace Ally MacLeod, who had just been named as Scotland boss. He became manager of Celtic in the summer of 1978 before sampling English football with Manchester City and Aston Villa. He returned as boss again at Celtic Park in 1987 and guided the club to the centenary league and cup double the following year. Left in 1991. Owned a pub in Queen's Park, Glasgow, and is now a media pundit and national newspaper columnist.

John Clark

The dependable defender moved to Morton at the end of season 1970/71 before coming back to Celtic Park in a coaching capacity in 1973. Joined up again with Billy McNeill as his assistant at Aberdeen in 1977 before both returned as a managerial double-act at Celtic a year later. They remained in place for five years. He also had spells as boss of Cowdenbeath, Stranraer and Clyde and is now kitman at Celtic.

Jimmy Johnstone

Jinky's fourteen-year love affair with the club ended on 9 June 1975 when he was granted a free transfer. He joined Hamilton Accies briefly before moving to the States to play for San Jose Earthquakes. He later returned for spells at Sheffield United, Dundee (with Tommy Gemmell as his boss), Shelbourne, Elgin City and the junior club Blantyre Celtic, where he was player/coach for four months in 1980. Died after a brave battle against motor neurone disease on 13 March 2006.

Willie Wallace

Joined Crystal Palace in a double deal with John Hughes on 19 October 1971. The chunky frontman returned to play for Dumbarton before emigrating to Australia to sign for Apia. Came back to join Ross County before teaming up again with Tommy Gemmell at Dundee. Has since returned to Australia.

Stevie Chalmers

After almost eighteen years at the club, the Lisbon match winner left Celtic for Morton on 9 September 1971. He moved on to Partick Thistle and scored against Celtic in a 1–1 draw at Parkhead on 10 February 1973 while facing old Lisbon mates Bobby Murdoch, Celtic's scorer, Billy McNeill, Jimmy Johnstone and Bobby Lennox! Two years later he returned to Celtic in a backroom capacity and he is still a regular attender at Parkhead.

Bertie Auld

The midfielder joined Hibs on 6 May 1971, ending his second spell at the club. He became coach at the Easter Road side before managing Partick Thistle and then returning to Hibs as team boss. He also had spells as boss at Hamilton Accies, Partick Thistle, for a second time, and Dumbarton.

Bobby Lennox

The buzz-bomb frontman left Celtic in March 1978 for a six-month stay in the States with Houston Hurricanes. He was persuaded to return to Celtic by Billy McNeill and, after retiring from playing, joined the Parkhead coaching staff. He left the club in 1993. Like Chalmers, he is a keen golfer and is also a regular attender at games.

Squad Members

John Fallon

Moved to Motherwell on 29 February 1972 and then on to Morton after a spell at Fir Park. He finally joined Blantyre Celtic as a coach.

Ian Young

The safety-first right back joined St Mirren on 1 May 1968 – just under a year after the Lisbon triumph. He was at Love Street for two years before having a stint as coach of Saltcoats Vics.

David Cattanach

The utility defender quit to join Falkirk on 1 January 1972 and, two years later, retired early to concentrate on business. He ran a glazing firm along with Alex Smith, his former Stirling Albion boss who then went on to lead St Mirren and Aberdeen to Scottish Cup successes in the eighties. Cattanach now owns a restaurant bar in Falkirk.

Willie O'Neill

Played the opening four games of the glorious European Cup run before being ousted by Tommy Gemmell. He joined Carlisle United in 1969 before injury forced him to retire two years later. Has worked in the pub trade.

Jim Brogan

The adaptable defender – who also played rugby later in life – left Celtic after thirteen years to join Coventry City on 4 June 1975. He returned to have a spell with Ayr United before retiring on 1 November 1977 to concentrate on off-field matters. Has had interests in the car and pub businesses.

John Cushley

Billy McNeill's stand-by joined West Ham United two months after the European Cup victory. He also had stints at Dunfermline and Dumbarton. He rejoined Celtic in 1978 before moving to Dumbarton and Clyde as a coach. Has also worked in the media.

Charlie Gallagher

The cultured playmaker left Celtic for Dumbarton on 1 May 1970 on a free transfer. He had three seasons at Boghead before retiring from the game in 1973.

Joe McBride

The much-travelled goalscorer moved to Hibs on 11 November 1968 and proved he was far from finished, netting two goals in the Edinburgh club's 2–0 league success over Celtic at Easter Road on 19 September 1970. He went on to play for Dunfermline and Clyde before retiring in 1972.

John Hughes

Yogi was an instant hit when he joined Crystal Palace on 19 October 1971. Shortly after signing, he scored a remarkable solo goal against Sheffield United that was replayed time after time by *Match of the Day*. He had a spell at Sunderland alongside his brother Billy before spending four years as coach of the Scotland junior side. Now in the pub trade.

20

THE ROAD TO THE FINAL

First Round – first leg
28 September 1966, Celtic Park

Celtic 2, Zurich 0

On the evening of 28 September 1966, in the east end of Glasgow, Tommy Gemmell wasn't to know it but he was just about to have a major say in Celtic conquering Europe.

The raiding defender's reputation of being the possessor of a pulverising long-range shot obviously hadn't worked its way through to Switzerland. If it had, Celtic would, most assuredly, have struggled to make the breakthrough against an extremely competent Zurich outfit. It was still goalless after the hour mark and the fans were beginning to get more than just a little bit anxious. The Swiss defence was doing its job well and the main threat of Joe McBride was being blunted.

This was Celtic's first-ever European Cup game and they wanted to mark it with something special. Gemmell was the man to provide that ingredient. As the clock ticked round to the sixty-fourth minute, John Clark thwarted a Swiss breakaway and passed a neat ball out to Gemmell, who was playing at right back that evening with Willie O'Neill on the left. Gemmell, a few yards inside enemy territory, nodded the ball forward and must have been surprised that there wasn't a posse of defenders immediately swarming around him as he prepared to surge further forward. Zurich backed off and Gemmell didn't need to be asked twice about having a pop at goal.

Celtic fans, knowing what was about to happen, held their collective breath in anticipation. Tommy took a swift look up, got his eye-to-ball co-ordination absolutely right, summoned all the power in his frame and swung his mighty right boot at the spherical object.

The ball was a mere blur as it took off from about twenty-five yards. Goalkeeper Steffen Iten, who had looked safe and sound all evening, hardly moved a muscle as the missile zeroed in on its target before smashing into the rigging at his top left-hand corner. It was hit with such frightening pace that the Zurich No. 1 probably did himself a favour by not going anywhere near it.

Gemmell punched the air in delight, relieved team-mates bounded in his direction, Jock Stein, four days before his forty-fourth birthday, bounced out of the dugout and Parkhead was engulfed in delirium. Understandably, the Zurich heads went down.

They had played a cool and controlled game and always looked dangerous on the break. Now they were a goal adrift with almost half an hour still to play in an intimidating atmosphere.

Five minutes later, it got even worse for the visitors as suddenly Celtic's advantage had doubled. Clark, with the minimum of fuss, broke up a Swiss raid and passed the ball out to Gemmell who switched it inside to McBride.

The striker darted for the danger zone and played a wonderful one-two with Bertie Auld, whose cheeky back-heel completely wrong-footed the rearguard. McBride was another who would always have a go when he saw the whites of the goalposts and he did so again from the edge of the box.

It took the merest of touches off a desperate defender as it swept beyond the sprawling Iten but there is every chance it would have found the back of the net in any case.

The game ended in a controversial note, though, when it looked as though McBride had claimed a third goal. Certainly there was nothing wrong in the manner in which he scored and there was no question of him being offside. The referee blew for time-up and thousands of puzzled supporters emptied out of Celtic Park wondering if their favourites had won 2–0 or 3–0.

It transpired the fussy match official had blown his whistle just as the ball was crossing the line. So, Celtic had to settle for a two-goal lead to take to Zurich. In the end, it didn't matter.

Team: Simpson; Gemmell and O'Neill; Murdoch, McNeill and Clark; Johnstone, McBride, Chalmers, Auld and Hughes.

First Round – second leg
5 October 1966, Hardturm

Zurich 0, Celtic 3
(agg. 0–5)

Celtic confounded the European experts by attacking the Swiss on their own ground. They were expected to erect a fortress in front of Ronnie Simpson in an effort to hold on to their 2–0 first leg advantage. Someone forgot to tell Jock Stein!

Gemmell, torturer-in-chief in Glasgow, walloped in the opener in his usual booming style and it was all over when Bobby Lennox flicked on a right-wing corner for Stevie Chalmers to fire under the keeper's body.

Just to add to the flavour of the evening, Gemmell claimed his third goal over the two ties when he crashed in a penalty kick. Keeper Iten had learned from the first leg – he went the wrong way!

Team: Simpson; Gemmell and O'Neill; Murdoch, McNeill and Clark; Johnstone, Lennox, Chalmers, Auld and Hughes.

Second Round – first leg
30 November 1966, Malakoff Stadium

Nantes 1, Celtic 3

The French had made some persuasive boasts – to their fans, anyway – about what they would do with Celtic in the encounter at the Malakoff Stadium on St Andrew's Day. They had every intention of making certain the Scots would not be celebrating that night. They were wrong.

However, they did give Celtic a fright when they took the lead inside twenty minutes through the outstanding Magny. Jock Stein had always preached to his side to keep it tight within this period, especially away from home. Magny, though, pierced their barrier to turn the ball wide of Ronnie Simpson and suddenly Celtic were confronted with a mountain to climb. Their response was instant.

Joe McBride, so lethal and so full of energy, provided the leveller in the twenty-fourth minute when he latched on to a pass from Bobby Lennox and sent a piledriver flying past Castel.

Nantes, far and away the best French team for years, weren't quite in the mood, though, to down tools. They came back in fine style and Simpson had to make two superb saves before the interval to make sure it remained all square.

Jimmy Johnstone had already won over the French with his right-wing antics and left back De Michele was to be commended for not trying to boot the little winger out of the park. He stuck to his task but everyone knew he would be the happiest man on the pitch when the referee got round to blowing the full-time whistle, irrespective of the scoreline.

Stein had ordered Johnstone to take the ball for runs down the wing to stretch the French defence throughout the first half. With their superior stamina and fitness, Celtic were told to kill off their dangerous opponents in the second half. They followed their gaffer's orders.

Bobby Murdoch found some space to hit a telling through ball into the path of Bobby Lennox, whose speed carried him away from two startled defenders. The danger signals flashed for the French, but it was too late as Lennox took aim and let fly. Once more Castel was picking the ball from the back of his net.

Nantes must have known it was all over late in the match when Budzinski, otherwise an impressive performer, dallied on the ball and it was worked on to Stevie Chalmers who whacked it into the inviting net. Job done!

Team: Simpson; Gemmell and O'Neill; Murdoch, McNeill and Clark; Johnstone, Chalmers, McBride, Lennox and Auld.

Second Round – second leg
7 December 1966, Celtic Park

Celtic 3, Nantes 1
(agg. 6–2)

Jock Stein went on record before this game promising the Celtic fans that his team would attack. He said, 'We may be 3–1 ahead from the away leg but we are committed to attacking, entertaining football and we will show that again on this occasion.'

He and his team were as good as their word. Top scorer Joe McBride sat this one out through injury and Stein shuffled the pack with Charlie Gallagher coming in to bolster the midfield. Was he being cagey, after all?

Jimmy Johnstone provided the answer as he cantered into the penalty area and put Celtic 4–1 ahead on aggregate in the thirteenth minute. Georgin equalised with a fine effort that left Ronnie Simpson helpless. Astonishingly, the same player almost snatched another a few minutes later. His effort looked like looping over the head of Simpson but the veteran keeper scrambled back to grab the ball just as it was about to cross the line. Celtic players and fans alike breathed a sigh of relief. It remained 1–1 at the interval.

But Jinky was having one of his special evenings and he skipped through the French rearguard on the right touchline to pick out Stevie Chalmers with a perfect pass and he nodded in from close range.

It was all over a few minutes later when Johnstone treated the French to some déjà vu with an identical run down the touchline and a fine low pass across the box that was swept in by Bobby Lennox. Now for the quarter-final!

Team: Simpson; Gemmell and O'Neill; Murdoch, McNeill and Clark; Johnstone, Gallagher, Chalmers, Auld and Lennox.

Quarter-final – first leg
1 March 1967, Stadium of Vojvodina

Vojvodina Novi Sad 1, Celtic 0

Tommy Gemmell, so often the hero, was the culprit of the night as the Yugoslavs snatched a one-goal advantage to take to Glasgow for the return match. Everything was going according to plan as Celtic tried to snuff out the Slavs in midfield on a flint-hard surface that always threatened to conjure up the odd mistake or two.

Unfortunately, Gemmell became the villain of the piece twenty minutes from the end with a wayward pass. It fell between Bobby Murdoch and John Clark and that was all the darting Djordic needed to speed on to the ball. He squared it across to winger Stanic who drilled an unstoppable effort low past the out-rushing Ronnie Simpson.

The legendary Vujadin Boskov, later to manage some of the biggest teams in Europe, had ordered his team to give him a two-goal advantage and they poured down on Simpson as they tried to comply with his wishes.

Vojvodina had been tipped by many as the dark horses in that season's European Cup. They had beaten the highly rated Spanish outfit Atletico Madrid in a replay to reach this stage and that proved their pedigree. Their movement, strength and tactical knowledge displayed against Jock Stein's men merely underlined their many attributes. However, it is to Celtic's eternal credit that they refused to panic or fold in front of such impressive opposition.

However, the Slavs had to be content with Stanic's solitary effort as Celtic shut up shop with Simpson, Billy McNeill and John Clark bolting the back door.

Team: Simpson; Craig and Gemmell; Murdoch, McNeill and Clark; Johnstone, Lennox, Chalmers, Auld and Hughes.

Quarter-final – second leg
8 March 1967, Celtic Park

Celtic 2, Vojvodina Novi Sad 0
(agg. 2–1)

There have been many dramatic encounters at Parkhead over the years but surely none as tense and fraught as this nail-biting confrontation. Picture the scene with the game locked at 1–1 on aggregate and the clock fast running down towards full-time. Celtic forced a corner kick out on the right and Charlie Gallagher raced over to take it. Up went skipper Billy McNeill, scorer of so many precious goals, as the Slavs protected their penalty area. Behind them was the exceptional Ilija Pantelic, a goalkeeper rated by many as one of the best in the world.

It was a bitterly cold, frosty evening in the east end of Glasgow but no one was complaining. A crescendo of noise came up from the expectant crowd as Gallagher quickly appraised the situation and bodies jostled for position. It was all very frantic. Gallagher, in the team at the expense of Bertie Auld, swung the ball into the middle of the goal. Pantelic made his move off his line. McNeill, surging past defenders, timed his run. The ball seemed to hang in the air for an eternity before it finally found its destination – McNeill's head.

There was a dull thud, Pantelic looked back in horror, a defender tried to perform heroic acrobatics on the line but it was to no avail. Big Billy's header arrowed straight into the net and Celtic were in the semi-finals of the European Cup. Bhoys' Own stuff, no doubt about it.

Vojvodina wearily trooped forward to restart the game and the referee blew for time-up exactly *two seconds* later. Talk about leaving it late!

Celtic had levelled the tie just before the hour mark when Tommy Gemmell made amends for his first-leg loss of concentration that may have cost Celtic so dear. He used John Hughes as decoy as he bombed down the left wing and pitched over an inviting ball into the centre. Pantelic sprang from his line but the courageous Stevie Chalmers was even faster off the mark and he got there just ahead of the keeper to knock the ball into the gaping net.

And that set up the grand finale that still leaves the fans who witnessed it breathless if not as little awestruck. A marvellous and enduring moment in the history of Celtic Football Club.

Team: Simpson; Craig and Gemmell; Murdoch, McNeill and Clark; Johnstone, Lennox, Chalmers, Gallagher and Hughes.

Semi-final – first leg
12 April 1967, Celtic Park

Celtic 3, Dukla Prague 1

This was the night Celtic really began to believe they could become only the fifth team in history to win the European Cup.

It had seemed a dream too far – an achievement out of reach. Could they really emulate Real Madrid (6), Benfica (2), Inter Milan (2) and AC Milan (1) and conquer the playing fields of Europe? Was there the mere possibility that Jock Stein's men could become Europe's masters?

The evening of 12 April in a frostbitten east end of Glasgow was to prove eventful as Celtic nudged ever closer to their destiny. They were up against an experienced and highly rated Czechoslovakian side that had some world performers in their line-up – not least their captain and playmaker Josef Masopust.

Something – or someone – triggered Celtic that night. Willie Wallace had to sit out the previous round because he had not been signed in time to face Vojvodina. He was in the mood to make up for lost time and didn't it show as he put in a shift that wore down the rugged Czech rearguard?

He scored two, could have had two more and was a menace throughout the ninety minutes. The twin giants in the heart of the Czech defence were run ragged by Wallace, bought the previous December from Hearts for a snip at £30,000.

The game started with a fair bit of controversy when Stevie Chalmers had a goal disallowed. Tommy Gemmell flighted an inviting ball downfield, Wallace got a touch to Chalmers, he slipped it to Jimmy Johnstone, coming in from the right, and the little winger chipped it back for Chalmers to nod in at the near post. The referee ruled Johnstone's foot was high and cancelled the effort.

Johnstone got revenge in the twenty-eighth minute when he got one that did stand. It was a goal that started with a Ronnie Simpson kick-out and ended in the back of the Dukla net. The keeper launched one down the middle, Chalmers got a flick and it fell for Bertie Auld who teed it up for Wallace. His shot deflected off a defender into the path of Johnstone and he gleefully lifted it over the head of the out-rushing Dukla goalkeeper, Viktor.

But that was wiped out right on the stroke of half-time when the Celtic central defence got into a real muddle on their own eighteen-yard line. Strunc, a beanpole striker who always looked menacing, pounced and stroked the ball away from Simpson. Parkhead fell silent. A nervous half-time period ensued until Billy McNeill led out his troops for the second half.

Just before the hour mark, Gemmell thumped the ball forward and Wallace was running free of the Czech defence to get a wonderful touch off the outside of his right boot and send the ball soaring into the net for the second goal.

In the sixty-fifth minute, a desperate Dukla player clawed away a cross from Bobby Murdoch with his hand. Free kick! Up popped Bertie Auld. He dithered a bit to unsettle the defensive wall and then touched it sideways to Wallace who rattled a screamer into the net.

Dukla were there for the taking and Celtic went for more. Chalmers slashed one past the post, Wallace hit one just wide and Murdoch sent a left-foot sizzler just over the crossbar. Wallace even knocked one against the face of the bar from a Chalmers cross and Celtic had to be content with a 3–1 first-leg win.

Jock Stein had asked for a two-goal advantage. His team responded.

Team: Simpson; Craig and Gemmell; Murdoch, McNeill and Clark; Johnstone, Wallace, Chalmers, Auld and Hughes.

Semi-final – second leg
25 April 1967, Juliska Stadium

Dukla Prague 0, Celtic 0
(agg. 1–3)

Stevie Chalmers was the Celtic hero as they cemented their place in the European Cup Final. He was asked to play a lone role up front and the striker didn't shirk the challenge. His lung-bursting performance that afternoon at the Juliska Stadium is the stuff of which heroes are made. It was unlike Jock Stein, and he vowed never to repeat his tactics, but he put out a defensive formation to frustrate the Czechs. It worked but it could have backfired if Ronnie Simpson hadn't been alert in the early minutes of the match.

Strunc had a shot blocked and it dropped in front of Nedorost about ten yards from goal. His vicious volley flew goalwards and he had to step back in horror as Simpson took off to his left to touch the ball over the bar. It was the closest Dukla came to a goal that day.

Celtic, with Billy McNeill in commanding form, soaked up everything the Czechs could throw at them while Chalmers raced around chasing everything that dropped in Dukla's half.

McNeill recalled, 'What a game Steve had in Prague. We felt a bit sorry for him! At one stage, he got into a bit of bother and suddenly he was surrounded by about four of their players. We were too far away to lend him some support. Thankfully, the referee sorted it out.'

Next stop Lisbon!

Team: Simpson; Craig and Gemmell; Murdoch, McNeill and Clark; Johnstone, Wallace, Chalmers, Auld and Lennox.

21

ATTENDANCES, APPEARANCES AND GOALSCORERS

Attendances

Celtic were watched by a total of 354,361 spectators in their nine European Cup games. The highest attendance was the 74,406 who turned out to witness the 3–1 semi-final triumph over Dukla Prague at Celtic Park. The lowest was the 15,464 who attended their 3–1 victory over Nantes in France in the first leg of the second round. The Estadio Nacionale in Lisbon was a sell-out at 45,000.

Here is the breakdown:
Zurich: home – 47,604; away – 20,236
Nantes: away – 15,464; home – 39,120
Vojvodina Novi Sad: away – 24,000; home – 69,374
Dukla Prague: home – 74,406; away – 19,157
Inter Milan: neutral – 45,000

Appearances

Ronnie Simpson: 9 – Zurich 2, Nantes 2, Vojvodina 2, Dukla Prague 2, Inter Milan
Tommy Gemmell: 9 – Zurich 2, Nantes 2, Vojvodina 2, Dukla Prague 2, Inter Milan
Willie O'Neill: 4 – Zurich 2, Nantes 2
Jim Craig: 5 – Vojvodina 2, Dukla Prague 2, Inter Milan

Bobby Murdoch: 9 – Zurich 2, Nantes 2, Vojvodina 2, Dukla Prague 2, Inter Milan

Billy McNeill: 9 – Zurich 2, Nantes 2, Vojvodina 2, Dukla Prague 2, Inter Milan

John Clark: 9 – Zurich 2, Nantes 2, Vojvodina 2, Dukla Prague 2, Inter Milan

Jimmy Johnstone: 9 – Zurich 2, Nantes 2, Vojvodina 2, Dukla Prague 2, Inter Milan

Bobby Lennox: 7 – Zurich 1 (away), Nantes 2, Vojvodina 2, Dukla Prague 1 (away), Inter Milan

Willie Wallace: 3 – Dukla Prague 2, Inter Milan

Joe McBride: 2 – Zurich 1 (home), Nantes 1 (away)

Stevie Chalmers: 9 – Zurich 2, Nantes 2, Vojvodina 2, Dukla Prague 2, Inter Milan

Charlie Gallagher: 2 – Nantes 1 (home), Vojvodina 1 (home)

Bertie Auld: 8 – Zurich 2, Nantes 2, Vojvodina 1 (away), Dukla Prague 2, Inter Milan

John Hughes: 5 – Zurich 2, Vojvodina 2, Dukla Prague 1 (home)

Squad members not used: John Fallon, David Cattanach, Ian Young, John Cushley and Jim Brogan

Goalscorers

Stevie Chalmers – 5
Tommy Gemmell – 4
Willie Wallace – 2
Bobby Lennox – 2
Joe McBride – 2
Jimmy Johnstone – 2
Billy McNeill – 1

Goals for – 18
Goals against – 5

22

THE MEN AND THEIR MEDALS

Ronnie Simpson

League Championship: 4 (1966, 1967, 1968, 1969)
Scottish Cup: 1 (1967)
League Cup: 3 (1965, 1966, 1967)
European Cup: 1 (1967)
(**FA Cup with Newcastle United:** 2 (1952, 1955))

Jim Craig

League Championship: 7 (1966, 1967, 1968, 1969, 1970, 1971, 1972)
Scottish Cup: 4 (1967, 1969, 1971, 1972)
League Cup: 3 (1967, 1968, 1969)
European Cup: 1 (1967)

Tommy Gemmell

League Championship: 6 (1966, 1967, 1968, 1969, 1970, 1971)
Scottish Cup: 3 (1965, 1967, 1969)
League Cup: 4 (1965, 1966, 1967, 1968)
(**League Cup with Dundee:** 1 (1973))
European Cup: 1 (1967)

Bobby Murdoch

League Championship: 8 (1966, 1967, 1968, 1969, 1970, 1971, 1972, 1973)
Scottish Cup: 4 (1965, 1967, 1969, 1972)
League Cup: 5: (1965, 1966, 1967, 1968, 1969)
European Cup: 1 (1967)

Billy McNeill

League Championship: 9 (1966, 1967, 1968, 1969, 1970, 1971, 1972, 1973, 1974)
Scottish Cup: 7 (1965, 1967, 1969, 1971, 1972, 1974, 1975)
League Cup: 6 (1965, 1966, 1967, 1968, 1969, 1974)
European Cup: 1 (1967)

As a manager

League Championship: 4 (1979, 1980, 1982, 1988)
Scottish Cup: 3 (1980, 1988, 1989)
League Cup: 1 (1982)

John Clark

League Championship: 3 (1966, 1967, 1968)
Scottish Cup: 3 (1965, 1967, 1969)
League Cup: 4 (1965, 1966, 1967, 1968)
European Cup: 1 (1967)

Jimmy Johnstone

League Championship: 9 (1966, 1967, 1968, 1969, 1970, 1971, 1972, 1973, 1974)
Scottish Cup: 4 (1967, 1971, 1972, 1974)
League Cup: 5 (1965, 1966, 1968, 1969, 1974)
European Cup: 1 (1967)

Willie Wallace

League Championship: 5 (1967, 1968, 1969, 1970, 1971)
Scottish Cup: 3 (1967, 1969, 1971)
League Cup: 2 (1967, 1968)
(League Cup with Hearts: 1 (1962))
European Cup: 1 (1967)

Stevie Chalmers

League Championship: 4 (1966, 1967, 1968, 1969)
Scottish Cup: 3 (1965, 1967, 1969)
League Cup: 4 (1966, 1967, 1968, 1969)
European Cup: 1 (1967)

Bertie Auld

League Championship: 5 (1966, 1967, 1968, 1969, 1970)
Scottish Cup: 3 (1965, 1967, 1969)
League Cup: 4 (1966, 1967, 1968, 1969)
European Cup: 1 (1967)

Bobby Lennox

League Championship: 10 (1966, 1967, 1968, 1969, 1970, 1971, 1972, 1973, 1974, 1979)
Scottish Cup: 8 (1965, 1967, 1969, 1971, 1972, 1974, 1975, 1980)
League Cup: 4 (1965, 1966, 1967, 1968)
European Cup: 1 (1967)

23

NICKNAMES

Celtic liked to play the name game back in 1967 and everyone – with the odd exception of Stevie Chalmers – had a peculiar nickname.

Faither
Ronnie Simpson – the oldest man in the team at thirty-six.

Cairney
Jim Craig – after a television series *This Man Craig* in which Scottish actor John Cairney took the lead role.

Big Tam
Tommy Gemmell – obvious, really.

Chopper
Bobby Murdoch – an exceptionally gifted midfielder who sometimes doubled up as Jimmy Johnstone's on-field minder.

Caesar
Billy McNeill – he started off being called Cesar after the American movie star Cesar Romero who, apparently, was the guy designated to drive the Rat Pack around Hollywood in their heyday. The Rat Pack, of course, consisted of the likes of Frank Sinatra, Dean Martin, Sammy Davis Junior and Peter Lawford. As Billy was the only one who possessed a car in this particular footballing Rat Pack, he got the job of chauffeuring the likes of Pat Crerand and Jim Baxter around the haunts of Glasgow. Later it would be said that Caesar was in deference to his poise and character.

Luggy
John Clark – he picked this one up and no one was too sure why or who started it. The fans also sometimes called him The Brush for the sterling work he did in defence, cleaning up after everyone.

Jinky
Jimmy Johnstone, of course – all was explained as soon as you saw him in action.

Wispy
Willie Wallace – his soft, whispering type of voice was what the players latched on to for this one.

Stevie
Stevie Chalmers – he didn't lend himself to an odd moniker but the newspapers had a field day in November 1968 when he scored a hat-trick in a 5–0 win over Arbroath. Di Steveano was the contrived headline as Celtic were reported to be interested in bringing the great Alfredo Di Stefano out of retirement at the time. It never happened and eventually Chalmers became plain Stevie again!

Ten-Thirty
Bertie Auld answered to this one. Bertie? Thirty? Get it?

Lemon
Bobby Lennox – he picked this one up early in his career. Once again, a lot of thought went into it!

The rest of the squad also picked up nicknames with possibly the cruellest of them all being the one that substitute goalkeeper John Fallon found himself lumbered with – **Peter**. Seems innocuous enough until you discover it was taken from the TV character Peter Brady, who played *The Invisible Man*! Apparently, John's team-mates weren't too enamoured on one occasion when he wasn't where he should be while defending his goal.

John Hughes answered to **Yogi** after the cartoon character Yogi Bear – just take a look at the juggernaut Hughes in action and all will be explained.

Bridie was Charlie Gallagher, **José** was Joe McBride and **Pumper** was Willie O'Neill. Pumper? We are reliably informed it was because he took up pole position in the team bath and so was able to pump in the hot water exactly where he was situated.

24

FACTS

✤ It cost exactly £42,000 to assemble the Lisbon Lions. The only two players who cost transfer fees were Willie Wallace (£30,000 from Hearts) and Bertie Auld (bought pre-Stein for £12,000 from Birmingham City).

✤ Celtic had a remarkable 42 goal attempts against Inter Milan with 26 on target. There were 19 efforts inside the penalty area with 23 outside the box.

✤ Celtic forced 10 corner kicks against Inter Milan who didn't have a single one. Jock Stein's side were caught offside seven times as against the Italians' two. Both sides committed 20 fouls each.

✤ The Celtic coach travelling from Estoril to Lisbon for the final was delayed because of traffic congestion. It eventually got to the Estadio Nacionale just 45 minutes before kick-off.

✤ Billy McNeill made 69 European appearances for the club between 1962/63 and 1974/75.

✤ Jimmy Johnstone scored 16 goals in 64 European games between 1963/64 and 1974/75.

✤ Willie Wallace claimed 13 goals in only 26 European appearances between 1966/67 and 1971/72.

FACTS

❧ Bobby Lennox became the last of the Lions remaining at the club after Billy McNeill, at 35, announced his retirement following the 3–1 Scottish Cup Final win over Airdrie in 1975.

❧ It is a popular misconception that Rangers were the first team to beat the Lisbon Lions. The Ibrox side did, indeed, win 1–0 on their own ground in a league game on 18 September 1967 with a goal from Orjan Persson. However, David Cattanach was in the Celtic line-up that afternoon in place of Jim Craig.

❧ Kiev Dynamo were the first side to overcome the Lions when they won 2–1 in Celtic's first defence of the European Cup at Parkhead. Celtic had Bobby Murdoch sent off as they drew 1–1 in Russia but still went out on a 3–2 aggregate. Bobby Lennox scored both goals. John Hughes replaced Stevie Chalmers for the second leg.

❧ An end of an era was witnessed at Celtic Park on 1 May 1971 when the Lions appeared together for the last time. Ronnie Simpson, who had already announced his retirement, was in the line-up as Billy McNeill led the team out but Faither was replaced before the start by Evan Williams. Celtic beat Clyde 6–1 with three goals from Bobby Lennox, two from Willie Wallace and one from Stevie Chalmers.

❧ Bertie Auld, praised by many as Celtic's architect-in-chief of their win over Inter Milan, left the club on a free transfer for Hibs on 6 May 1971. Shortly afterwards Stevie Chalmers and John Clark left for Morton and, within a year, Tommy Gemmell had joined Nottingham Forest, Willie Wallace and John Hughes moved to Crystal Palace and Jim Craig signed for South African side Hellenic.

THE LISBON LIONS

✿ Jock Stein bought Willie Wallace from Hearts and he became a direct replacement for the unlucky Joe McBride who was ruled out for the remainder of the campaign after injuring a knee against Aberdeen at Pittodrie on Christmas Eve, 1966. Wallace and McBride would only play three games alongside each other. The prolific McBride still finished the season as Scottish football's top scorer with 35 goals in all competitions.

✿ Tommy Gemmell and John Clark were Celtic's only ever-presents in the triumphant 1966/67 season. They played in all 62 games. Captain Billy McNeill turned out 61 times.

✿ A total of 21 players were used during the season. In all five competitions won by the club, they scored 196 goals in 62 games. They won 51 and drew 8. They lost three times – to Vojvodina in the first leg of their European Cup quarter-final in Yugoslavia and twice to Dundee United, 3–2 home and away. They conceded 48 goals in total.

✿ Celtic claimed 111 goals as they retained their title. The goalscorers were: Stevie Chalmers (23), Joe McBride (18), Willie Wallace (14), Bobby Lennox (13), Jimmy Johnstone (13), Tommy Gemmell (9), Bertie Auld (7), John Hughes (6), Bobby Murdoch (4), Charlie Gallagher (2). There were two own goals from George Miller (Hearts) and Bobby Wilson (Dundee).

✿ Celtic claimed the Scottish Cup with a 2–0 win over Aberdeen at Hampden on 29 April 1967 where Willie Wallace hit both goals. They played six games in all, including a semi-final replay against Clyde. They scored 20 goals and conceded 3. The Celtic team in the final was: Simpson; Craig and Gemmell; Murdoch, McNeill and Clark; Johnstone, Wallace, Chalmers, Auld and Lennox. Attendance: 127,117.

FACTS

♣ A goal from Bobby Lennox gave Celtic a 1–0 triumph in the League Cup Final over Rangers at Hampden on 29 October 1966. The club played ten games in all in the competition, winning them all and scoring 35 goals in the process. They conceded seven. The Celtic team in the final was: Simpson; Gemmell and O'Neill; Murdoch, McNeill and Clark; Johnstone, Lennox, McBride, Auld and Hughes. Stevie Chalmers replaced Hughes in the second half. Attendance: 94,532.

♣ Celtic won the Glasgow Cup with a 4–0 victory over Partick Thistle on 7 November. Bobby Lennox (3) and Stevie Chalmers were the goalscorers. George Niven was in goal for the Firhill side – he had been the Rangers keeper beaten seven times when Celtic won the League Cup in 1957/58. The Celtic team in the final was: Simpson; Gemmell and O'Neill; Murdoch, McNeill and Clark; Chalmers, Gallagher, McBride, Lennox and Auld. Attendance: 31,000.

♣ Bobby Lennox started the Glasgow Cup competition with a hat-trick in the 4–0 victory over Rangers at Ibrox where Billy McNeill opened the scoring. Celtic also beat Queen's Park 4–0 in the second round at Parkhead with goals from Joe McBride (2), Bobby Lennox and Charlie Gallagher.

♣ Three goalkeepers turned out for Celtic throughout the season – Ronnie Simpson (60 appearances), John Fallon (1) and Bent Martin (1).

♣ Stevie Chalmers netted Celtic's first league goal of the season when they beat Clyde 3–0 at Shawfield on Saturday, 10 September 1966. He also got the club's last competitive goal of the season with the winner against Inter Milan.

✤ Bobby Lennox brought the curtain down on a marvellous season when he netted the winner in the 1–0 triumph over Real Madrid at the Bernabeu Stadium in Alfredo Di Stefano's testimonial match on 7 June.

25

THE GREATEST-EVER CELTIC TEAM

Seven of the Lisbon Lions were voted into The Greatest-Ever Celtic Team by the supporters in an official millennium poll. The magnificent seven were Ronnie Simpson, Billy McNeill, Tommy Gemmell, Bobby Murdoch, Jimmy Johnstone, Bertie Auld and Bobby Lennox. The four non-Lions who also won a place in the historic line-up were Danny McGrain, Paul McStay, Henrik Larsson and Kenny Dalglish. The team (in a typically attacking 3–3–4 formation) read: Simpson; McGrain, McNeill and Gemmell; Murdoch, McStay and Auld; Johnstone, Larsson, Dalglish and Lennox.

26

1967 – IN THIS YEAR . . .

A ticket for a stand seat at the Celtic v. Inter Milan game was £2.38 (or, as it was then, £2 7s 6d) with a place on the terracing costing 50p (10 shillings).

A pint of beer was 10p (2 shillings).

The average semi-detached villa in Scotland cost £4,012.

A new Austin Morris was £700.

A two-piece suit from Burton's would have set you back £16.50 (£16 10s).

And a daily national newspaper was 4d (under 2p).

The first-ever Super Bowl took place in Los Angeles with Green Bay Packers beating Kansas City Chiefs 35–10.

The Beatles released the *Sgt Pepper's Lonely Hearts Club Band* LP.

One of the top-selling singles was 'If You're Going to San Francisco (be sure to wear some flowers in your hair) by Scott McKenzie. He sounds Scottish but was born Philip Blondheim in Jacksonville Beach, Florida, on 10 January 1939.

Two other big singles were 'A Whiter Shade of Pale' by Procol Harum and 'I'm a Believer' by The Monkees.

Top movies were the James Bond film *You Only Live Twice* and *The Dirty Dozen*.

One of the most-watched TV programmes was the Western *Bonanza*.

Jock Stein's first signing for Celtic after Lisbon was Pat Mc-Mahon. Chelsea had also wanted the inside forward came from the junior club Kilsyth Rangers. He later moved to Aston Villa.

Alex Ferguson handed in a transfer request at Dunfermline and was signed by Rangers.

The bookies' odds for the European Cup Final were 13/8 Celtic, 11/8 Inter Milan and 5/2 for a draw. One Glasgow bookie admitted, 'Money is pouring in on Celtic to win.'

Jock Stein advertised the Skelly Ford garage with the slogan: 'I can trust them.'

Anderston councillor John Dunne defied a Glasgow Corporation ban on going to Lisbon to support Celtic. He claimed the reason for his visit to Portugal was to go on a religious pilgrimage to Fatima – just outside Lisbon!

Scotland beat world champions England 3–2 at Wembley with Ronnie Simpson making his international debut at thirty-six.

Manchester United won the English First Division title.

Bayern Munich won the European Cup-Winners' Cup, beating Rangers 1–0 with a Franz Roth goal in extra time. A crowd of 69,480 watched the action in Nuremberg.

Yugoslavia's Dinamo Zagreb won the Inter-Cities Fairs Cup (now the UEFA Cup) with a 2–0 aggregate victory over the two legs against Leeds United.

West Ham signed Kilmarnock's Bobby Ferguson for £65,000 – a record British fee for a goalkeeper.

Spurs beat Chelsea 2–1 to win the FA Cup.

And Celtic Football Club won the European Cup. Well, as Bobby Lennox quite rightly points out, we all like a happy ending!